D0011160

JOHN M. GOTTMAN, PH.D.,

JULIE SCHWARTZ GOTTMAN, PH.D.,

& JOAN DECLAIRE

THREE RIVERS PRESS · NEW YORK

Ten Lessons

to Transform

Your

Marriage

AMERICA'S LOVE LAB EXPERTS

SHARE THEIR STRATEGIES FOR

STRENGTHENING YOUR RELATIONSHIP

Published in the United States by Three Rivers Press, an imprint of the Crown Publishing
Group, a division of Random House, Inc., New York.
www.crownpublishing.com

Three Rivers Press and the Tugboat design are registered trademarks of Random House, Inc.

Originally published in hardcover in the United States by Crown Publishers, an imprint of the
Crown Publishing Group, a division of Random House, Inc., New York, in 2006.

Library of Congress Cataloging-in-Publication Data
Gottman, John Mordechai.
Ten lessons to transform your marriage : America's love lab experts share their strategies for
strengthening your relationship / John M. Gottman, Julie Schwartz Gottman, and Joan DeClaire.
p.   cm.
1. Marriage.   2. Marital conflict.   3. Married people—Psychology.   I. Title: Ten lessons to
transform your marriage.   II. Gottman, Julie Schwartz.   III. DeClaire, Joan.   IV. Title.
HQ734.G7133 2006
306.81—dc22

2005019645

ISBN 978-1-4000-5019-2

Printed in the United States of America

DESIGN BY ELINA D. NUDELMAN

10   9

First Paperback Edition

To our parents—Lina and Solomon Gotthelfsman,
and Selma and Marvin Schwartz—
in celebration of their long-lasting marriages

—JMG and JSG

Contents

Contents

Acknowledgments

Special thanks to Catherine Romano and the staff at *Reader's Digest* for their collaboration on "The Love Lab" column, upon which this book is based. Thanks also to Virginia Rutter, who provided screening and logistical support for this effort, and to Sybil Carrere, Alyson Shapiro, Amber Tabares, and Janice Driver for making our laboratory work successful.

We also wish to express our continuing gratitude to the people and organizations that help to fund our marriage and family research. These include Bruce and Jolene McCaw, founders of the Apex Foundation and the Talaris Research Institute; Craig Stewart, president of the Apex Foundation; Dan and Sally Kranzler, founders of the Kirlin Foundation; Ron Rabin, executive director of the Kirlin Foundation; Peter Berliner and the Paul G. Allen Family Foundation; Molly Oliveri of the National Institute of Mental Health (NIMH); and a grant from NIMH titled "Basic Processes in Marriage."

In addition, thanks go to the staff of the Gottman Institute: Etana Dykan, Linda Wright, Venita Ramirez, Stacy Walker, Candace Marshall, and Belinda Gray. With great dedication and commitment, they have supported us to serve more than five thousand couples and to train more than fourteen thousand clinicians.

Joan DeClaire wishes to express thanks to Louise Carnachan, Carla Granat, and Debra Jarvis for their tremendously helpful comments on the manuscript. Her gratitude also goes to Wendy Townsend, Bob Heffernan, and the members of the "Artists' Group"—Nan Burling, Louise Carter, Rebecca Hughes, Wendy Slotboom, and Jan Short Pollard—for their never-ending support and encouragement.

And finally, thanks to all the couples who have so generously volunteered for this and other research projects throughout the years.

From Predicting Divorce to Preventing It:

An Introductory Message from John and Julie Gottman

It's been more than a decade since John and his colleagues at the University of Washington (UW) first announced their discovery: Through the power of careful observation and mathematical analysis, the team had learned to predict with more than 90 percent accuracy whether a married couple would stay together or eventually divorce.

This discovery captured the imagination of many. If research psychologists could now pinpoint specific behaviors that lead to divorce, then perhaps people in troubled relationships could change those behaviors and save their marriages.But as any weatherman can tell you, the ability to predict trouble is not the same as the ability to prevent it. It's one thing to detect a storm brewing on radar; it's quite another to make those storm clouds disappear.

And yet that's the kind of work we at the Gottman Institute have been doing. Since 1994 we've been developing tools to help couples identify problems that are proven to destroy relationships—and to turn those problems around. By experimenting with various forms of therapy, we've been learning how to help husbands and wives improve their marriages and prevent divorce.

Through our workshops, therapy sessions, and books, couples are gaining the tools they need to build stronger friendships and manage their conflicts. As a result, they are learning to work through a whole host of problems common to marriage—problems such as these:

- *the stress of caring for a new baby*
- *exhaustion from working too hard*
- *loss of interest in sex and romance*
- *health problems*
- *recovering from an extramarital affair*
- *struggles with depression*
- *arguments over housework and finances*
- *changes that come with retirement*
- *the loss of a job, an identity, or a lifelong dream*

And once again we're achieving some exciting results. Our studies show that 86 percent of people who complete our marriage workshops say they make significant progress on conflicts that once felt "gridlocked." And after one year, 75 percent of husbands and 56 percent of wives who attend our workshops and therapy sessions feel their marriages move from a broken state to a functional one. Even simply reading our books can make a difference. One study showed that 63 percent of husbands and wives who read John's 1999 bestseller, *The Seven Principles for Making Marriage Work,* reported that their marriages had changed for the better and were still improved a year later.

These numbers are a big improvement over other forms of marital intervention. For example, acclaimed marriage researcher Neil Jacobson conducted an evaluation of one of the most highly regarded therapy methods and showed that only 35 percent of couples using it improved their marriages.

What's behind our success? We believe it's the science. The tools we've developed—and that you'll see real couples using in this book—aren't based on our beliefs or whims about marriage. They are grounded in decades of work John and his colleagues have been doing at the Family Research Laboratory, originally located at UW and now part of our Relationship Research Institute in Seattle. The Love Lab—as we've come to call it—is a research facility where husbands and wives are screened, interviewed, and observed interacting with each other. Researchers use video cameras, heart monitors, and other biofeedback equipment to determine people's stress levels during conversations with their partners. This information is then coded and mathematically analyzed. By collecting and analyzing such data on thousands of couples—and tracking their progress over time—we've learned an enormous amount about the dynamics of marriage. And, ultimately, we've been able to determine which interactions lead to lasting happiness, and which interactions lead to emotional distance and divorce.

In the bestselling book *Blink* (Little Brown, 2005), journalist Malcolm Gladwell refers to our process as "thin slicing." Simply put, this means we're able to quickly determine a great deal of information about a couple from analyzing a very thin slice of data collected in one short lab session. The reason our swift analysis works is because each thin slice of data is actually grounded in a tremendous amount of "thick slicing"—i.e., huge volumes of data that we've been collecting and validating on thousands of other couples for more than thirty years.

To help everyday couples use these discoveries to improve their own marriages, we established the Gottman Institute, which provides therapy and workshops for husbands and wives, as well as training for marriage therapists. Combining John's extensive research findings with Julie's thirty years of experience as a clinical psychologist, we've developed a body of advice that's based on two surprisingly simple truths:

1. Happily married couples behave like good friends.

In other words, their relationships are characterized by respect, affection, and empathy. They pay close attention to what's happening in

3

each other's life and they feel emotionally connected. One of John's studies of couples discussing conflict demonstrated this well. It showed that spouses in happy, stable marriages made five positive remarks for every one negative remark when they were discussing conflict. In contrast, couples headed for divorce offered less than one (0.8) positive remark for every single negative remark.

2. Happily married couples handle their conflicts in gentle, positive ways.

They recognize that conflict is inevitable in any marriage, and that some problems never get solved, never go away. But these couples don't get gridlocked in their separate positions. Instead, they keep talking with each other about conflicts. They listen respectfully to their spouses' perspectives and they find compromises that work for both sides.

With this book, we give you an intimate view of ten couples who learned to work through serious problems that were threatening their marriages—problems like infidelity, overwork, adjustment to parenthood, unresolved anger and resentment, and a loss of interest in sex. You'll learn a bit about each couple's background and how they perceived the problems they brought to the Love Lab. You'll also read parts of the conversations that occurred when we asked husbands and wives to talk to each other about their problems.

For each couple, we present two dialogues, one that took place before we counseled them and one that happened after they heard our advice. In addition, you'll see a commentary alongside each dialogue titled "What We Noticed." This gives you a therapist's perspective on the interaction so that you might learn to detect some of the most common stumbling blocks that occur in relationships. You may notice, for example, places where a few words spoken in haste can take a conversation—and a marriage—down a dangerous path. You may learn to spot behaviors proven by John's research to damage relationships. These include a set of particularly poisonous patterns of interaction we call "the Four

Horsemen of the Apocalypse." Our studies have shown that, left unchecked, these behaviors can send couples into a downward spiral that ends in divorce. The Four Horsemen are

* CRITICISM. Often, criticism appears as a complaint or episode of blaming that's coupled with a global attack on your partner's personality or character. Criticism frequently begins with "you always" or "you never."

* DEFENSIVENESS. These are the counterattacks people use to defend their innocence or avoid taking responsibility for a problem. Defensiveness often takes the form of cross-complaining or whining.

* CONTEMPT. This is criticism bolstered by hostility or disgust. Think of somebody rolling their eyes while you're trying to tell them something important about yourself. Contempt often involves sarcasm, mocking, name-calling, or belligerence.

* STONEWALLING. This happens when listeners withdraw from the conversation, offering no physical or verbal cues that they're affected by what they hear. Interacting with somebody who does this is "like talking to a stone wall."

Our commentary also indicates the places where these couples make great strides—i.e., where they say or do something that strengthens the relationship by making them feel closer, encouraging compromise, or healing old wounds. Examples of such positive behaviors include

* SOFTENED START-UP. This is the ability to start talking about a complaint or a problem gently, without criticizing or insulting your partner. When one spouse does this, the other is more willing to listen, making compromise possible.

* TURNING TOWARD YOUR PARTNER. Close relationships consist of a series of "emotional bids"—that is, your partner

reaches out for emotional connection with a comment, a question, a smile, or a hug. You can choose to

1. *turn away, ignoring the bid*
2. *turn against, reacting with anger or hostility*
3. *turn toward, showing you're open, listening, and engaged*

Our research shows that habitually turning away or turning against your partner's bids harms your marriage. But consistently turning toward your partner strengthens emotional bonds, friendship, and romance.

* REPAIRING THE CONVERSATION. This is an effort to de-escalate negative feelings during a difficult encounter. A repair can be an apology, a smile, or bit of humor that breaks the tension and helps you both feel more relaxed.

* ACCEPTING INFLUENCE. Partners who are open to persuasion from each other generally have stronger, happier marriages. Being stubborn or domineering has just the opposite effect. Our studies show that a husband's willingness to accept influence from his wife can be particularly helpful to forming a strong, happy marriage.

Such concepts may seem familiar to people who have read John's previous books or attended our workshops. The difference with this book is that it invites you right into the Love Lab. Reading it, you spend time with ten couples who agreed to let us share their stories so that the work we did together might also help others. (For privacy, we've used fictional names and changed some identifying characteristics, but the situations and the conversations you'll read are real.)

Unlike books that simply *tell* you how to change your marriage, this book actually *shows* you how that transformation happens—how real couples talking about truly difficult problems can change the dynamics of their conversations; how they can stop having the same painful, destructive interactions over and over again and move on to a more peaceful coexistence. You see how they take the tools we suggest and use them to build back that sense of affection and romance that attracted them to each other in the first place.

In addition, each chapter provides quizzes you can take to see if you and your partner face the same problems these couples are overcoming. And we offer exercises you can do to make the same kind of progress these couples do.

As you read about these couples' progress, you may notice that many of the changes they make are small, simple adjustments—not big, complicated ones. A husband may, for example, learn to ask his wife more questions about how she's feeling. Or a wife may learn to express more appreciation for all the work her husband's been doing. We might advise a couple to stop and take a break to calm down when they're in the middle of a heated discussion. Or we might give them strategies for going to a deeper level in their conversations, sharing their hopes and dreams.

While the changes we suggest may not always seem like a big deal, our research shows that small, positive behaviors, frequently repeated, can make a *big* difference in the long-term success of a marriage. You could compare this work to piloting a plane cross-country. A turn of a few degrees over Ohio may seem like a small adjustment—merely fine-tuning. But in the long run it determines whether you end up in San Francisco or Los Angeles. So it is with a long-term relationship. When both partners commit to making small but consistently positive shifts in their interactions, they can take their marriage to a much happier place. And it's easier to assimilate small changes, rather than big ones.

Whether you're currently in a distressed relationship or you simply want to make a strong, happy relationship even better, we believe this book can help. It will show you what it's like to work with an effective therapist to improve your marriage. And it will also give you insights and tools you can use to make progress with or without counseling.

We hope that as you read this book, you find it comforting that you're not alone in your desire to make marriage better; that the challenges you and your partner may face are *not* insurmountable. And don't be surprised if you recognize yourselves in the situations and dialogues that follow. Our work has shown us that every couple is unique, but we also see many, many similarities. And that's a great sign that we can all learn from one another.

Best wishes,
John and Julie Gottman

CHAPTER 1

"All You Ever Do Is Work"

Sam remembers that falling in love with Katie was easy. The newest member of his coed softball team, she was "attractive, intelligent, and fun."

Holding on to her was harder. Soon after their first date, Katie left for a two-year Peace Corps job in Paraguay. Sam kept the courtship alive by sending Katie passionate letters. He would join her in South America at the end of her stint, he promised, and they would spend several weeks touring exotic destinations together.

Katie consented. "He was nice, fun, and witty," she recalls. And traveling with a man would feel safer than traveling alone. "But I thought he was crazy for writing those letters. We didn't even know each other!"

Ten years of marriage and three kids have certainly changed that. In Love Lab interviews and questionnaires, Katie and Sam reveal that they understand each other quite well. They also see eye to eye when it comes to tricky issues around parenting and finances.

But the Minneapolis couple has some serious challenges, too. During our initial meeting, Katie complains that Sam works far too much. She says he puts in so many hours at his job as a scientist for a small

What's the Problem?

- Katie's complaints about Sam's work slip into criticism.
- Sam defends himself and launches a counterattack.
- Katie gets defensive, angry, and more critical.
- Cycle of criticize/defend/countercriticize continues.
- Sam withdraws.
- Katie feels alone and frustrated.

What's the Solution?

- Learn to complain without criticizing.
- Hear the longing in each other's complaints.
- Express appreciation for each other.

biotech firm that he often has no energy left for the family. "Sam can be a great dad," Katie says. But when he takes time off, he's often too preoccupied and tired to play with their kids, aged six years, four years, and eighteen months, she explains.

Katie works part-time as a biochemist herself, so she understands how compelling Sam's work can be. But she feels strongly that, for the sake of their marriage, Sam needs to strike a better balance between work and family.

Katie also wants more of Sam's attention herself. After they put the kids to bed, he often disappears into his basement office until the wee hours, she complains. She'd like him to come to bed with her and cuddle. Whatever happened to the guy who wrote those passionate love letters, she wonders. Why can't he understand that she'd still like to see his romantic side?

Meanwhile, Sam's got his own complaints. Katie doesn't seem to appreciate how hard he works for the family's benefit. He feels that all he gets from her are criticism and demands. She should understand that when he's grappling with a difficult problem at work, it's hard for him to just "turn his brain off" and focus on the family, he explains. If he's going to relax, he needs more "down time," more solitude. Katie's requests for attention just make him want to withdraw.

Such complaints are common among couples who juggle demanding jobs with raising children. There really are just twenty-four hours in each day, and partners are bound to disagree over the way each person spends time. Since such conflicts aren't likely to disappear, the couple's challenge is to learn to live with their differences without harming the relationship. By the time Katie and Sam visited the Love Lab, however, they were beginning to lose confidence in their ability to get along.

"When we try to talk about our problems, we get angry so quickly," says Katie. "And then Sam can't stand to be in the same room with me, so he leaves. It just makes me crazy."

"Usually some trivial issue causes a disagreement," adds Sam. "And then, because we can't communicate, it just flares."

To learn more about the way they handle conflict, we ask Sam and Katie to talk to each other about a disagreement for ten minutes. We videotape the conversation. We also have them wear electrodes on their hands and abdomens so we can measure any physiological signs of stress, such as increases in heart rate, while they're talking. After the conversation, we analyze the tape and physiological data for information about the way their interactions are affecting their relationship.

On the next page, you'll see some excerpts from that conversation. In the left-hand column, you can read what Sam and Katie say. We recommend that you read that first. Then you can go back and look at the notes on the right-hand side for some of our observations about the conversation. Like "color commentary" from a sports announcer, these notes on the right may give you a little more insight into the successes and errors of this, a marital team. Comments preceded by a plus (+) sign indicate that the statement is having a generally favorable effect on the interaction. Comments preceded by a minus (−) sign indicate a generally negative effect. As you read, see if you can detect patterns in their interaction. Pay attention especially to moments when Katie or Sam goes from complaining to criticism, and what effect that has on the other person. Then read our analysis at the end of the dialogue and the advice we give.

11

What They Say	*What We Notice*
Katie: You were working so much of the time last summer. It felt like even when you were physically present, you weren't emotionally present. And I am really scared of that happening again.	+ Starts gently. + Complains without blaming him. + Talks clearly about her feelings.
Sam: The work is so important to me. It defines who I am.	− Doesn't respond to her expression of feelings. − Slightly defensive. + States his need.
Katie: I know. And when it heats up again, I don't want the same thing to happen. We were angry at each other all the time.	− Quickly dismisses his heartfelt statement. + Uses "we"; shows she shares responsibility for the problem.
Sam: Yeah. I remember that.	+ Validates her statement.
Katie: I don't want to go back there. So I would really like to figure out a way for you to still be able to be part of the family even when your work is busy and stressful. Then you could get the appreciation that you need from me, which you didn't get this last summer because I was so angry at you. I was so lonely because you were so not there.	+ Takes responsibility for part of the problem. + Tries to repair problems. + Expresses her feelings. − Slightly critical at the end.

What They Say	What We Notice
Sam: Yeah, when I'm busy with work, it's just in my head all the time.	+ Clarifies.
Katie: And so the family is just supposed to take a backseat.	− Criticizes with sarcasm.
Sam: No.	− Slightly defensive (short response).
Katie: We're just supposed to live without you for months.	− Criticizes.
Sam: No.	− Defensive.
Katie: Because you were physically there, but you were not emotionally present for a long time.	− Criticizes.
Sam: I'm not disagreeing. But I don't feel like you respect my work. You don't value that I'm working really hard. It's like everybody wants a piece of me. You just want another piece of me.	− Defensive. + Expresses his feelings. − Complaint turns to criticism.
Katie: That's reasonable for me to want a piece of you. You're my husband! You're supposed to be my best friend, my confidant, my support.	− Defensive. − Criticizes him again. − Doesn't respond to his complaint.

continued

What They Say	What We Notice
Sam: You want my support, and I wasn't getting any support from you. All I got was more demands.	− Defensive. − Countercriticizes.

After a while, the conversation moves into Katie's complaint about bedtime.

What They Say	What We Notice
Katie: I would love to go to bed together at the same time.	+ Starts gently. + Avoids blaming.
Sam: And I often get in bed and talk to you for a little bit and then I want to go off and watch the TV or . . .	− Slightly defensive. + States his need (to watch TV).
Katie: That's not really getting in bed with me. When you lie on top of the covers and I'm under the covers. I mean, I don't know if the physical stuff means anything to you, but it does to me.	− Interrupts. − Ignores his stated desire. + Clarifies her need.
Sam: Even though the physical stuff—is just touching?	+ Asks a question to clarify her need.
Katie: Yeah.	+ Validates.
Sam: It means something to me.	+ Validates, clarifies his feelings.

What They Say	What We Notice
Katie: I want to put my head on your bare shoulder.	+ Further clarifies her need.
Sam: I think you want me to be there to go to sleep. Which I would like to do, but I want to also have some downtime by myself.	+ Restates her needs. + States his own need of wanting time alone.
Katie: And you do get downtime by yourself. I mean, without staying up till three in the morning.	– Slightly defensive.
Sam: Yeah. Some evenings I do, but that's not the way it usually is. Usually, by the time the kids are in bed, you want to talk, and you want to talk all evening.	– Defensive. – Criticizes her needs.
Katie: Sam, that's not true. I can't remember an evening where we sat and talked all evening.	– Defensive.
Sam: That's what you would like.	– Criticizes.
Katie: But I can't remember one where we have actually done it. What I'd really like is just to feel connected to you.	– Defensive. + Expresses her need.
Sam: Yeah.	+ Validates.

continued

15

What They Say	What We Notice
Katie: Part of it is that I would really love to cuddle and we would probably have a better love life. And part of it is that when you stay up so late at night, you're exhausted.	+ Expresses her needs.
Sam: Yeah. OK. So you want more of me. You want me to be—	+ Restates her needs.
Katie: Emotionally there. You can be so much fun with the kids. You can actually be this wonderful father. And I love seeing you that way. And when you're exhausted, you're short with the kids. You have no patience. You yell at them.	− Interrupts him. + Expresses appreciation. + Expresses her needs. − Criticizes him.
Sam: The thing is, I would like to change all of that stuff. But I feel compelled to stay up late. I feel compelled to—	+ Expresses his feelings.
Katie: But those are all choices you make. You're the only one that can control your life.	− Interrupts him. − Criticizes.
Sam: I know. But when you're being antagonistic instead of being supportive of me changing, it isn't helping.	− Defensiveness. − Counterattack. − Blaming.

Our Analysis: A Cycle of Criticize/ Defend/Countercriticize

What patterns do you notice in Sam and Katie's interactions? Here's what we see:

On the positive side, Katie does a great job at the beginning of the conversation by bringing up problems in a gentle, nonconfrontational way—something we call "softened start-up." This is essential for couples who want to connect emotionally and build understanding. She also states her needs without blaming Sam. She simply describes how his behavior (working long hours; staying up late) affects her and how she feels about it.

To his credit, Sam initially responds to Katie's complaints by taking some responsibility for their problems. But he never really acknowledges Katie's feelings of loneliness and frustration. Then, after a few exchanges, the real trouble begins: Katie's complaints turn to criticism. In other words, she goes from simply revealing *her* feelings to making negative statements about *his* faults. Instead of describing specific problems, she paints the dispute as long lasting and global. ("We're just supposed to live without you *for months.*" ". . . you were not emotionally present *for a long time.*") We also notice a bit of hurtful sarcasm sneaking into her tone with statements like "The family is supposed to take a backseat."

Sam's response is typical for a partner under attack. He doesn't empathize or express understanding. He simply defends himself and eventually starts launching a counteroffensive. ("You want my support, and I wasn't getting any support from you.") This, in turn, causes Katie to become defensive, setting up an all-too-common cycle of criticize/ defend/countercriticize—a pattern that can cause arguments to escalate out of control.

Fortunately, such escalation doesn't happen for Katie and Sam in this conversation. That's because Katie does a masterful job of pulling the plug after just a few exchanges; she agrees with Sam that she has indeed been demanding. ("Right," she responds, "you're absolutely right.") This temporary cease-fire allows Sam to tell Katie more about his needs, and Katie—thank goodness—listens. It doesn't take long, however, for the criticism and defensiveness to creep back into their exchange. And by the end of the conversation, Katie's frustration is palpable and Sam is withdrawing. If this conversation occurred in their bedroom instead of our lab, Sam probably would be headed for the basement and some downtime, leaving Katie to seethe.

Our Advice

We suggest that Katie and Sam try a second conversation about their differences. Only this time we give them three specific pieces of advice:

1. COMPLAIN WITHOUT CRITICIZING

Katie and Sam both have valid complaints. Katie feels she needs more help with parenting and more romantic attention from Sam. Sam feels he needs more respect from Katie for all the hard work and the financial support he's providing. So the most important change we recommend for Katie and Sam is to learn to express those needs without criticizing each other's character or personality. Constant criticism can be very harmful to a relationship. Unchecked, it can even put marriages on a downhill course that ends in divorce. But if Katie and Sam can learn to state their needs in a more healthy way (see "Healthy Complaining Versus Harmful Complaining" on page 25), they can break the cycle of criticize/defend/countercriticize that's causing prolonged and contentious arguments.

Avoiding criticism is particularly important if you're married to somebody who is highly sensitive to others' disapproval. Through our interviews, we learn this may be true for Sam, who was raised in a military family—a culture that some psychologists believe makes kids quite vulnerable to criticism. (See "The 'Oversensitive' Partner," page 29.) Both Sam and Katie report that Sam seems to take even the most minor negative statements to heart, as though he were bracing himself for the blow that hasn't happened yet, but seems sure to come.

To help Sam cope with this sensitivity, we advise Katie to ask Sam questions about his behaviors. By showing genuine interest in his desire to work so much, for example, she may help him to open up to her so they can discuss the issue more deeply. This, in turn, may eventually lead to better understanding and a solution to their conflict.

2. LOOK FOR THE LONGING IN EACH OTHER'S COMPLAINTS

It's clear to us that Sam wants more understanding and appreciation from Katie. And although Katie doesn't always express it, it's also clear to us that she appreciates Sam very much. That's why she wants to spend more time with him. She wants to enjoy his sense of humor, she wants to share the fun of raising their kids together, and she wants to share more intimacy in bed.

The trouble is, Sam isn't hearing that longing. All he's hearing is Katie's irritability and discontent. When Katie says, "I love to feel your skin and cuddle with you," all Sam hears is, "Once again, she thinks I'm inadequate."

Our advice for Sam is to listen more closely to the longing in Katie's complaints. And if he's not sure what she's longing for when she complains, ask questions. "What does spending time together in bed at the end of the day mean to you?" he might ask. "Tell me why this is important."

Katie might ask Sam more questions about his complaints as well—questions like "What would it mean for you to feel that I respect and support your work? Why is that important to you? What would it look like?"

3. EXPRESS AND ACCEPT APPRECIATION

Both Katie and Sam say they feel unappreciated in their marriage, which is too bad, since both of them are working harder than ever, and they're doing it for the sake of their shared interest—their family. This seeming lack of appreciation is common for many young, busy

19

couples—especially during periods of high stress at work, or unusually tough family demands. Operating in survival mode, each partner feels exhausted and may not have the extra energy it takes to say, "Thanks for doing the taxes," or "I really appreciated that you got up at two a.m. to feed the baby." But when partners don't hear expressions of appreciation, they feel taken for granted and their feelings of stress just get worse.

This seems to be true for Katie and Sam when he's working long hours and she's caring for the kids on her own. So we suggest that they make a more conscious effort to notice good deeds the other does. We tell them to try to "catch each other in the act of getting it right." Then speak up. Tell each other that you see and appreciate the good things each is bringing to the family.

While we notice that Katie expresses quite a bit of appreciation for Sam, he doesn't necessarily hear and internalize the appreciation that she offers. We suspect that's because Katie's praise is often coupled with criticism. (Remember how she starts to tell him he's a "wonderful father" only to conclude, "You have no patience. You yell at them.") This contrast is a testament to the terrible negative power of criticism, which may be undoing all of Katie's best intentions to build Sam up.

Another problem is that Sam has a hard time accepting Katie's appreciation. "I don't understand her love for me sometimes," he tells us. "I don't know where it comes from." So here's another piece of advice for Sam: Give yourself the benefit of the doubt. Even if Katie's love seems irrational to you at times, open yourself up to it. When she expresses appreciation, make a mental note and repeat that conversation in your mind. Over time, you may learn to accept this fact: You are truly worthy, and you are truly loved.

Here are some excerpts from a second conversation, where Sam and Katie try out our advice:

What They Say	What We Notice
Katie: I want to hear more about why your work is so important to you.	+ Opens with a supportive question.
Sam: First, I want to tell you something that you probably don't know. I like that you want to cuddle with me. I appreciate that you want that.	+ Expresses appreciation.
Katie: I'm glad you like it, because I like it, too.	+ Expresses gratitude, appreciation.
Sam: Now, about my work, I get a sense of self-worth from doing the complex and technical stuff.	+ Responsive, expressing his feelings.
Katie: So is that why your mind doesn't let go of it?	+ Open-ended, exploratory question.
Sam: When I'm thinking about something, it's just what my mind does. It's not a conscious thing. It's just that my mind takes me there.	+ Responsive, clarifying.
Katie: Do you get the self-worth from your work even when your work is not as time-consuming and demanding?	+ Exploratory question.

continued

What They Say	*What We Notice*
Sam: Yeah, but it doesn't have to do with recognition from other people. It has to do with me feeling like I've done a good job for myself. That's where my self-esteem comes from. It's important to me that I've come up with an elegant solution or whatever.	+ Responsive, expressing his feelings.
Katie: That must feel good.	+ Communicates empathy and approval.
Sam: Yeah, it does feel good. I appreciate you asking me about it. It feels really nice.	+ Expresses appreciation and feelings.
Eventually, the topic shifts to bedtime.	
Sam: I would like to devote time to you each evening. What holds me back is I feel like it's an obligation instead of something I'm doing because I want to do it. I feel like it's being demanded of me as opposed to something I'm giving freely.	+ Expresses willingness to meet her need. + Honestly expresses that he feels obligated by her demand. + Not blaming.
Katie: I really do appreciate the fact that you want to spend some time with me in the evening. But I think even if I said, "Can I have a half hour of your time?" you would still hear criticism. Even if I don't say, "We haven't done it all week," you might still hear, "God, I haven't done that. She doesn't think I do that enough."	+ Expresses appreciation. + Honestly expresses fear that he won't be able to hear her needs without thinking she's criticizing him.

What They Say	What We Notice
Sam: That's true. You're right. I am very likely to hear that. But over time, if we practice, I think we probably can do better.	+ Accepts responsibility and expresses hope.
Katie: Is there something else I should say that would help?	+ Good exploratory question.
Sam: If you would tell me what you want without focusing on what my behavior has been in the past—that would go a long way. Even if you did that, I might hear my own subtext of criticism for a while. But I could practice trying to listen more to your words. Maybe you could joke about it. That might click in my mind, "She really is trying to keep it positive."	+ States need for her to avoid focusing on the past. + Accepts responsibility. + Expresses willingness to find solution.
Katie: So what if I just make it more light— add some joke to make it more positive?	+ Good summarizing, clarifying.
Sam: Yeah, that would go a long way, I think.	+ Validating.

By the end of the conversation, Sam and Katie seem relieved. Katie's questions show that she is genuinely interested in Sam's experience. This, in turn, encourages him to open up to her. The validating remarks and statements of appreciation they share keep the conversation on a positive track so that they can talk peacefully and productively about their problems. Noticeably absent are statements of criticism and defensiveness.

For the first time, Katie can see how the criticism in her complaints affects Sam and their relationship. And she understands that even when she's not being particularly critical, Sam may still hear her words in that way.

Sam explains that he now realizes how much he wants to respond to Katie's longing. "When I don't feel criticized, I want to give you what you want, what you need," he tells her.

One Year Later

We check back with Sam and Katie a year later, and here's what we find: Sam is still working long hours and Katie still wishes he wouldn't. Are we surprised? Not at all. Sam and Katie's differences over Sam's work are a classic example of what we call a "perpetual issue"—i.e., a disagreement that will never go away. (For more about this, see the section titled "Don't Get Gridlocked over Perpetual Issues" in chapter 10.)

Every long-term relationship has its share of perpetual issues. In fact, our research shows that some 69 percent of all marital conflicts can be categorized as never ending. What can change, however, is a couple's willingness to accept their differences and to improve their skills at solving problems that result.

That's one way Sam and Katie have changed over the past year. Katie says she has learned to accept Sam's passion for his work and his long hours as part of who he is. "So now I make a conscious effort not to give him a hard time about it, because that's what he wants to do," she says.

Sam, in turn, appreciates the changes in Katie. "The criticism is just not there anymore and that makes a huge difference to me," he reports.

Sam is also seeing Katie's needs from a new perspective. "Before, when she would ask me not to work, I felt like she was attacking me. Now I'm more likely to take a breath and remember that she just wants to be with me, that's all. She's just asking for some of my time." As a result, he says he feels less defensive and more willing to do what she's asking.

HEALTHY COMPLAINING VERSUS HARMFUL COMPLAINING

It's a myth that happily married people don't complain about each other's behavior. In fact, it would be ludicrous to expect two human beings to live together without complaints. We all have our own idiosyncratic needs, desires, rhythms, and habits. And these needs are bound to collide, producing strong emotions.

Constantly stifling your complaints is not a good idea. Doing so can cause you to hold on to angry, resentful feelings toward your partner. You may develop a state of mind we call "negative sentiment override," where your bad thoughts about your partner and relationship overwhelm and override any positive thoughts about them. You may start to stockpile your grievances, keeping track of each offense your partner commits. In the meantime, your bad feelings fester and grow, resulting in one of two outcomes: You either distance yourself emotionally to avoid the pain or you lash out. Meanwhile, your offending partner, who rarely hears a negative word from you, is in the dark. There's little chance for your partner to improve his or her ability to meet your needs because your partner doesn't know what's wrong— that is, until you hit your limit and explode with a barrage of grievances you've been saving up.

There is an alternative to either stifling or exploding, however. Partners can learn to express their needs (i.e., complain) in ways that are respectful, clear, specific, and immediate. There are many benefits to this approach. For example, your partner is more likely to hear your complaint and respond to it if you express it in this way, and complaining in a healthy way actually helps to solve problems, build intimacy, and strengthen the relationship.

Here are examples:

Healthy Complaining	*Harmful Complaining*
Share responsibility for the problem: "We haven't been able to afford a vacation in two years. Maybe we should work out a better budget."	**Blame the problem on the other person:** "It's all your fault that we can't afford a vacation. You waste our money on stupid things."
Describe the problem in terms of your perception, opinion, or style: "I'm just more conservative about money and I think you spent too much for that pair of shoes."	**Describe the problem as a matter of absolute truth:** "Anybody can see that's too much money to spend on a pair of shoes."
Focus on a specific problem, tackling one at a time: "You set your glass on the coffee table last night and now there's a ring."	**Stockpile complaints:** "You haven't done the laundry in two weeks, the lawn needs mowing, and you never cleaned the garage like you said you would."
	Make broad, sweeping statements: "You never take me anywhere."

Healthy Complaining	Harmful Complaining
Focus on the present:	**Dig up past grievances:**
"You said you would help Sean with his homework, but you're still watching TV."	"You didn't cook one meal the whole time I was putting you through law school."
Focus on partner's actions and how those actions make you feel:	**Criticize your partner's personality or character:**
"I thought we were going to have a romantic evening together, and you invited your mother. I feel so hurt and disappointed."	"I thought we were going to have a romantic evening together, and you invited your mother. How can you be such a clueless, insensitive dolt?"
Pick a time to complain about the problem when partner can listen and respond.	**Complain at times when partner is distracted by pressing matters such as a deadline or caring for small children.**
Tell partner about your needs and desires:	**Don't complain. Expect your partner to mind-read, to guess your needs and desires.**
"I feel so tired that I need to just cuddle with you right now. Maybe tomorrow we can make love."	She moves away from his touch with no explanation.

continued

27

Healthy Ways to Respond to a Complaint	Harmful Ways to Respond to a Complaint
Rephrase the complaint so the complainer knows you understand: "So you're upset because I'm an hour late."	**Ignore the complaint altogether.**
Ask questions for a better understanding: "Do you want me to call you if I'm going to be late?" "You say you want more of my attention. Do you feel like we don't talk enough?"	**Belittle or criticize your partner for complaining:** "I can't believe you're upset because I'm an hour late. You're such a control freak." "You want more of my attention? You want me to sit here and stare at you all day?"
Acknowledge the feelings behind your partner's complaint: "I forgot it was Valentine's Day. You must feel hurt and angry."	**Defend yourself:** "I forgot it was Valentine's Day because I was so focused on my training. I've got to make a living, you know!"
	Use sarcasm or criticism: "What do you want me to do—cancel my training because it's Valentine's Day?" "If you had a real job, you wouldn't have time to obsess about Valentine's Day."
Take responsibility for the problem: "You're right. I should have been nicer to your mom."	**Deny responsibility for the problem:** "It's not my fault that your mom is so touchy."

THE "OVERSENSITIVE" PARTNER

Some people seem to react very strongly to complaints and criticism, making it hard for their partners to talk about needs that aren't being met. Such high sensitivity is often the result of patterns set in childhood. People who grow up in families with problems such as substance abuse or emotional, physical, or sexual abuse, for example, may be more sensitive to criticism than others. That's because small children are so naturally egocentric that they falsely believe their actions can cause or prevent family problems and instability. *("If I'm just good enough, Mom won't yell at me." "Dad would still be here if I hadn't talked back to him.")* Kids from military families, where a parent sometimes has to leave unexpectedly, may experience the same type of problems. *("If I can just make Dad happy, maybe he won't ship out again.")* What's the result when kids constantly feel responsible for unfortunate circumstances beyond their control? They grow up feeling compelled to defend themselves, to say constantly, "It's not my fault." If they hear a complaint, they automatically brace themselves. They prepare to fight back whether they're under attack or not.

This can be a real struggle in a close partnership or marriage. What starts out as a simple conversation about one person's needs can easily turn into a full-fledged battle. An example:

"We need to balance the checkbook."

"I'm not the one writing all those checks!"

"I thought you wrote one to the hair salon just yesterday."

"So now I'm supposed to cut my own hair, is that it?"

What's the solution? If you're the highly sensitive partner:

29

* Listen carefully to the words your partner is saying when stating a need or making a request. Your partner may not be as critical as you first think.

* Be aware of times that you automatically react by defending yourself. Can you think of a different reaction instead?

* See what happens when you take a deep breath and agree. *("OK. Let's balance the checkbook tonight.")*

* Try asking your partner to tell you more about the need or complaint. *("Why do you like to balance the checkbook every two weeks?")*

If your partner is highly sensitive:

* Take extra care to avoid criticism when stating your needs. (See section called "Healthy Complaining Versus Harmful Complaining" on page 25.)

* If your partner responds defensively, avoid responding the same way.

* Respond to defensiveness by clarifying your statement of need. *("I'd just like to balance the checkbook to make sure that we don't get overdrawn.")*

When One Partner Works Too Much

Katie's complaint that Sam works too much is a common one. Many people believe their relationships would improve if their partners would stop working long hours and start putting more energy into the marriage. And in many cases, the complaining partner is right. Strong marriages require two partners who are willing to give their time and attention to each other.

If you're the overworking spouse, you may be reacting to pressures in the workplace—a demanding boss, for instance, or your employer's threat to lay off less productive workers. Maybe you're under financial stress; you feel that you've got to work long hours simply to make ends meet.

Or perhaps your own attitude toward your work makes you feel compelled to work long hours. Like Sam, you may feel that your profession is your identity, that your job is "who I am." If this is true for you, you probably feel most comfortable when you're in the workplace, doing your job, and doing it well. There's nothing wrong with this, of course. In fact, for many people, it's ideal. But if you find that you're consistently putting in so many hours that your spouse feels emotionally disconnected from you, your attitude toward work may be putting your marriage at risk.

What can couples do to change this dynamic? You may find it helpful to have a conversation like the one that Sam and Katie had—one that explores two sets of questions.

1. To the spouse who is overworking, questions include:

- *What does your work mean to you?*

- *What pleasure or satisfaction does work bring to you?*

- *What need does working fulfill in your life?*

- *Does your work relate to some personal legacy you'd like to contribute to the world?*

2. To the spouse who is complaining about overwork, questions include:

- *What does your spouse's absence mean to you?*

- *What positive things do you miss about your partner when he or she is gone so much?*

- *What are you longing for in terms of emotional, physical, intellectual, or spiritual connection with your partner?*

continued

As you explore these questions, remember to avoid criticizing your partner's position, or defending your own. Listen carefully and express appreciation for the contribution each person brings to the marriage.

If you're the spouse who is complaining about your partner's long hours, try to express your longing in a positive way.

If you're the spouse who is working long hours, listen carefully to your partner's complaint, zeroing in on the yearning behind it. As you talk, don't focus on the behaviors that your spouse would like to eliminate—habits like evening meetings, cell-phone calls, or work-related e-mail during a family vacation. Instead, visualize the experiences your spouse might like you to have as a result of working less—perhaps a romantic vacation, relaxing evenings at home, or better relationships with the kids.

The key is to help the overworking spouse to understand this: *Your life is valuable far beyond what you contribute as a worker and a wage earner. You are also loved, appreciated, and needed as a friend, lover, confidant, co-parent, traveling companion, and so on.*

Couples who can share this sense of appreciation toward each other feel a strong sense of emotional connection. This, in turn, makes it easier to discuss conflicts related to work. Some may see their conflict in a new light and choose to make big life changes. Others may decide to maintain the status quo as Katie and Sam did, but they do so with a better acceptance of each other's feelings about the issue of work. When couples experience less criticism and more appreciation, a happier marriage becomes possible—*despite* the ongoing difference of opinion about how much work is too much.

The exercise at the end of this chapter, called "What's Your Mission? What's Your Legacy?" may also help. It's designed to assist couples in clarifying and communicating their priorities in life, including the value work holds for individual partners.

Quiz: Is There Too Much Criticism in Your Relationship?

The following quiz can help you see how well you and your partner state your needs (i.e., complain) without resorting to harmful criticism. Take the quiz twice. The first time, answer the questions for yourself. The second time, answer the questions the way you believe your partner would answer them.

PARTNER A		PARTNER B
T/F		T/F
_____	1. I often feel attacked or criticized when we talk about our disagreements.	_____
_____	2. I often have to defend myself because the things my partner says about me are so unfair.	_____
_____	3. When I complain, I think it's important to present many examples of what my partner does wrong.	_____
_____	4. When my partner complains, I often just want to leave the scene.	_____
_____	5. I think it's important to point out when problems are not my fault.	_____
_____	6. I often feel insulted when my partner complains.	_____
_____	7. I think my partner should know what I need without my having to say it.	_____
_____	8. I often feel as though my personality is being assaulted.	_____
_____	9. When I complain, I think it's important to show my partner the moral basis for my position.	_____
_____	10. I often think my partner is selfish and self-centered.	_____
_____	11. I am not guilty of many things my partner accuses me of.	_____
_____	12. Small issues often escalate out of proportion.	_____

continued

PARTNER A		PARTNER B
T/F		T/F
____	13. My partner's feelings get hurt too easily.	____
____	14. I often feel disgusted by some of my partner's attitudes.	____
____	15. My partner uses phrases such as "you always" or "you never" when complaining.	____
____	16. I think it's helpful to point out ways my partner can improve his or her personality.	____
____	17. When I complain to my partner, I think it's helpful to mention examples of other people who do things the way I'd like them to be done.	____
____	18. I often think to myself, "Who needs all this conflict?"	____
____	19. If I have to ask my partner for a compliment or a favor, then it really doesn't count.	____
____	20. I often feel disrespected by my partner.	____

SCORING: If you have more than four "true" answers either time you take the test, you may have a problem with too much criticism in your relationship. Use the tips in the section titled "Healthy Complaining Versus Harmful Complaining" to reduce the criticism.

Exercise: Listen for the Longing Behind Your Partner's Complaints

Below is a list of common marital complaints. Often partners complain because they long for something good or healing to happen in their relationship. Here are some examples of such complaints, followed by the positive desire the complainer has for the relationship:

Complaint: Why do you always let the garbage pile up like this?

Longing: I wish that we could feel more like teammates taking care of our house.

34

Complaint: You never call me during the day.

Longing: I wish we could feel close to each other, even when we're apart.

Complaint: I'm tired of making dinner every night.

Longing: I'd like to go out to dinner with you, as we did when we were dating.

Now, see if you can imagine the positive desire behind the following complaints. Take turns reading a complaint out loud and have your partner supply the longing behind the complaint.

Complaint: It seems like so long since we've had any fun.

Longing: _____

Complaint: We haven't had sex in weeks. What's wrong with you?

Longing: _____

Complaint: I never seem to get personal presents for my birthday.

Longing: _____

Complaint: I'm just too tired to go grocery shopping.

Longing: _____

Complaint: If you keep spending like this, we'll go bankrupt.

Longing: _____

Complaint: I hate it when your mother drops by without calling first.

Longing: _____

Now list some complaints you commonly hear from your partner. Then each of you write a statement about the longing that's behind that complaint.

Complaint: _____
Longing: _____

Complaint: _____
Longing: _____

Complaint: _____
Longing: _____

Complaint: _____
Longing: _____

Complaint: _____
Longing: _____

Complaint: _____
Longing: _____

Exercise: What's Your Mission? What's Your Legacy?

This exercise comes from Julie's experience counseling patients with terminal illness. She saw that most people, in the face of their own deaths, have little trouble setting priorities. They know what matters most.

Through our workshops, we've learned that visualizing the end of your own life may have similar benefits. You come to understand your own values better. And that helps you make choices about how to spend your time.

Read the following questions and jot down your ideas. Then discuss your ideas with your partner.

1. Imagine that a doctor has just told you that you have only six months to live. How would you choose to spend that time?

2. Imagine opening the newspaper the day after you die and seeing your own obituary. How would you like that obituary to read? How would you like people to think of your life, to remember you? What legacy would you like to leave behind?

3. Using ideas from steps one and two, write a mission statement for your life. What is your purpose? What is your life's meaning? What are the most important things you'd like to accomplish? What elements of your current life matter most to you? What matters least?

CHAPTER 2

"Will We Ever Get Over Your Affair?"

Maybe it was good fortune that David wanted most in a wife. That's certainly what attracted him to Candace when they first met at a church youth group when they were both sixteen years old.

"We were playing poker and Candace drew four aces and the joker," David recalls. "That really made an impression on me!"

Candace remembers the teenaged David as a soft-spoken, gentle boy. That notion never changed. "I've always thought of him as a good person, the sweetest man there is," she says. "He's really kind to me—my sweetheart and my best friend."

So imagine Candace's shock when, at forty, she learned that David was having an affair.

"It happened about two years ago," says David, a Pittsburgh-area real estate salesman. He'd been under a lot of pressure at the time. He had just invested—and lost—most of their retirement savings in a land deal that went sour.

"I hadn't fairly consulted with Candace, and I felt so bad about it," David said. Then he met a woman at his office who was willing to listen. "She really sympathized with me and I got involved with her. I never thought it was going to go that way, but unfortunately it did."

Candace found out about the affair in a phone call from the woman's husband. Feeling shattered, she confronted David. He didn't try to deny it. In fact, he confessed and ended the relationship with the other woman right away.

Then David and Candace went to work, doing everything they could think of to get their marriage back on track. Over the next two years they read every book they could find about healing their marriage. They went to marriage workshops. They even began co-teaching a class on marriage at their church. Still, it seemed a struggle to recover from the emotional upheaval the affair had caused. While David wrestled with feelings of guilt, Candace felt haunted by a recurring sense of betrayal.

Neither partner reports having had serious problems in their marriage prior to David's fling. Married at nineteen, the couple had two sons in their first four years together. David's sales job required lots of travel to other states, so he took his young family with him. Both he and Candace remember those early years as happy times, traveling by car, staying in motels, enjoying their time together. After

What's the Problem?

- David and Candace avoid conflict; they don't share negative feelings.
- When Candace brings up a problem, David gets stressed.
- Instead of expressing understanding, David tries to reassure Candace that everything is OK.
- Candace feels unheard, frustrated.
- Candace gets stressed and shuts down.
- Emotional distance grows—a problem that contributed to David's affair.

What's the Solution?

- Say what you're feeling, what you need, even if it's difficult to handle.
- Listen and respond to each other's feelings and needs before you rush to reassure and before you try to solve problems.
- Recognize when you're stressed, and take steps to relax.
- Expect more, not less, from your marriage.

39

the boys started school, Candace went to college and became a nurse while David concentrated on starting his real estate business.

Candace tells us they always tried to be "realistic" about marriage. "As you age, those big, passionate, 'teenage crush' feelings naturally go away—that's to be expected," she says. So, by their late thirties, she wasn't surprised that their romantic feelings for each other had waned. Having a strong friendship seemed good enough.

When she learned of David's affair, however, all of her ideas about a passionless marriage went up in smoke. "Now I could see that David still had the capacity for romance," Candace explains. "Passion doesn't have to go away just because we're growing older."

David swears he has totally recommitted to his marriage, and Candace seems to trust that that's true. Still, she finds herself wanting more from him than she ever needed before. In the aftermath of the affair, she needs to know on a much deeper level that she's number one.

David seems eager to reassure Candace, but he also admits that he has a hard time conveying his romantic feelings for her. Why? Both believe their hectic lifestyle is part of the problem. David claims they're always so busy trying to "get their ducks in a row" that they never take time for each other.

But we suspect there may be other obstacles to greater emotional intimacy. To find out, we ask Candace and David to talk to each other about a recent conflict. They start by discussing an incident that happened in the hotel room that morning, just before they came to the Love Lab.

What They Say	What We Notice
Candace: This morning I asked if you would massage my feet after you made your telephone calls. But it would have just thrilled my heart if you would have done the massage first. It would have made me feel like I was more important than the calls.	+ Good start; clearly expresses feelings. + States her need.
David: The problem is, you said, "You can do it after you call the office." And I already had my schedule planned out. But I wouldn't have minded doing that for you.	− Defensive. − Ignores her feelings of disappointment. − Responds with his own complaint. + Expresses willingness to respond to her request.
Candace: But that would have interrupted your plans.	− Doesn't acknowledge his willingness. − Slightly defensive. − Backs away from expressing her needs.
David: You said up front that it was OK for me to do these other things first. Then you seemed to get irritated. That's *my* source of irritation. You want me to read your mind. But I think we do pretty good over all, don't you?	− Slightly defensive. + States his complaint. − Tries to sweep the problem under the rug by praising the relationship. − Still doesn't acknowledge her feelings of disappointment. + Asks for reassurance, but is he asking for the suppression of emotion?

continued

What They Say	What We Notice
Candace: *(Nods yes.)*	− Stifles her feelings. − Doesn't respond to his attempt to deny their problems.
David: There are just certain things that we have problems with. Maybe we just need more communication.	− Minimizes her feelings. + Hesitantly refers to the problem again. − Tries prematurely to put a lid on the problem.
Candace *(through tears)*: I just feel . . . it makes me very sad when I am not your highest priority.	+ Tries again *(courageously)* to communicate her needs and feelings.
David: Do you feel like I do this a lot?	+ Asks a question without being defensive.
Candace *(wiping tears away)*: Most of the time you make me a high priority.	+/− Reassures him, but backs away from discussing her need.
David *(softly)*: Can you give me an example of when you think I don't?	+ Invites feedback without being defensive.
Candace: *(She sighs and says nothing.)*	− Still stifles her expression of sadness.

What They Say	What We Notice
David: I try to be flexible and I think I am. But if I don't understand, then maybe I'm not listening as well as I should.	– Somewhat defensive. +/– Takes responsibility, but in a general, vague way.
Candace: I don't know why I'm so tearful today. *(Long silence.)* I've lost my train of thought, I think.	– Stress causes her to "flood"; becoming upset interferes with her thinking and communication. – Doesn't ask for what she needs.

Our Analysis: Sidestepping Difficult Feelings Blocks Emotional Intimacy

On the surface, this couple seems to be handling their differences well. They show lots of concern and affection for each other; their tone is sweet and caring. Looking more closely, however, we can see the source of emotional distance: David and Candace are so intent on avoiding bad feelings that they're sidestepping issues that really need discussion. And David, especially, seems to be in such a rush to reassure Candace, he misses opportunities to demonstrate just how much he really cares.

Optimistic by nature, David and Candace have always placed a high value on getting along. And after David's affair threatened the security of their relationship, being accommodating and reassuring feels more important than ever. But when couples consistently avoid problems, they develop a habit of squelching their negative feelings. This creates emotional distance, which is a high price to pay for avoiding conflict. The price includes a sense of loneliness and a lack of romance. It's hard to be passionate toward your spouse when you don't feel close anymore.

Still, Candace has decided she will use this visit to the Love Lab as an opportunity to tell David what she needs. And in the dialogue above, she bravely states that she wants his physical affection, starting with a foot massage. Despite his initial defensiveness about the way Candace makes her request, David shows that he's open to her request. But he doesn't acknowledge how Candace is feeling in the moment. For example, he doesn't say, "I can see that you felt sad when I didn't stop and pay attention," or "I'm sorry that I missed your cue. That must have hurt your feelings."

Our guess is that David feels it's too risky to engage Candace in a conversation about her sadness. His heart rate, which we measured via electrodes attached to his chest and fingers, shows this may be true. At the beginning of the conversation it was already 100 beats per minute, which is higher than average—perhaps because he finds it stressful to be in the lab, poised to talk about problems. But it jumps even higher, up to 121 beats per minute, when Candace starts telling David about her disappointment. Such spikes are a sign of "diffuse physiological arousal," or "flooding." In other words, emotional stress has caused the many parts of his nervous system to become so overloaded that it's difficult for him to think straight and communicate, so he tries to put a lid on the conversation. But his attempts to reassure Candace and to repair the interaction don't do the trick because he's jumping to the conclusion. "I think we do pretty good, don't you?" he asks Candace. But nothing has happened yet to make *her* feel that things are pretty good.

What's the result? Candace doesn't seem to notice consciously that her needs have been dismissed. By all appearances, David is being his old sweet, reassuring self. So, despite her sadness, she nods, as if to say, "Yes, everything is just fine." But her heart is telling her something different, so she tries once more. ("It makes me very sad . . .") Only this time she doesn't wait for him to dismiss her feelings. She does it herself. Our heart monitor tells us her pulse is racing at 154 beats per minute, which causes her to clam up, full of tears. With her heart rate at this level, she's probably secreting the hormone adrenaline, as well. This interferes with her ability to think clearly, and she withdraws. The interaction leaves both of them feeling hurt, frustrated, and confused because they can't see where they've gone wrong.

Our Advice

1. TELL YOUR PARTNER WHAT YOU NEED, EVEN IF IT FEELS DIFFICULT

It's clear to us that David and Candace need to do a better job of stating their needs to each other. Although Candace makes a strong bid for getting more attention from David, she backs down when David tells her everything is OK. She may be doing this because she wants so badly to get her marriage back on solid ground, but it's having just the opposite effect.

As Candace told us earlier, she and David gradually started to expect less romance in their relationship over time, believing that would make them happier in the long run. "Don't expect much and you won't be disappointed," they might have said. But now she sees that their strategy has backfired. And it's not surprising, considering what marriage researcher Donald Baucom has found. His studies show that couples who have high expectations for romance and passion in their relationships are more likely to have these qualities in their marriages than are those who have low expectations; and those with high expectations have happier marriages as a result.

Candace's habit of letting David off the hook does not make things better for this couple. Instead, it creates more distance. If Candace wants to grow closer to David, she's going to have to make sure she's heard by him, even if it creates the potential for more conflict. Avoiding the conflict will only make matters worse for them.

By the same token, David needs to let Candace know what's in his heart. Imagine what might have happened if David had been more open with Candace when he lost their retirement money. Imagine if he'd been able to tell her, "I feel terrible about this. I need your understanding. I need your forgiveness. I need your support." He badly wanted such sympathy at the time, but instead of turning to Candace, he turned to somebody outside the marriage for support. Because he was not able to express his deepest feelings to his wife, his marriage became prone to an affair long before the affair ever started. As marriage researcher Shirley Glass discovered, when partners avoid talking to each other about their deepest feelings, they put their marriage at risk for infidelity.

David and Candace say they understand this in hindsight. And they tell us they really want to change the way they interact. They want more emotional intimacy, they want to feel closer. But after twenty-three years of avoidance, how do they start sharing intense feelings with each other now?

One key is to believe that you can trust your partner to be receptive and nonjudgmental when you start to speak. You want to feel "safe" that your partner will listen carefully and with an open mind. She won't dismiss your feelings. He won't judge, criticize, or offer unsolicited advice. Once you achieve this sense of trust, you feel freer to stay with your feelings in the conversation and express them to your partner as they come up. Emotional flooding becomes less of a problem, which means you're less likely to withdraw.

To help Candace and David experience this, we suggest that they try another conversation in which they take turns at expressing what they need emotionally from the relationship and telling each other how they feel about the need. When it's one partner's turn, the other partner's job is to simply listen and ask questions that can lead to better understanding.

We give them some guidelines. We advise Candice, "Stick to your guns and don't withdraw. If David responds with reassurances that don't change—or even acknowledge—the way you're feeling, let him know that. You don't have to be unkind about it. You can simply hold your ground and say, 'I really want you to understand my feelings here.' "

2. "BROADCAST" YOUR FEELINGS AS THEY COME UP

To David we say, "When it's your turn, think about the emotions you're feeling and tell Candace about them as they come up. It's kind of like being a play-by-play radio broadcaster. Candace can't *see* what's going on inside your heart and your head. To help her follow the game, you've got to announce the plays." We explain that this may seem a little strange after twenty-three years of being the strong, steady, silent type in this relationship, but it gets easier with practice.

3. POSTPONE PROBLEM SOLVING UNTIL AFTER YOU FEEL CONNECTED

We encourage them both to stay with the strong emotions that may surface as they talk. Don't try to draw conclusions prematurely; doing so will be counterproductive.

And, finally, we advise them to avoid problem solving at this point. This conversation is not about solving problems; it's about opening a door to emotional intimacy and feeling closer to each other. Problem solving can come later.

David agrees to go first. Here's what happened.

What They Say	What We Notice
David: I need for you to open up and tell me what you're thinking. A lot of times, we just share facts. And sometimes when you start talking about feelings, you shut down. That really bothers me.	+ Starts gently. + Focuses on her feelings. − Still, he's not saying much about his own feelings, his own needs.
Candace: So you're saying you want me to tell you what I'm thinking and feeling? That's what you need from me?	+ Clarifies. *continued*

What They Say	*What We Notice*
David: Yeah. Like with the foot massage, it would have helped if you had just said, "I need some time with you right now. I need to feel connected to you. And you could help me feel connected by putting this lotion on my feet."	+ Expresses what he wants from her without blaming, without defensiveness.
Candace: Are you saying that it would have been better if I had said, "I need to spend some time with you right now"?	+ Clarifies his request. + Looks for reassurance that he means what he's saying.
David: Possibly. I think you were trying to help me get my work done when that's not really what you wanted. You didn't want me to do this massage as just another part of my routine, just another one of my obligations. And I keep telling you, you're not just another obligation.	+ Shows he understands her feelings. + Encourages her to ask for what she needs, even if it's not convenient for him.
You want to feel important, like you're number one. And I want to make you number one. This morning, if you had told me honestly that that you needed to have an emotional connection—instead of expressing it as you did—then I think I would have reacted differently. Does that make sense?	+ Tells her she's important to him. + Expresses his willingness to be influenced by her. + To connect, asks for her validation.
Candace: It makes a lot of sense.	+ Validates his attempt to connect.

What They Say	What We Notice
David: After I made the phone calls and you said, "Well, it's not important. I don't need it now," I felt bad, because then I realized that the massage wasn't something that you wanted me to just schedule in.	+ Talks about his feelings, expressing his regret that he didn't meet her needs.

(Now it's Candace's turn to talk while David listens.)

What They Say	What We Notice
Candace: I need to know from you that I am number one. I would like you to do that almost automatically. Instead of putting me in the schedule when I ask you to, I would like you—all on your own—to say, "Let's spend a little time together." I need for you to just be sweet and romantic. You know?	+ Clearly states what she wants—for him to initiate time for connection, not just respond to her.
I like to be touched. And when I'm stressed, or when I'm grieving, or when I have a problem and I need to explain things to you, I need you to physically touch me.	+ Clarifies what she means by "sweet and romantic"; i.e., she states specific need for physical affection.
David: Do you think that's something I don't do enough of?	+ Asks for more information.
Candace: It's just what I need.	+ Sticks with her statement of needs. – Still avoiding conflict by not saying, "Right. You don't do it enough."

continued

What They Say	What We Notice
David: OK.	+ Good feedback.
Candace: I need you to listen to me, but mostly to touch me. Rub my skin. It makes me feel loved. It makes me feel that you're paying attention to me. *(She tears up.)*	+ Goes deeper, telling him about her most intense needs and feelings. + Her willingness to share tears gives her communication emphasis (like writing something in italics).
David *(sweetly)*: I understand that. You wish that I would anticipate those things more frequently.	+ Expresses his understanding by reflecting back what he hears.
Candace: That's true.	+ Affirms that he gets it.
David: That's a common complaint, I think. That you say, "Why don't you just think of this yourself? Why do I have to tell you?" That kind of bothers me. That you believe I should automatically think of these things. Is there a way to resolve that?	+ Expresses that he understands. + Expresses his complaint. + Shares responsibility for finding a solution. − May be slipping into problem solving a little too early.
Candace: I guess I just want you to know me well enough to know some of the things that I like. I'd like to know me that well. *(She chokes up again.)*	+ Sticks with expressing her need. + Expresses her deepest need: for David to know her so well he understands what she needs.

What They Say	What We Notice
David: So that when I see you're under a lot of stress, that I would touch you more, or rub your shoulders, or give you a massage, or whatever.	+ Clarifies her need, showing that he understands. + Shows that he accepts her influence.
Candace: And it really irritates me when I see you taking care of everything else, when I haven't been taken care of. That bothers me.	− Misses the chance to acknowledge him for understanding. + Continues to go deeper, courageously expressing her anger as well as sadness.
David: Yeah. But when you're feeling that way, I need to know somehow. Maybe we can work out some kind of signal.	+ Expresses his need to be reminded. + Expresses willingness to find a solution together.

This time around, Candace has done a better job of expressing her needs, and David is much less likely to brush aside her concerns with premature reassurances. We got the sense that he was willing to stay with Candace as she talked about her sadness and her longing. This willingness allowed Candace to go deeper, which is essential to building a stronger bridge of emotional intimacy in the marriage. It's conversations like this that allow people to feel that their partners know and understand them.

In our session after this conversation, Candace talked more about wanting David to anticipate her needs *without being told*. This raises questions common to many couples in conflict: Is it fair to expect your partner to "read your mind"? Should your partner "automatically" know that you want a massage, a gift, a compliment, or sex? Unless your partner is telepathic, it might be hard to guess what you need moment by moment, so how could such mind-reading possibly work? And yet some people feel that having to ask for affection or sex takes all the romance out of it.

Our response is to encourage couples to look at the longing behind their dilemma. What Candace craves, and what most people long for, is to know that they are a top priority in their partners' lives. They want to know that they are not just another obligation, another "duck" to line up in a row. (This is especially important to Candace because during David's affair, she was *not* number one.)

While Candace can't get David to read her mind, she can expect him to make a conscious effort to place a high priority on her needs and desires. By paying close attention, he might notice when she's feeling down and acknowledge that. He might think of her during the day and come up with expressions of affection to delight her. This could be a phone call "just to say hi," a quick note via e-mail, or an unexpected kiss. He might simply ask her from time to time, "Candace, what do you need from me?" If he does these things out of his own initiative—and not because Candace is asking for them—his efforts can go a long way toward healing their relationship.

In this second conversation, David does a much better job of responding to Candace's feelings. But there's still a big piece missing—discussion of *David's* needs. Noticing this, Julie quizzes David about his omission: "I know you need Candace to tell you what she wants, but where is David in all of this? Don't you need anything from Candace? Do you need her to touch you? Do you need to share your feelings with her? Do you need her to listen to you while you tell her how it felt to lose $50,000?"

"Yeah," David answers quietly. "I need that, too. And that was the problem back when I lost the money, when I had the affair."

"When it was your turn to speak about your needs, you asked Candace to let you be a better listener," says John. "But what do you, David, need directly?"

"I haven't thought about that too much," David answers.

This isn't surprising. Like many men in our culture, David has learned to ignore his emotions and focus instead on problem solving and accomplishment. So when his wife brings up difficulties in their relationship, his first instinct is to analyze the problem quickly as she presents it and to seek the solution. David successfully resisted this inclination in the second conversation. But he draws a blank when we say, "Tell Candace how *you're* feeling. Tell Candace what *you* need emotionally."

He's aware of feelings of "stress" related to his relationship with Candace, but it's just a vague sense of negative stimulation going on inside. He has no language to express it.

"Maybe I need to just say what I'm thinking," David offers.

"That would be a good place to start," Julie responds. "Take your thoughts and broadcast them. Make them external, rather than just hearing them on the inside. The expression of emotions will come eventually."

Julie also advises him to pay attention to physical sensations that come up. "Do you feel tension in your throat? Your chest? Your stomach? Is that physical sensation a sign of sadness? Anger? Fear? Once you start to get a handle on this, tell Candace what you're noticing. Say, 'When we talk about this, I feel this tightness in my throat.'"

Such simple statements could be a window into David's emotional life, a way for Candace to know that he needs her comfort and understanding. That gives her something she can respond to. Also, Candace can help by occasionally asking David, "What are you thinking? What are you feeling? What do you need from me right now?" After twenty-three years together, it can be challenging to find new ways to grow closer. But such exchanges could open new doors.

Candace and David leave the lab knowing they have a lot of work ahead, a lot of healing to do. But their shared affection and commitment to strengthening their marriage is evident. We believe it will see them through.

One Year Later

Candace and David both report they've made major improvements—especially at expressing what they need. And David is getting much better at listening to Candace; he's less likely to cut her off with empty reassurances.

"Rather than just trying to smooth things over, we're actually listening and talking to each other," says David.

This, in turn, means that Candace doesn't get emotionally flooded as easily and she's less likely to withdraw from the conversation.

Candace says she still wishes David would be more passionate, more romantic. She would like more spontaneous expressions of affection from him. And David agrees he could do more to meet Candace's expectations. But, overall, both say they're feeling less lonely in their marriage, more in sync.

"On a scale of one to ten, our marriage used to be a four or five," says Candace. "Now I'd say we're at about nine."

THE HAZARDS OF
AVOIDING CONFLICT

For most of their twenty-three years together, David and Candace had the type of relationship we call a "conflict-avoiding marriage." In such marriages, spouses would rather sidestep disagreements than explore conflicts and the potentially difficult emotions that might surface. If they find themselves in opposite corners over an issue, they're most likely to "let it go." Rather than argue, they say things like "Let's just agree to disagree."

There was a time when relationship experts believed that conflict-avoiding marriages were fraught with trouble. They believed that unless partners consistently aired their grievances and worked out their conflicts, the marriage would be unstable. But research we conducted in the 1980s comparing various styles of marriage proved this wasn't true. We learned that as long as both partners were comfortable sidestepping difficult issues, conflict-avoiding marriages could be just as stable as marriages where partners faced their problems head-on. Conflict-avoiding couples can get by for years, simply by ignoring or minimizing their differences. Some problems in these marriages get resolved by "letting time take its course"; other conflicts never go away. Still, these couples stick together, finding happiness in their basic shared philosophy of marriage. They reaffirm what they love and value in their relationships, accentuate the positive, and accept the rest. This allows them to bump into areas of disagreement, resolve very little, and keep feeling good about each other.

But there are some distinct dangers to this emotionally distant style of marriage. One is that partners don't get to know each other as well as couples do when they are more open to exploring their emotional differences. They're more apt to keep quiet about their dissatisfactions and their unmet needs. Some may develop a secret "inner life" that they keep from their partners. And if they meet someone outside the marriage with whom they can share this hidden side, they may be at risk for an extramarital affair.

The hazards of a conflict-avoiding relationship often become apparent when couples face crises such as serious illness, a death in the family, job loss, or acute financial trouble. In the midst of such life-altering experiences, people need a blueprint for talking through feelings of grief, sadness, or anger, and finding comfort in their relationships. Couples who have habitually sidestepped such tough feelings may lack such a blueprint. Consequently, crises cause them to become even more emotionally distant from each other. They begin to live parallel lives, sharing the same space, but never interacting in meaningful ways. Couples in these circumstances often report feeling terribly lonely in their marriages. And some turn to sexual relationships outside their marriages for comfort and support.

That's what happened to David and Candace. Their conflict-avoiding style of marriage served them well for twenty years—until David's financial problems upset their world. Unaccustomed to sharing his troubles with Candace, he turned instead to a coworker for understanding. And in an emotionally charged atmosphere of secrecy and grief, he stepped over a line he never intended to cross; he became intimate—first emotionally, and then physically—with somebody other than Candace.

How can conflict-avoiding couples steer clear of such risks? We recommend they learn to share strong emotions like anger, sadness, and fear with each other rather than suppress them. We advise couples to practice telling each other what they are feeling and what they need—even if such expression brings conflicts to the surface, where they have to be acknowledged and managed.

We recognize this may be a struggle. Some people, like David, have trouble identifying what they're feeling, so they find emotional expression very difficult. The exercise on page 65 ("Identifying Your Feelings") may help.

Others may feel uncertain about the way their partners might react to negative expressions of emotion or strong statements of need. The exercise called "Give Me a Clue" in chapter 9 might give you some insights. And some may fear that negative emotions, if expressed, will result in escalating arguments that spin out of control and endanger their marriage.

If you're struggling to face conflict in your marriage, you may find the courage you need if you

* Focus on the long-term well-being of your relationship. Learning to express feelings, state needs, and address conflicts will help to build intimacy and strengthen your relationship so that it can weather hard times. If you learn to do this under everyday circumstances, you'll have that blueprint in place when you face the major crises that inevitably come up in everyone's life.

* Try discussing conflicts using the mediation exercise developed by social theorist Anatol Rappaport, which is described in the chapter 9 section called "A Blueprint for Handling Conflict."

* Keep in mind that you can get help from professional counselors or clergy if it seems as though problems are getting out of hand.

* Reaffirm the strengths of your relationship as you work through conflicts. This can be done by asking each other such questions as these:

   1. *What values do we share about the importance of our relationship?*

   2. *What do we believe is a fair way for couples to settle their differences?*

   3. *Can we identify other couples we both admire who have solved tough problems in their marriages? If so, what can we learn from their marriage?*

* Keep your expectations for happiness in your marriage fairly high. If you and your spouse expect to feel fulfilled and satisfied with your relationship, you'll be more motivated to work toward that standard.

THE AFFAIR-PRONE MARRIAGE

Before David's affair with a coworker, he and Candace would have described their marriage as happy. That's not surprising. Although research shows that people dissatisfied with their marriages are more likely to stray than those who are content, a happy marriage is no guarantee against extramarital affairs.

Research also points to certain characteristics that are most often linked to infidelity. Some of these factors have to do with the individual. Being raised in a family where having affairs is considered normal is one example. Having the type of personality that values excitement and risk taking over marital stability is another. Your social environment also has a big impact. If you're surrounded by coworkers and friends who believe that affairs are OK, you're less likely to stay true to your partner. The nature of your marriage is an important factor as well. People who feel emotionally distant from their spouses are more likely to look outside the marriage for a sense of closeness.

In her book *Not Just Friends* (The Free Press, 2003), marriage researcher Shirley P. Glass presented a compelling description of the way many happily married people unwittingly make their marriages vulnerable to affairs. The problems often start when coworkers form secret emotional attachments to each other by crossing small boundaries that are needed to protect their marriages.

"One way to determine whether a particular friendship is threatening is to ask, *Where are the walls and where are the windows?*" Glass wrote. "In a committed relationship, a couple constructs a wall that shields them from any outside forces that have the power to split them up. They look at the world outside their relationship through a shared window of openness and honesty. The couple is a unit and they have a united front to deal with children, in-laws, and friends. An affair erodes their carefully constructed security system. It erects an interior *wall of secrecy* between the marriage partners at the same time that it opens a *window on intimacy* between the affair partners. The couple is no longer a unit. The affair partner is on the inside, and the marital partner is on the outside."

Glass said keeping track of walls and windows can help you determine whether an outside relationship is a potential threat. "When a friend knows more about your marriage than a spouse knows about your friendship, you have already reversed the healthy position of walls and windows," she wrote.

By describing it this way, Glass not only shows how natural it is for people to get caught up in extramarital affairs, she also shows that it's possible to recover from an affair and/or to make you marriage affair-proof.

Couples in conflict-avoiding marriages like David and Candace's may be especially prone to affairs, according to Glass's analysis. That's because when something occurs in a conflict-avoiding couple's life that raises new issues (i.e., a baby is born, or one spouse is stressed at work), the partners keep from expressing difficult feelings or stating new needs in order to "keep the peace." But this lack of sharing can cause one or both partners to feel lonely. Meanwhile, the lonely partner may happen to have an intimate or exciting conversation with somebody outside the marriage. This partner may know on a gut level that they should let their spouse in on this development and the feelings it brings up. They could say something like "I had the most intense conversation with Chris at the office today. And it made me realize that you and I haven't talked like that in a long time, and that worries me." But, as we all know, a revelation like this may lead to a heated argument— something the conflict-avoiding couple wants to avoid at all costs. So the lonely partner puts off discussing the situation. And as a result, he or she now has *a secret*. As Glass would put it, the walls and windows in this marriage have been reversed and a boundary has been crossed— and that's just the beginning.

This is exactly what happened to David and Candace. When David began confiding in his coworker about the way he had secretly lost the retirement funds he and Candace shared, he constructed a wall of secrecy between himself and his wife. At the same time, he opened a window of intimacy with his coworker. She now knew more about the current state of David's marriage than Candace did. And Candace knew nothing about David's new relationship at work. It was the perfect setup for an extramarital affair.

Once Candace discovered the affair and confronted David, however, the dynamics changed. He realized that he didn't want to lose his marriage. So he did exactly what Glass recommended. He ended the affair and cut off all contact with the woman at work. Now he and Candace were back together again, behind that secure wall of intimacy that marriage should create, and the coworker was on the outside, where friends and acquaintances belong.

Breaking off the affair, however, was not enough to heal David and

Candace's marriage completely. According to Glass, the betrayal and deception that usually go along with an extramarital affair can create a post-traumatic stress reaction in the betrayed partner. To help this partner heal from the trauma, the couple needs to do a great deal of talking. The partner who had the affair needs to patiently answer all of his or her spouse's questions about the extramarital relationship—how it started, how it was maintained, and what it meant for their marriage. While such discussions are difficult, Glass's research shows they're essential to helping betrayed partners cope with the trauma and loss of trust inherent to infidelity.

For David and Candace, talking about the affair was painful, but it helped them to create a window of emotional intimacy from which they can view the shared circumstances now affecting their marriage.

Couples who want to heal the damage that affairs create usually benefit from working with a marriage counselor. In fact, several studies have shown that marital therapy can be quite effective in helping couples to recover from an affair. Researchers David Atkins and Andrew Christensen found that while couples who have experienced infidelity typically start therapy in a more unhappy state than other distressed couples, they also make quicker gains over the course of six months with a therapist.

Our own work has shown that shared therapy can create a safe space for the betrayed partner to express pain and get the answers he or she needs. At the same time, a trained therapist can steer that partner away from expressions of rage that would be harmful to their relationship. The therapist can also help the couple avoid "the Four Horsemen," that is, the four types of emotional expression that our research has proven to be dangerous in marriage—criticism, defensiveness, contempt, and stonewalling.

Instead, the couple focuses on communication that helps to rebuild feelings of fondness and admiration. Partners may be encouraged to say why they want to stay in the marriage, what they once admired and still love about each other. They can work on getting to know each other in a more emotionally honest way. This, in turn, eliminates one factor that puts marriages at risk for affairs—emotional distance.

Quiz: Do You Avoid Conflicts, or Do You Talk About Them?

Although our research shows that conflict-avoiding marriage can be a stable marriage, it can also lead to emotional distance, which sometimes puts couples at risk for affairs.

This list of questions can help you determine whether you (Partner A) and your spouse (Partner B) are more likely to avoid conflicts in your marriage or to talk about them.

PARTNER A		PARTNER B
T/F		T/F
____	1. I often hide my feelings to avoid hurting or inconveniencing my spouse.	____
____	2. When we disagree, there's not much point in analyzing our feelings and motivations.	____
____	3. Time takes care of most of our conflicts.	____
____	4. When I'm angry, I prefer to be left alone until I get over it.	____
____	5. During a disagreement, there's not much point in trying to figure out what's happening on a psychological level.	____
____	6. I think it's usually inappropriate to show strong signs of anger, sadness, or fear.	____
____	7. I just accept the things in my marriage that I can't change.	____
____	8. We've learned not to talk about issues that cause disagreements.	____
____	9. Talking about disagreements just makes matters worse.	____
____	10. There are some areas of my life that I prefer not to discuss with my partner.	____

continued

PARTNER A   **PARTNER B**

T/F   T/F

___ 11. There's not much point in trying to persuade my partner to   ___
     see things my way.

___ 12. Thinking positively solves a lot of marital issues.   ___

___ 13. Anger doesn't solve anything.   ___

___ 14. I prefer to work out negative feelings on my own.   ___

___ 15. In our marriage, there's a fairly clear line between the   ___
     man's role and the woman's role.

___ 16. We turn to our basic religious or cultural values for help   ___
     resolving conflict.

___ 17. It's hard for me to show when I'm angry, sad, or afraid.   ___

___ 18. Expressing negative feelings is selfish; it just brings your ___
     partner down.

___ 19. Expressing sadness, anger, or fear makes you appear weak   ___
     and ineffective.

___ 20. The best way to get over negative feelings is to ignore   ___
     them until they go away.

___ 21. We hardly ever disagree.   ___

SCORING. Count the number of items you and your partner marked as "true." If either of you scored eight or more, you may prefer a style of marriage that avoids conflict.

If one or both of you find you prefer this style, you may need to work harder at staying emotionally close and guard your relationship against extramarital affairs.

Recognize also that you may face conflicts that simply have to be addressed. When this happens, the mediation exercise described below has proven especially helpful for people who would just as soon not fight.

Exercise: Calm Down to Avoid Flooding

Like many people, David and Candace often experience "flooding" when they're emotionally upset. That is, their bodies release stress hormones into the blood, causing their breathing rates to increase and their hearts to race faster. It's all part of the "fight or flight" alarm system that we human beings inherited through evolution to mobilize our bodies to react in emergency situations.

Although flooding may be a natural response to stress, it's rarely helpful in marital interaction. In fact, research links the tendency to flood under stress with higher rates of marital distress and divorce. For example, in one of our studies comparing couples who divorced with those who stayed married, husbands in the divorcing couples have heart rates that are 17 beats per minute higher than those of their counterparts in stable marriages.

Flooding makes it harder to think, listen, and communicate effectively. One partner may fail to hear the other's attempt at humor or reconciliation, for example. Flooding also gets in the way of empathy or creative problem solving. It can cause people to feel "out of control."

To avoid such problems, many couples steer clear of stressful conversations altogether. They don't talk about conflicts or difficult emotions that come up in their relationships. But conflict avoidance can lead to emotional distance and loneliness, which isn't good for relationships, either.

An alternative is to develop a ritual of taking breaks when one or both of you are upset. This ritual can help you to calm down and to cope creatively with conflict rather than run away from it. Here are some tips for developing a ritual that works for you:

1. NOTE PHYSICAL SENSATIONS THE NEXT TIME YOU AND YOUR PARTNER EXPERIENCE CONFLICT. Do you feel tension in your jaw, forehead, neck, shoulders, or other parts of your body? Does your breathing become faster or shallower? Are you finding it difficult to concentrate on what your partner is saying? Is your heart beating faster than normal?* These feelings may be signs that you are flooding.

---

* In general, a rate over 100 beats per minute indicates that a person's heart is racing too fast for assimilating information and communicating effectively. An athlete's limit is typically lower—about 80 beats per minute.

2. SUGGEST TAKING A BREAK WHEN YOU'RE FLOODING. Do this without blaming or judging. See it as part of a positive solution. Over time you may develop a simple word or signal that communicates, "Let's take a time-out" in a thoughtful, caring way.

3. SET A SPECIFIC TIME TO RETURN TO THE ISSUE THAT'S CAUSING DISTRESS. Your break should last at least twenty minutes, because that's how long it takes for the body's nervous system to recover from the release of stress hormones. Agree with your partner on a time to resume talking. Don't postpone your discussion indefinitely; that can just lead to more distress farther down the road.

4. DURING YOUR BREAK, DO SOMETHING YOU FIND SOOTHING. Go for a walk, take a hot bath, or do some gardening, for example. Or you may want to practice these steps to self-soothing:

- Focus on your breathing. Take several breaths, inhaling and exhaling deeply and evenly. Your stomach should expand when you breathe in, and contract when you breathe out.

- Scan your body to find areas of muscle tension. Consciously make those areas more tense, hold the tension for a moment, and then relax.

- Imagine those relaxed muscle areas as heavy.

- Imagine those relaxed, heavy muscles as warm.

- Now that your body is relaxed, visualize an image or idea that makes you feel calm.

5. AVOID DISTRESSFUL THOUGHTS ABOUT YOUR PARTNER DURING THE BREAK. Repeating statements in your mind like "I don't have to take this from him," or "Why does she always do this to me?" will keep your stress level elevated and won't help you to calm down.

6. ONCE YOU'RE SURE YOU FEEL CALMER, GET BACK TOGETHER WITH YOUR PARTNER AND TALK ABOUT THE CONFLICT IN A RESPECT-FUL, ATTENTIVE WAY.

Exercise: Identifying Your Feelings

Sharing emotions doesn't come easily for some people—especially if they've been raised to ignore or discount feelings. Even those who *want* to tell their partners how they're feeling may discover they can't find the words.

We advise people to start by paying attention to physical signs of emotion in their bodies. The next time you're in an emotionally charged situation—an argument, for example, or a conversation when your part-ner is expressing a great deal of sadness—ask yourself these questions:

- What physical sensations am I feeling right now?

- Do I feel tension or discomfort in my jaw, throat, neck, chest, or other part of my body?

- Is there an emotion linked to this feeling? Is it anger? Sadness? Fear?

- What can I say to my partner about what I'm experiencing right now?

What you say can be as simple as "I feel very angry right now." And what if you're not certain about what you're feeling? You can express that, too. You can say, for example, "I'm not sure what I'm feeling, but I get this tight feeling in my chest when we talk about this."

Below is a list of words you can use to express what you're feeling. Some people in our workshops have found it helpful to write words like these on index cards and thumb through them when they're feeling strong emotions. In this way, they can find just the right word to express emo-tions, whether negative or positive. If you have trouble identifying the exact negative emotion, start with the word *upset,* and for positive emo-tions start with the word *good.*

NEGATIVE FEELINGS

sad	bored	fed up	fearful
crabby	put down	bitter	disgusted
grouchy	ashamed	restless	bewildered
anxious	guilty	trapped	puzzled
nervous	sorry	confused	upset
angry	frustrated	tired	

POSITIVE FEELINGS

happy	peaceful	grateful	joyful
stimulated	connected	centered	calm
warm	intrigued	appreciated	thrilled
loving	excited	energized	content
relaxed	strong	confident	loved
sexy	good		

Exercise: The Marital Poop Detector

David and Candace admitted that they tried to keep expectations for their marriage "realistic" as they grew older. This may have been a mistake. Research shows that people with the highest expectations for marriage usually wind up with the highest-quality partnerships.

One way to hold your marriage to high standards is to assess regularly how things are going. That way, you can detect small problems before they grow into big ones.

The following questionnaire, which also appeared in John's book *The Seven Principles for Making Marriage Work* (Crown, 1999), has proven to be a great tool for helping couples to do just that. We call it "the marital poop detector" because it helps you to sniff out problems at the first sign of trouble.

We recommend that you think about these statements often. Check as many as you believe apply. If you check more than four, plan to discuss these issues with your partner sometime within the next three days.

1. I have been acting irritable lately.

2. I have been feeling emotionally distant.

3. There has been a lot of tension between us.

4. I find myself wanting to be somewhere else.

5. I have been feeling lonely.

6. My partner has seemed emotionally unavailable to me.

7. I have been angry.

8. We have been out of touch with each other.

9. My partner has little idea of what I am thinking.

10. We have been under a great deal of stress, and it has taken its toll on us.

11. I wish we were closer right now.

12. I have wanted to be alone a lot.

13. My partner has been acting irritable.

14. My partner has been acting emotionally distant.

15. My partner's attention seems to be somewhere else.

16. I have been emotionally unavailable to my partner.

17. My partner has been angry.

18. I have little idea of what my partner is thinking.

19. My partner has wanted to be alone a lot.

20. We really need to talk.

21. We haven't been communicating very well.

22. We have been fighting more than usual.

23. Lately, small issues escalate.

24. We have been hurting each other's feelings.

25. There hasn't been very much fun or joy in our lives.

CHAPTER 3

"After All the Crises in Our Lives, We Don't Feel Close Anymore"

Mike and Maria arrive at the Love Lab exhausted. Parents of eighteen-month-old Tess, the Southern California couple has endured a litany of stressful events over the past two years. Maria's sister died from a complicated illness just six weeks before Tess was born. Then Mike, forty-three, was diagnosed with a heart defect that required open-heart surgery. Now Maria, thirty-nine, is struggling with a demanding new job as an officer for a financial services company. And Mike has the pressure of making a profit with his newly opened restaurant—a business he financed with investment from friends.

Reviewing the couple's questionnaires, we see that their lives are long on drudgery and short on fun. They have big concerns about their health because each has recently gained more than fifty pounds. Both have snoring problems, made worse by their weight gain, so they're sleeping in separate rooms. Feeling exhausted and unattractive, they've lost their interest in romance. In fact, it's been months since they've even attempted to have sex.

But it hasn't always been this way. In fact, when we ask Mike and Maria to talk about the way they met ten years earlier, they become

What's the Problem?

- Mike and Maria are dealing with grief, stress, and exhaustion.

- They have a crisis-driven habit of keeping a lid on feelings.

- They need deeper emotional intimacy, more sharing.

- Overworking, overeating, no exercise, and no fun have resulted in weight gain, loss of energy, sex, and romance.

What's the Solution?

- Reprioritize! Make big lifestyle changes, not small ones.

- Take time for relaxation, exercise, and romance.

- Go deep. Talk about your feelings.

- Connect emotionally before trying to solve problems.

suddenly energized and animated. Maria's face seems to light up in a rush of vivid, happy memories.

"It was one of those beautiful Friday nights in July—the first night of a three-day music festival," she recalls. "A beautiful setting. Gorgeous weather. Great music floating all around." Having arrived with a group, she and a girlfriend spotted Mike across an outdoor venue crowded with fans. In a silly mood, the two women started a game of paper, scissors, rocks to determine who would make a play for Mike. "We were both so interested in this cute guy with nice, long legs," Maria remembers. "Then he turns and starts walking straight toward us through the crowd. I took it as a sign from God!"

Maria didn't know that Mike had arranged to meet a friend in her group who was standing right behind her. Nor did she know that Mike was married at the time— although unhappily. That's why he kept his distance that weekend. But seven months later, after Mike's divorce was final, he found Maria through a mutual friend.

"Our first phone conversation lasted three hours," Maria recalls.

"We decided to have dinner later that week, but we couldn't decide where," Mike explains.

"So he called me back three nights in a row and we talked for hours each time," Maria says. "There was so much to say, we never did decide on a restaurant."

"Finally, we just had dinner at Maria's place," says Mike, smiling broadly. "Great conversation. Great wine."

"And extraordinary sex," adds Maria with a sigh. "For many years. We had a wonderful sex life. We're very earthy, very sensual people. And that was such a big part of our initial attraction—which is why we miss it so much now."

So how can they get it back? The first step, we tell them, is to acknowledge the cumulative effect of all the stress—both good and bad—that they've been through recently. They've had a baby, started new jobs, and survived Mike's heart surgery. All the while, they've been grieving the death of Maria's sister, whom they dearly loved. Individually, these are huge events that can take a toll on any marriage. Happening all at once, the impact has been devastating.

From this discussion, Mike and Maria move almost immediately into their concerns about their physical health. They see how the stress of the past two years has kept them from exercising and taking care of themselves. "The health issue ties into all our other problems," Mike explains. "If we were feeling healthier, we'd have more energy and feel more attractive, which would aid our sex life considerably."

Maria agrees. But because they devote nearly all their energy to their jobs and their daughter, there's no time for exercise or recreation.

"We've talked about taking better care of our health, and we've made a lot of plans," says Maria. "But we don't follow through."

Because this issue seems to loom so large for them as a couple, we suspect that a discussion about it may reveal a lot about their relationship with each other. So we ask them to talk about it one more time.

What They Say	What We Notice
Maria: The real issue is our health. And I'm assuming that if we pay attention to that . . .	+ Immediately frames the issues as a team effort.
Mike: A lot of other things will fall into place.	+ Validates.
Maria: Exactly. Energy level. Feeling attractive to each other. When we work together on something, we not only get the work done, but we do enjoy it more.	+ More good teamwork, a bid to join him in feeling connected.
Mike: Maybe that's the key, then. Because a lot of time when I have tried to lose weight, I've tried to do it on my own. But it's like a smoker trying to quit when there's another smoker in the house.	+ Accepts the bid. − Starts looking for the solution ("the key") before they've talked about their feelings; it's too early for this.
Maria: I know. We certainly haven't intentionally sabotaged each other, but it hasn't been as easy as it could have been.	+ Accepts some responsibility for the problem. + Avoids blaming.
Mike: And it does kind of work that way, intentionally or not.	+ Also avoids blaming.

What They Say	What We Notice
Maria: Diet and food is a big deal. But the bigger deal for me is getting into the routine of exercise. How are we going to do that? I got the membership started at the Y, but how do I push back against all the other pressures—like work—so that I actually make the time to do it? Once I get into the routine and start it, I believe I can sustain it. But it's overcoming huge inertia to start doing it.	— Continues in problem-solving mode, but it's still too early. — Not sharing feelings first.
Mike: For me, too. The problem is, we come up with so many great ideas and never follow through with any of them.	+ Validating. + Starts to express the despair he really feels.
Maria: I know. That's what I want help on. How do we actually hold each other accountable without saying "gotcha"?	+ Acknowledges his feelings. + Expresses desire for teamwork without criticism. — Goes back to trying to solve the problem.
Mike: Right. Maybe we could all get up at the same time so we could work out at least every other day.	+ Validating. — Still focusing on problem solving without exploring feelings.
Maria: In the morning? I need to get in to work earlier than you do. Getting up at 5:00 a.m. to work out is possible, but probably not very likely.	+ Clarifying. — But starting to offer resistance. — Resisting this solution.

continued

What They Say	What We Notice
Mike: And my best time for working out is morning. Because I don't get home until seven at night.	– More problem solving.
Maria: You're not going to get to bed at a reasonable hour if you go to the gym then.	– Resisting this solution, too, contributing to a feeling of hopelessness.
Mike: Exactly. Nor is Tess. Nor are you, if we're trying to do it together. So how about if we get up in the morning and at least have breakfast together? Then you go to work, and I'll take Tess to the daycare at the gym.	– Trying to be creative, and still problem solving, even though it's not working.
Maria: Then I'd take her to the daycare in the afternoon again? I don't like that.	– Still more resistance.
Mike: Oh God. Could we do it alternating days?	+ Starts to express frustration. – But jumps right back into problem solving.
(Silence. They stare straight ahead, looking absent, tired, bored.)	– No feelings; no emotional connection.
Mike: Heck! I don't know how to solve that one. But I know exactly what you mean. We need to spend time with Tess. And it needs to be good time. Right now if we're coming home and we're dead to the world, it isn't a good time!	+ Expresses frustration over this seemingly impossible situation. + Expresses shared values.

Our Analysis: Stress Creates Emotional Distance and Hinders Romance

First, we tell Mike and Maria how remarkable they are. It's unusual to see so much respect and acceptance when couples are dealing with a frustrating situation like this one. Under similar circumstances, many couples fall into a trap of blame, criticism, and defensiveness. But Mike and Maria don't take that destructive path. Instead, their habits of listening and responding to each other with respect reinforce their solidarity. They've got a terrific friendship.

Still, this conversation reveals some real problems. "There was very little emotion when you talked to each other," John tells them. "I felt like I was watching two people who had just had an 'emotion-ectomy.'"

We also notice how they zero in on problem solving before they've discussed their feelings. Mike, especially, seems intent on immediately brainstorming solutions. But each time he offers an idea, Maria responds with reasons why it won't work. She's not being belligerent; she's just trying to be realistic. They both appear very tired, as well. That's not a great state of mind for generating creative solutions. So eventually they fall silent, as though dealing with this issue is just too much.

"That moment of silence illustrated your dilemma in a really dramatic way," John tells them. "You seemed to be coming to the realization that you can't find time to exercise unless you take time away from the other things you're most committed to—your jobs and your daughter. No wonder you feel stuck."

What's the answer? Only Mike and Maria can say. But this much we know: They're going to have to bring some new insight and new energy to their situation. And that insight and energy have to come from a place of deeper emotional intimacy, more sharing. They've got to tell each other how they feel about the difficulties they've been going through.

We ask them to consider—once again—all the upheaval they've had in their lives in the past two years: a new baby, a death in the family,

Mike's heart surgery, Maria's new job, starting a new restaurant, and so on.

We also explore their family history and how that colors their response to stress. One of five children from a troubled marriage, Maria describes herself as the highly competent middle child who always made certain that her siblings' needs were met. She was also the most gifted intellectually—a distinction that had its costs. "My father always said to me, 'Of those to whom much is given, much is expected,' " she remembers. The pressure motivated Maria to do well in school and at work, but it also felt like a burden.

"As a young person, you were asked to play the role of this shining hero who cared for everyone, this superstar who made the family look good," suggests Julie. "And when you keep trying to play that role today, it doesn't leave much room for expressing your own needs or taking care of yourself."

Meanwhile, Mike is feeling tremendous pressure as well. His best friends have invested their savings in his business, so he'd better make a go of it.

So here we have two people who love each other profoundly, going through an extraordinarily stressful period of their lives. But instead of talking to each other about the feelings they're experiencing— emotions of grief, fear, anger, anxiety, frustration, and more—they carry on with a calm, brave stoicism, as if major transitions have caused no ripple, nothing is amiss.

What's the result? Emotional distance, a loss of intimacy, and the death of passion. Mike and Maria have become terrific teammates— sharing the responsibility of caring for their daughter and supporting their household. But they have lost their identity as lovers.

We know that Mike and Maria have the capacity to connect emotionally. Their vivid memories of their dating relationship—with its long, heartfelt phone conversations, deep sharing, and passionate sex— tell us so. But because of all the crises and change they've faced in recent years, they've developed a habit of pushing their feelings aside.

Instead, they have focused squarely on solving the serious problems that each day presented, believing they had neither the time nor the inclination for long, heartfelt conversations.

What's more, those same stressful life circumstances have led to poor health habits—overworking, overeating, getting no exercise, and gaining weight at an alarming rate. Their situation—especially considering Mike's heart condition—is putting their marriage, and perhaps Mike's life, at risk.

Our Advice

"View this as a wake-up call," John tells Mike and Maria. "You're in a marital crisis and you've got to treat it like one. Now is the time to make big changes in your life, not small ones. If you don't, things are not going to get better in your marriage. They're only going to get worse."

Mike and Maria's primary problem is the need to connect emotionally on a regular basis. But to do that, they've got to clear away the obstacles. They've got to reprioritize their lives, making room for rest, relaxation, better physical health, romance—and, ultimately, sex. And they've got to do it now.

To help them accomplish this, we recommend a broad-based prescription of lifestyle changes:

1. *Set better boundaries on the job so you can work less and enjoy life more.*

2. *Schedule weekly two-hour "dates" away from your child, where you can talk one-on-one without interruption.*

3. *Schedule quarterly romantic getaways together, leaving your child with a relative or babysitter.*

4. *Get on a healthy food plan.*

5. *Start exercising regularly.*

6. *Get medical advice about your snoring so that you can sleep better.*

And because they're so obviously exhausted, we also recommend that they take a vacation alone together as soon as they possibly can.

"You're both committed to your work, but if you're burning your- selves out, you're not being creative," John advises.

"And you're both such devoted parents," adds Julie. "But that means you'll want to stay healthy to watch your child grow older. So it's absolutely essential that you take care of yourselves for her sake."

Mike and Maria's reaction to our advice is positive. "You've just signed our permission slips," says Maria. "I'll tell them, 'I can't be at the board meeting; I'll be digging my toes in the sand.' "

And, presumably, there will be time for long, heartfelt talks as well. To help Mike and Maria practice, we suggest that they try talking about their health issues once again. Only this time we suggest that they postpone the problem solving. Determining logistics, like who's going to the gym when, can come later. What's most important is for them to focus on sharing their deeper thoughts and feelings about the issue.

Maria suggests this won't be easy for her: "There's this fear of being overwhelmed, that I'm opening up Pandora's box, rather than just loosening the tension on a spring."

Julie acknowledges Maria's fear: "The emotion may feel like a tidal wave. But emotions also ebb. They wax and wane in a natural way. You don't have to be afraid of them."

"But if you try to suppress them," adds John, "you often end up with this low-level depression or irritability. You pay a price for it."

"For me, that price is overeating," Maria admits.

John suggests the reason that Mike may have difficulty talking about his emotional needs, as well. "Here Maria is providing for the family while your new business may or may not work. So you wonder, 'Where do I come off, talking about my needs?' "

"You've hit the nail on the head," says Mike. "This immense disparity in our income is very tough."

"But we're asking you to put aside that tendency to keep your feelings hidden," says John. "Because the only way to be present with Maria is to get real about what you need and what you feel. Staying hidden is causing you both to become emotionally disengaged. And it's robbing you of your romance, your sex, your passion. You've got to become more vulnerable. You've got to say what you need."

Mike and Maria agree, and the two begin a second conversation, starting with a discussion of how their weight is affecting their health.

What They Say	What We Notice
Mike: Looking in mirrors is rather painful.	+ Good disclosure of his feelings.
Maria: Oh, I know. It's like a science fiction movie.	+ Validating. + Humor helps.
Mike: With bad casting.	+ More humor.
Maria *(laughing)*: I know. It is all those feelings of being a failure and being disgusting and just thinking, "Where do I start?" The problem is so big. Literally. *(Laughs)*	+ Good disclosure of her feelings. + Humor continues.
Mike *(sighs)*: Well.	+ More expression of feeling, perhaps sadness, without words.

continued

What They Say	*What We Notice*
Maria: So it's that sense of hopelessness. Having tried a couple times before to really get serious about losing weight.	+ Empathizes with him, putting feelings into words.
Mike: I feel disgusted because I quit smoking. So I know I've got the willpower to nail it. And here it is again. You know? It's bloody ridiculous!	+ Reveals more feelings—disgust, frustration, anger.
Maria: So you just feel annoyed with yourself and disgusted.	+ Summarizes his feelings, showing that she's listening.
Mike: I'm just flat-out angry with myself. Because there's no way that I should have allowed myself to get back into this shape, excuses or not. You know? Because if there's anybody who should know the meaning of being in shape, it's me. It's me.	+ Expresses more feelings. + Takes responsibility for the problem.
Maria: I know. It is scary. I've tried to just tell myself that everything is fine now. "He's fixed. You know, he's not going to die." *(She starts to cry.)*	+ Validates his expression. + Opens up emotionally, revealing her own fears, deepening the intimacy.
Mike: I have to tell you, I have not been that sure. I have felt the exact opposite. I have felt that my time is limited. I've felt that I am not going to be around long. You know? Whether I fix the weight or not. And it scares the hell out of me.	+ Joins her in this deeper emotional space, telling her what he fears, establishing that they're on common ground.

What They Say	What We Notice
Maria: Yeah. And it scares me for ourselves. It really scares me for Tess.	+ Continues to join him in this deep emotional space.
Mike: It scares me for that reason, too. And it scares me for you. I can't imagine doing what you did—how you watched me go through that.	+ Continues sharing feelings. + Tells her he admires her.
(They talk about the way Maria and his friends supported him through his heart surgery.)	
Mike: I get freaked out about your health, your weight, too. Tess can't . . . I can't . . . afford to lose you.	+ Continues sharing feelings. + Corrects himself to make it an even more profound statement of love.
Maria: So in addition to fearing the ultimate— that we're going to die prematurely because of not taking care of ourselves—there's just the reduced quality of life that we experience right now.	+ Continues sharing, broadening the topic. − Intellectualizes a bit, probably because she feels the need to lighten up.
Mike: Ummhmm.	+ Shows he's listening.
Maria: It feels like a huge loss.	+ Strong statement of feeling. + Avoids blaming.

continued

What They Say	*What We Notice*
Mike: And that actually gets me angry sometimes. At both of us, I mean. Because, it's like, damn it, this is important!	+ Strong statement of feeling. + Accepts responsibility for problem.
Maria: Right.	+ Validates his feelings, accepts what he's saying.
Mike: This is important for us.	
Maria: I know, and I make myself last on the list.	+ Validates what he's saying. + Accepts responsibility for the problem.
Mike *(flip, joking)*: Don't do that!	+ Uses humor that expresses empathy for her dilemma.
Maria *(laughs)*: I never learned how to put myself first. I never learned how to make it OK that I wasn't taking care of everything and everyone else around me. *(In tears.)* So it feels like I'm shirking my duty.	+ Responds to his humor. + Good insight. + Strong expression of emotion.
Mike: Ummhmm.	+ Shows he's listening.
Maria: And there are things that are left undone.	+ Expresses her worry.

What They Say	What We Notice
Mike *(sweetly)*: You know, I figure there is always something that's going to be left undone. We ain't gonna die with clean underwear.	+ Reassurance that she does fine. + Humor.
Maria: I will. *(Laughs.)*	+ Accepts his humor and returns it.
Mike: Thanks. *(Laughs.)*	+ More healing humor.
Mike: I just so much want to see us get back to where we were. You know? We do have to make time for us.	+ Brings the conversation back to the central issue—their intimacy and their feelings about it. + Avoids blame.
Maria: I know. I just miss that feeling of—just being in your arms.	+ Loving expression of her own need.
Mike: Yeah. I miss it, too. It's so much a part of what we were. The thing I really miss is that sense at the end of the day that it's OK. It's OK now. You can go to sleep.	+ Matches that loving expression with his own, making a deep connection.
Maria: I just remembered something that you said years ago—that your favorite times of the day were waking up and falling asleep with me.	+ More profound, loving expression. + Shares a loving memory of him, which incidentally helps him to tell her how much she means to him.

continued

What They Say	*What We Notice*
Mike: They still are. They still are. Believe me.	+ He responds with a deep, loving statement.
Maria: And I really don't want you to feel that you can't talk about how you're feeling. I know that I've conveyed a lot of that. As if I was saying, "What the hell do *you* have to feel resentful for?" "What the hell do *you* have to feel slighted about? Suck it up. I'm pulling every wagon in this relationship, so shut up and be grateful." And I am sorry for that, Mike.	+ Invites him to keep sharing feelings. + Takes responsibility for her part in creating emotional distance. + Apologizes for hurting him in the past.
Mike: It's OK. It really is OK. I understand. I think I had a pretty good idea of where it was coming from.	+ Accepts apology. + Expresses understanding.

By the end of this conversation, we're all fairly astounded at the depth of intimacy Mike and Maria have achieved.

"Until today, I had always assumed we were so good at talking about the whole picture," says Maria. "But now I realize we can go much deeper—that's not something we grew up knowing how to do."

They start off with humor, which softens the way to self-disclosure of difficult emotions like shame, fear, anger, and longing. Their willingness to be vulnerable to each other pays off richly. By the end of this short conversation, they've not only rekindled lost passion, but they're also starting to heal old wounds.

"This is the pathway for getting back to romance, passion, sex, and intimacy," says John. "And the great thing is, you have all the skills you need to do this at any time." "You also have all the love you need," adds Julie. "It never went away; it was there all along. You just have to remember to go to your emotions. It's almost like you have to imprint it on your brain: Feeling distant? Isolated? Lonely? Go to emotion. Go to empathy. Go to feeling."

One Year Later

When we follow up with Mike and Maria a year later, it's obvious that they answered the wake-up call. They've made a number of positive lifestyle changes that are reflected in their relationship and their physical health.

First, they're spending more time together just relaxing. In fact, when an opportunity came up to buy a small beach cabin a few hours from their home, they jumped at it. Now they're getting away to their computer-free, cell-phone-free hideaway at least one weekend a month.

"I had to realize that I have one of those jobs that's never done, and my family is more important," says Maria.

Mike had to make some changes in his job, too. Now he's got a manager to cover the restaurant on the weekends he leaves town.

Usually, they take two-year-old Tess along, but sometimes she stays with Maria's mom—giving Mike and Maria more time for conversation and romance.

Maria and Mike have also been finding time to exercise regularly. Mike goes to the gym midmorning after taking Tess to daycare. He also takes long walks on weekends at the beach. Maria sometimes stops at the gym at the end of the day before she picks up Tess. But she's also does a lot more physical activities with her daughter—like bouncing on a small indoor trampoline or dancing along to a "run, hop, and march" video. When Maria walks on the beach, Tess often accompanies her in a backpack.

The result of all this increased activity? Mike has lost ninety pounds and Maria has lost seventy.

But perhaps the biggest burden they've released is their stoicism.

"The session with the Gottmans made us realize that we had been through an incredible amount of change all at once and we hadn't really adapted to it very well," says Mike.

Adds Maria, "Keeping a lid on our feelings helped us to maintain forward momentum in our lives, but there was a price to pay for not acknowledging the extent of our pain."

So now the couple is making a conscious effort to share their feelings about life events—past and present. They're also sharing more appreciation, affection, and trust.

"We're definitely having more fun, less drudgery," says Mike. And the romance? "It's returning," he reports.

HOW A LITTLE SELFISHNESS CAN HELP YOUR MARRIAGE

All of us face major stress at some point in our lives—such challenges as a serious illness in the family, adjusting to parenthood, or a demanding new job. And most of us respond by giving more. After all, that's what we're taught. In a crisis, you step up to the plate. You do more than your share. You put others' needs before your own. Such tendencies are not only admirable; in many cases they're essential to a family's survival.

Things tend to get worse, however, when people adopt such crisis-mode behavior beyond the crisis—when they turn self-denial into a habit, when self-neglect becomes a lifestyle. As Mike and Maria experienced, ignoring the body's needs for physical activity, sleep, and a healthy diet results in exhaustion and illness. Overwork and continual self-sacrifice lead to resentment, emotional distance, and loss of sexual intimacy. So although it may sound crazy to people who value hard work and devotion to family, our advice is this: You need to be a little more selfish.

Taking time for physical activity is the great example. Mike and Maria firmly believed that their daughter's needs must come first, so spending time at the gym seemed frivolous. By skipping daily exercise, they could give that extra hour each day to Tess. Of course, during much of the time they spent with their daughter, they felt exhausted and out of sorts. And that's not the kind of parents they wanted to be. When they decided to take more time to themselves for exercise, however, the dynamic changed. Yes, Tess is now spending a bit more time in daycare, but now she's got a healthier, happier mom and dad— which is something every child needs.

The same principle applies to pursuits that bring you sheer pleasure—activities such as music, sports, crafts, gardening, or spending time with friends. When responsibilities mount, such "indulgences" are usually the first to go. But outlets like these can also be some of the most revitalizing. They provide you with the energy you need to navigate hard times.

So what's a good response when your partner says, "I'm going for a run," or "I want to practice the piano"? Try this: "Great! I'll watch the kids. And when you get back, I'll take my turn."

It's also important to make time for relaxation together as a couple. We suggest that parents plan a weekend getaway without the kids every few months. And we strongly recommend that couples plan "dates" at least twice a month—even if it's just to go to a pub or coffee shop for an hour or two.

The point is to plan for uninterrupted time together when you can reconnect. If you've been going through a particularly trying time with family or work issues, it helps to talk about that and how it's changing your perspective, making you feel. (See the exercise on page 93: "Keep Your Love Map Up-to-Date.") And if you find that you spend most of your time talking about the kids or your jobs, that's fine—as long as you each take the opportunity to share your feelings and be heard about the things that matter most in your lives. While such conversations are important at any time in your marriage, they can be especially valuable as you weather stressful periods or times of big transition. They allow you to stay in touch with each other.

That way, the storm brings you closer together instead of driving you apart.

Quiz: How Much Stress Have You Had Lately?

Evaluating how much stress they had recently experienced helped Mike and Maria see their marriage from a new perspective. Their problems weren't caused by a lack of love, or by a lack of trying. They had simply been overwhelmed by the pressures of a new baby, new jobs, Mike's illness, Maria's sister's death, and more. Once they acknowledged this, they felt motivated to make big changes to reduce stress and to take better care of themselves and their relationship.

The following test is a common one, developed by researchers Thomas Holmes and Richard Rahe to help people measure stress in their lives and to determine whether that stress might be putting them at risk for illness. Take this quiz with your partner to see how you score.

Keep in mind that people adapt to stress in different ways. Some have a high tolerance and don't seem to be bothered much physically or mentally by the kinds of events listed in the test. Other people can be very sensitive to stress, and they may experience negative effects at levels even lower than this test would indicate. The test is simply meant to show you how you might compare to the average.

If you have a high score (say, 300 or above) and your marriage is distressed, it may be that your relationship is not the source of your pain and unhappiness. Rather, your troubles could be based on an unfortunate set of circumstances you've been going through. Stress at high levels can erode your sense of perspective and interfere with good communication and emotional communication. If you think that might be the case in your marriage, talk over this list of stresses with your partner and take a critical look at your lives. Consider what you've both been going through, where you are now, and what you might want to do to reduce stress in the future.

Circle those events you have experienced in the past year. Then total the number of points assigned to those items you've circled.

Event	Score
Death of a spouse	100
Divorce	73
Marital separation	65
Imprisonment	63
Death of a close family member	63
Major personal injury or illness	53
Getting married	50
Dismissal from work	47
Marital reconciliation	45
Retirement	45
Major change in health of family member	44
Pregnancy	40
Sexual difficulties	39
Gain of new family member (birth, adoption, elderly relative moving in)	39
Major business readjustment (merger, reorganization, bankruptcy)	39
Major change in financial state	38
Death of a close friend	37
Change to a different line of work	36
Change in number of arguments with spouse	35

continued

Event	Score
Major mortgage	32
Foreclosure of mortgage or loan	30
Major change in responsibilities at work	29
Son or daughter leaving home	29
Trouble with in-laws	29
Outstanding personal achievement	28
Spouse begins or stops work outside home	26
Beginning or ending formal schooling	26
Change in living conditions	25
Revision of personal habits	24
Trouble with boss	23
Major change in work hours or conditions	20
Change in residence	20
Change in schools	20
Major change in recreational activities	19
Major change in church activities	19
Major change in social activities	18
Minor mortgage or loan	17
Major change in sleeping habits	16
Major change in number of family get-togethers	15
Major change in eating habits	15
Vacation	13
Christmas season	12

Event	Score
Minor violation of the law (traffic ticket, etc.)	11

SCORING:

Less than 150 points = low risk of developing stress-related illness

150–300 points = medium risk of developing stress-related illness

More than 300 points = high risk of developing stress-related illness

Exercise: Steps to a Healthier Lifestyle

As Mike and Maria's story shows, taking care of your health is important to a happy marriage. But changing your habits around diet, exercise, work, and relaxation can be challenging. Mike and Maria's experience also shows that it *can* be done, however—especially if you attend to the emotional issues that may be keeping you from making self-care a top priority. Once those matters are addressed, you feel more motivated to follow through on basic advice for healthier living.

Research on behavior change shows that people who set goals, make a plan, and then track their progress have the most success. We recommend you consult with your personal physician on a regular basis, and especially if you're starting a new exercise program or food plan. If you're ready to make some positive changes, the following tips and questions may help:

Tips for Goal Setting

- *Make your goals specific.*
- *Make your goals measurable.*
- *Think about the pros and cons of making healthy changes.*
- *Break big goals into little ones.*
- *Ask for support.*
- *Anticipate obstacles and have a backup plan.*
- *Make a daily plan and track your progress.*
- *Reward yourself for short-term and long-term success.*

91

1. WHAT LONG-TERM GOAL WOULD YOU LIKE TO ACHIEVE? Think about it in a way that's *specific* and *measurable*. (*Example:* Don't say, "We need to talk more." Say, "Let's schedule a date every other Saturday morning. We'll use the time to go to the coffee shop and just talk. Then we'll go for a jog, or hang out together at the bookstore.")

_____

_____

2. MAKE A LIST OF PROS AND CONS OF ACHIEVING THIS GOAL.

Pros	Cons
Example: Regular dates will help us feel closer to each other.	*Example:* It will be expensive to hire a babysitter each week.

For each "pro" on your list, close your eyes and imagine achieving this benefit. For each "con," consider how you'd respond to a friend with the same concern.

3. WHAT SMALLER STEPS CAN YOU TAKE TO ACHIEVE YOUR LARGER GOAL? (*Example:* If your main goal is to "get in shape," smaller steps might be "Work out with weights for thirty minutes three times a week; run or swim for forty minutes two times a week.")

_____

_____

_____

_____

4. WHAT OBSTACLES CAN YOU FORESEE? HOW CAN YOU BREAK THROUGH OR GET AROUND THESE OBSTACLES? It pays to have a backup plan. (*Example:* If your goal is to exercise and you usually walk outdoors, think of what you'll do when the weather is just too lousy. Will you go to a gym? An indoor pool? Walk the mall?)

_____

_____

_____

_____

5. NAME THREE PEOPLE YOU CAN COUNT ON TO SUPPORT YOU IN THIS CHANGE.

1. _____

2. _____

3. _____

Contact them and ask for their encouragement. Call them when you need a boost.

6. HOW WILL YOU REWARD YOURSELF? Make a list of things you enjoy that also support your changes. Think of rewards for both short-term and long-term achievements.

- Rewards for meeting my one-week goal (*examples:* massage, lunch at my favorite restaurant, a music CD, flowers for my desk):

_____

_____

_____

_____

- Rewards for meeting my one-year goal (*examples:* a trip to Mexico, season tickets, a week off to do whatever I want):

_____

_____

_____

_____

7. HOW WILL YOU KEEP TRACK OF HOW YOU'RE DOING EACH DAY?
Will you jot down notes on a calendar or in your Palm Pilot? How about a
star on your calendar for each day you meet your goal? Would you find it
helpful to keep a special journal related to this issue?

_____

_____

_____

_____

Whatever method you choose, try to

- Review your goals daily, remembering the reasons you want to
  make changes.

- Decide on your intentions for the day. (*Examples:* "I'll stay away
  from the doughnuts at the staff meeting," or "We'll spend at least
  fifteen minutes of uninterrupted time tonight talking about our day.")

- Review what happened the day before: Were you successful at
  meeting your goal? What worked? What didn't? What could you do
  differently today to have more success? Use this information to re-
  vise your goals as needed.

Exercise: Keep Your Love Map Up-to-Date

In John's book *The Seven Principles for Making Marriage Work* (Crown,
1999), we introduce the concept of "love maps"—our term for the part of
your brain where you store important information about your partner's life.
These maps hold details about your partner's life history, daily routines,
likes, and dislikes. Our research shows that couples who maintain accu-

rate and detailed love maps of each other's lives have happier marriages. They're also better prepared to weather difficult life passages, such as having a baby or losing a parent. Such important life events can change individuals' whole view of themselves and their place in the world. That's why it's especially important to keep your love maps up-to-date during times of transition. Doing so may allow you to grow closer during challenging periods rather than to drift apart.

Below is a list of questions to help you update your love maps. To benefit from this exercise after stressful or life-changing events, set aside some uninterrupted time when the two of you can take turns asking and answering these questions at a relaxed pace. As your partner searches for honest answers, do your best to listen and respond in an open and supportive way.

- How has this event (change, transition, loss, stress) changed how you feel about your life?

- How has it changed the way you feel about your role in your extended family?

- How has it changed the way you feel about your job?

- How have your priorities changed since this event occurred?

- How has it changed your views regarding religion, spirituality, or God?

- How has it changed the way your think about the future?

- How has it changed the way you think about serious illness or death?

- How has it changed your experience of time? Are you more concerned or less about what might happen in the future? Do you find you're paying more attention or less to things that are happening in the present moment?

- How has it changed your relationship with your friends or relatives?

- How has it changed what you need for yourself? (For example, are you less interested in material goods, more interested in emotional connection?)

- How has it changed your sense of security in the world?

- How has this affected your daily mood?

- What kind of support do you need from me as you enter this period of your life?

CHAPTER 4

"You Never Talk to Me"

Conversation wasn't a problem for Bob and Marilyn when they met at their small-town Iowa church in 1944. At age seventeen, Bob found fourteen-year-old Marilyn "very attractive, very jolly, and very talkative."

Whatever Bob didn't say during their wartime courtship, he conveyed in other ways. He came home on leave from the army with Marilyn's name tattooed on his arm.

"All of our dating was closely chaperoned," Bob remembers. "We'd sit on the front porch swing near the window with Marilyn's mother sitting just inside."

"She would pass by pretty often," recalls Marilyn. "Then she'd come to the door and say, 'All right, Marilyn, it's time to come in.'"

But one night before his leave ended, Bob borrowed a car from Marilyn's brother and took her out for a spin. Alone with Marilyn at last, Bob asked her to marry him.

"It took me about a minute to decide," says Marilyn. "I thought he was wonderful."

The couple wed shortly after the war, and had their first of three daughters one year later. For nearly their entire life together, they lived

What's the Problem?

- Bob and Marilyn criticize and insult each other.
- Each launches counterattacks of more criticism, more contempt.
- Over time, the marriage feels unsafe, so they withdraw and quit talking.
- Stonewalling and silence lead to more bad feelings, more criticism.

What's the Solution?

- Say "what I want" rather than "what I don't want."
- Resist the urge to respond with countercriticism, countercomplaints, or stating "what I want" in return.
- Instead, simply listen.
- Respond to criticism with the honest question, "What do you want?"
- Express appreciation to each other for listening and responding.
- Take steps to nurture positive thoughts and feelings about each other.

a sort of parallel existence. Marilyn was in charge of the kids, the household, and the family's social life. Bob focused on his sales career outside the home. With Bob's retirement, however, those lines have now intersected, and the adjustment has been hard.

Marilyn, now seventy-two, says her biggest complaint is that Bob won't talk to her. "Whenever I go out someplace, he always asks, 'What did you do?' And I used to tell him everything," she says. Recently, however, she noticed Bob doesn't do the same. "He comes home and I ask, 'How'd it go?' And he'll say, 'I golfed.' That's it. No detail. No communication. Nothing."

Feeling hurt, Marilyn decided, "That's not right. Why should I share the details of my life with him if he doesn't care enough to share his life with me?"

But Marilyn's not the only one feeling injured. "When I retired, it seemed like Marilyn took all the pent-up things she didn't like about me—and she dumped on me all at once," Bob, seventy-five at the time of our first interview, told us.

Marilyn agrees that Bob's retirement seemed like a turning point. "Now that we're together all the time, when I try to talk to him, he gets very defensive, very angry. I don't know how to deal with it."

"I get the feeling that she resents me being around," Bob says. "It's like I'm interfering, like I'm no longer needed."

It's not surprising that Bob and Marilyn's problems have come to a crisis at this point in their lives. Like other major transitions in a couple's life—the first baby, kids leaving home, and so on—retirement often brings marital difficulties into sharper focus. Problems that once seemed possible to ignore suddenly feel intolerable.

To better understand how Bob and Marilyn get along, we ask them to talk to each other about this problem they have talking.

What They Say	What We Notice
Bob: I'd like to know what you expect from me, as far as improving communications.	+ Asks her what she needs.
Marilyn: I'd like you to just plain talk to me—like you do other people. You just ask me questions. "What'd we get in the mail?" Or, "What's for lunch?" That's not communicating. It's not telling me how you feel.	+ Responds in a clear, specific way. − Slightly critical.
Bob: Yeah, but when I ask questions, you get resentful. Like when you get off the phone with your sisters, I ask questions because you never volunteer to say anything. I just want to be part of what's going on.	− Critical. − Defensive; takes no responsibility. − Globalizes the problem with "you never . . ." + States his need to be involved.

continued

What They Say	What We Notice
Marilyn: Well, when you're talking to someone, and I say, "What did they say?" you don't tell me. You say, "They were just talking." You don't tell me one thing.	− Counterattacks with a righteously indignant form of defensiveness.
Bob: I do, too. I tell you what happens on the golf course, how we got caught in the rain.	− Defensive; still taking no responsibility. − Not accepting influence.
Marilyn: You're mentioning one time when Fred was there. I'm talking about when we're alone. There's no communication, Bob. We go days without saying a word. If you go outside to work in the garage, and I say, "What are you doing?" You say, "Nuthin'." You make me feel shut out of your life totally. I don't know how you feel and I don't know how you think. The only time I know how you feel is when you become very angry at me. And I was—	+ Acknowledges that he did share some detail once. − Becomes defensive and critical again. − Imitation ("Nuthin' ") expresses contempt. + Complains in a specific way. + Tells him how she feels. − Criticizes him again at the end.
Bob: Well, I get angry because I know you're not listening to me. You start finishing my sentence and telling me what I'm thinking.	− Interrupts. − Countercriticizes.
Marilyn: But when you want to talk, you go on for ten minutes and I'm not supposed to say one word.	− Defensive. − Countercriticizes and ups the ante; she's unhappy that he doesn't express his feelings and that he talks too much when he does.

What They Say	What We Notice
Bob: You don't interrupt your sisters like you do me.	– Another criticism.
Marilyn: My sisters and I interact, Bob. With you, I'm supposed to sit and listen to you go on and on and on.	– Criticism and contempt.
Bob: Because I lose my train of thought when you interrupt me.	–/+ Although he's defensive, he tells her something important about himself.
Marilyn: Well, that's mutual.	+ Adds her own self-disclosure, shows they're in the same boat.
Bob: And when I do that, I get angry. Not at you, necessarily—just at my inability to express myself. A lot of the times you tell me, "That's stupid," when it may be stupid to you, but it's the way I wanted to express myself.	+ More self-disclosure. + Starts to try to repair the interaction. – Criticizes her, which interferes with his ability to repair.
Marilyn: And what about when I'm trying to express myself? You get angry at me and you get up in my face. And then you'll storm outside.	– Cross-complaint. – Defensive, critical.
Bob: That may be true, but I still don't like it. That's why I try to get away from it.	+ Some acknowledgment, taking some responsibility. + Tell her about his feelings; could repair the interaction.

continued

101

What They Say	What We Notice
Marilyn: I don't like it, either.	+ Expresses her feelings.
Bob: Well, me neither. I don't like to be called names.	+/− Still trying to repair, but turning back to criticism.
Marilyn: I don't like to be called names, either.	− Defensive. − Counterattacks.
Bob: I don't call you names, Marilyn.	− Defensive.
Marilyn: Bob . . .	− Defensive.
Bob: You *always* call *me* names.	− Escalates the criticism.
Marilyn: Please don't say that, because you *do* call me names.	− Defensive. − Critical.
Bob: Do you remember saying, "It's never going to change"? When you say that, I don't know where to go because it leaves no possibility.	+ Good switch to self-disclosure, letting her know how desperate he feels when she's so fatalistic.
Marilyn: Well, this has been going on our whole married life. And there have been times you've said, "I will change," but you don't. I'm willing to have closeness and companionship, but it's not there. I'm sorry, it's not there. I wanted it.	− Criticizes with global statements that go right to the heart of his fatalism. − Denies responsibility for their problems.

What They Say	What We Notice
Bob: I don't know how to change it, because I don't think you understand how I feel when you totally reject me by calling me names and telling me it's never going to change.	+ More self-disclosure. − Turns to criticism.
Marilyn: You keep talking about me calling you names, and—	+ A genuine inquiry; she wants to understand why he's saying this.
Bob: You do that. You call me a liar. You call me by my dad's name because you know it insults me. You don't understand what that does to me. It leaves me feeling that I'm totally unwanted. And I don't want to be rejected by the person I love. I could stand it from people in the world. But from the person that I love, it just does something to me on the inside. And I guess that's when I become angry, because I've—	− Interrupts her. + Specific complaints that lead to more description of how deeply hurt and rejected he feels. + Reveals his love for her, an attempt at repair that could have healing results.
Marilyn: You were angry before. And the last few years, I have tried to fight back. I thought, "I'll call you names, because you call me names."	− She counterattacks; his repair attempt fails.
Bob: What names have I called you?	+ A genuine inquiry; he's still trying.
Marilyn: You know.	− Bitterness.
Bob: No, I'm asking.	+ Stays with the inquiry. *continued*

103

What They Say	What We Notice
Marilyn: You have called me names for years.	− Criticism.
Bob: What names have I called you? I do not remember calling you names.	+ Stays with the inquiry.
Marilyn: You would say words that we were taught not to say.	−/+ Responds to his inquiry, but with veiled criticism, moralizing.
Bob: I wasn't calling you—	− Defensive.
Marilyn: What names am I calling you, then?	− Interrupts/defensive.
Bob: Well, you call me stupid.	+ Responds with specific complaint.
Marilyn: Well, you call me stupid, Bob.	− Defensive in a reactive way; not really taking in what he's saying.

Our Analysis: Attacks and Counterattacks Make the Marriage Unsafe for Conversation

Bob and Marilyn's conversation continues like this until we call a cease-fire and join them in the lab. "Was that similar to the kinds of discussions you have at home?" Julie asks as she takes a seat.

"Yeah," Bob answers sadly, and Marilyn nods. She looks sad, too, and it's little wonder. Both have said what they want from each other—somebody to talk to, somebody to listen, an end to all the painful insults and name-calling. But the trouble is, they've expressed their needs in extremely negative ways—by hurling criticism and accusations at each other.

To find out how these patterns developed in their marriage, we ask Bob and Marilyn to tell us a bit about their families. Bob describes his father as angry, judgmental, and unforgiving, and Marilyn chimes in.

"I think that figures into a lot of our problems," she says. "I can see Bob's dad in him and there are times when I tell him, "I wish I never knew your dad. It might be easier that way."

"That must really hurt Bob when you say that," John offers.

"I'm sure it does," says Marilyn, "and I mean it because I usually say it when we're in a big, big fight."

Later on, we talk about Marilyn's development from a quiet young woman who was afraid to speak her mind, to someone who became quite vocal about her needs.

"How did that happen?" John asks.

"I don't know," Marilyn replies.

But Bob has an answer. "Marilyn has always been very aggressive, very domineering," he says with a wry chuckle. "The whole family knows it."

John observes that Marilyn might be insulted by Bob's remark, but Bob is not about to apologize. Instead, he says, "I know she would be insulted. I just don't understand why she doesn't see it."

Despite such hostility, however, Bob and Marilyn show a vulnerability and tenderness toward each other that makes us realize how much they want to change.

"I don't want to grow old and not have a secure, loving feeling," Marilyn tells us. "I want a relationship where, when you hurt, the other person knows it. And when you're happy, they'll know that too."

Bob reflects on better times, but seems to fear what may be in store: "If we can't somehow learn to relate to each other without being so hurtful, I'm afraid that all our joys in this life will be obliterated."

There's good reason for Bob to worry. Their conversation has demonstrated three of the four behaviors that we call "the Four Horsemen of the Apocalypse"—behaviors that almost always lead to the deterioration of marriages. Bob and Marilyn have shown us criticism, contempt, and defensiveness. As for the fourth horseman, stonewalling—that's what their whole conversation was about: the way they withdraw and refuse to share the details of their lives with each other.

For Bob and Marilyn to find a better way to relate, they'll need a deeper understanding of how they're hurting each other. So Julie asks them to reflect on what just happened.

"Bob, when you said Marilyn was aggressive, you kind of laughed about it," says Julie. "It may have felt like a joke, but that joke also expresses contempt—like you're putting yourself above her and trying to make her feel ashamed of herself.

"And likewise for you, Marilyn. When you say Bob is 'just like his father,' that strikes him as a putdown, an assault on the person he's trying to be in this world. That's very painful and he's asked you not to do it."

Over time, such attacks cause people to feel psychologically unsafe in their marriages. With so much criticism and contempt in the air, neither partner feels like talking about things that really matter to them. They don't share their goals, their dreams, or their regrets. Bringing up topics like these feels too risky; they know all too well anything they say can and will be used against them. We saw a clear example of this in Bob and Marilyn's first dialogue, when Bob tried to tell Marilyn how hurt and rejected he felt. This would have been a great moment to reward his vulnerability with compassion, but instead Marilyn used it as an opportunity to attack him again. When people experience this kind of hostility repeatedly in intimate relationships, they learn to clam up and keep their emotional distance. Eventually they stop sharing even the smallest details. It's a lonely way to live.

Our Advice

Bob and Marilyn need to stop this cycle of attacking each other and defending themselves with counterattacks. That's the only way they are going to make their marriage feel safer and move out of their isolation.

After more than fifty years of marriage, it's not easy to change patterns of interaction. Still, we've seen couples at all ages change their marriages for the better, and we believe that Bob and Marilyn can do it, too.

For starters, we ask them to consider these simple steps:

1. TELL EACH OTHER WHAT YOU *WANT* RATHER THAN WHAT YOU *DON'T WANT*

For example, instead of saying, "I don't want you to call me names anymore," try saying, "I want to feel as if you respect me. As if I'm your friend."

This is easier if you focus on the present, rather than the past. Don't concentrate on what your partner didn't do five years ago, five weeks ago, or even five seconds ago. Think about what you want from your partner in the moment.

2. RESPOND TO EACH OTHER'S STATEMENTS OF NEED WITH OPEN-ENDED QUESTIONS

This may take some extra thought, especially while you're trying to break old patterns. Just remember:

- *Don't jump in by stating your own need. ("Yeah, well, I'd like to feel respected, too!")*

- *Don't react defensively. ("Oh, so now you're saying we're not friends anymore!")*

Instead, try to *truly listen* and *understand* what your spouse is saying. You might ask questions like "What could I do that would make you feel more respected?" Or "This seems important; tell me what my friendship and respect mean to you."

If you should find yourself reacting in a defensive way, stop. Take a deep breath to calm down. Then start again, this time with a simple question, such as "Can you tell me more about this?"

107

3. EXPRESS APPRECIATION TO THE SPOUSE WHO'S BEEN LISTENING

Tell your partner when you feel you've been heard. Say, "Thank you for listening to me."

These three simple steps can be used under just about any circumstances when partners need something from each other. Whether you're expressing a need for companionship, sex, a balanced checkbook, or help with the laundry, the dynamics are the same. State your needs clearly in a positive way; practice careful, active listening through open-ended questions; and show your gratitude.

In Bob and Marilyn's case, we anticipate that this formula might give them new hope that loving, respectful conversations are possible again. We want to demonstrate that they can talk about their needs without feeling as though they've got to defend themselves against attack.

Bob and Marilyn agree to try our advice in their second conversation. They decide to start by discussing what they want from each other in everyday interactions, such as sharing the computer.

What They Say	*What We Notice*
Marilyn: When I ask, "Do we have any interesting e-mails from anyone?" I would like for you to say, "Yeah, we've got one here from so-and-so," or maybe read it to me. That would make me feel more like part of the computer thing, because I'm not as involved in it as you are.	+ Good start: explaining a specific need.
Bob: Would you like me to tell you when there's something in there you'd be interested in?	+ Genuine request for more information; not defensive.

What They Say	*What We Notice*
Marilyn: Yeah. Just say, "There's a message here from Bill." And when I'm at the computer, I'd like you to be more willing to help me out—show me the things that I forget to do.	+ Good response, focused on her specific need; avoids focusing on what he doesn't do for her.
Bob: Do you want me to do this at any particular time?	+ Asks for more information.
Marilyn: No, just when you're at the computer. I would like to know sometimes what you're doing.	+ Tells him more about what she needs.
Bob: I didn't know that you really wanted me to show you how to do it. And I appreciate you thinking that I might know something about it.	+ Expresses appreciation!
Marilyn: Well, yes. I feel like you know more about it. And when I'm trying to do my photos, just kind of help me along.	+ Acknowledges his competence; a compliment! + Explains more about what she needs.
Bob: I'd be glad to help you. Of course, I haven't gotten into the photo reproduction as much as you have. So I'm not sure about offering you instructions on something that you've been doing longer than I have.	+ Responds with willingness to help her. + Acknowledges her competence; a compliment!

continued

What They Say	What We Notice
Marilyn: Sometimes I forget things, and you can figure out what I've done wrong.	+ Tells him she needs him and that he's capable; another compliment.
Bob: I don't think you're doing things wrong. It's just that you learn by doing. But I'd be glad to offer information, as much as I can.	+ Reinforces his belief in her competence. + Expresses willingness to help.
Marilyn: I think it'd be more fun for us if we did it together. That'd make me feel more a part of your life.	+ Expresses optimism in their relationship. + Expresses her need to feel closer to him.
Bob: I think that's probably true.	+ He agrees with her optimism!
(They switch roles, talking about something Bob wants.)	
Bob: When we're planning to go somewhere, I'd like to get some idea of what you think needs to be done before we go. So then I can work within that framework.	+ Also a good start; expresses a need while avoiding criticism.
Marilyn: Um, I don't understand what you mean.	+ Asks for clarification; avoids defensiveness.

What They Say	What We Notice
Bob: Before we go to the city to the doctor or whatever, I'd like to know what you have in mind so I can do my things around that schedule. Sometimes I feel like I'm in limbo. I don't know whether to go start some project. And it would help if you could let me know what you need to do and what I can do.	+ Describes his need in a more specific way.
Marilyn: Well, I will try to be aware of that, but we both know what time our appointments are. And I feel like there are certain things that have to be done before you leave the house, and . . . and I don't know . . . maybe if you'll tell me the things that you need to do.	+ Expresses willingness to be aware of his need. −/+ Starts to get defensive, but then stops herself and goes into a problem-solving mode instead. Good save!
Bob: A lot of the time, I start moving things toward the car before you're ready for them to be packed. So if I could just get some general outline . . .	+ Gives her more detail about what he needs.
Marilyn: Well, I'll try to be more aware of that, to let you know the things that need to be done before we can leave	+ She agrees to meet his need.
Bob: I appreciate that.	+ A genuine, heartfelt appreciation!

continued

111

What They Say	*What We Notice*
Marilyn: I know it can be a real hassle sometimes when we have doctors' appointments and a list a mile long. But it's something that we can work on together. I'll try to let you know what I have to do. I appreciate you thinking about it and wanting to make things better.	+ Acknowledges that they share the "hassles" of life together. + Expresses optimism in the relationship. + Expresses willingness to work together. + Expresses that she appreciates him!

When the dialogue is over, we rejoin the couple and John asks, "How did that feel, compared to your first conversation?"

"It felt better, like we were respecting each other's thoughts and ideas," says Bob.

Marilyn is impressed that they could make such an improvement just by discussing "small things" such as e-mail or setting out the luggage.

But this doesn't surprise us. "Here's the truth about marriage," says John. "It's the small positive things, done often, that make all the difference. You did everything right. You were saying what you need, you were asking good questions, you were expressing appreciation. These are things you have to keep in mind all the time. You have to do them as often as you possibly can. Doing so will prevent you from falling into criticism and contempt—which can destroy your relationship and make you very lonely."

At the same time, we recognize that Bob and Marilyn have been together for more than fifty years, and it's not likely they will change their patterns overnight. There will always be regrettable instances of criticism or insult, followed by blistering comebacks, and more hurt feelings. But if they make a commitment to switch to a more positive mode as often as they can, it will make a difference, John promises.

"Think about it like baseball," John suggests. "If a batter has a .300 average, he's having a terrific season—even though he's missing seventy percent of the balls! Communication in marriage can be like that—lots of missed opportunities, lots of failed attempts. But if you do your best and your spouse knows you're trying, batting .300 can work out just fine."

One Year Later

The following year presented lots of challenges for Bob and Marilyn. Two of Marilyn's siblings passed away, and so did one of Bob's brothers.

"When you're dealing with your grief, you sometimes get tense and short with each other, so it's kind of hard," says Marilyn. And yet she notices that they have been sharing more thoughts and feelings with each other than they did in the past.

"We also seem to be listening to each other better," Bob adds.

Bob says he appreciates how they can now talk about their needs in ways that are safe and nonthreatening. "You don't have to build a wall around yourself and leave all these problems unresolved," he explains.

True to our prediction, the couple says they still slip into their old habit of criticize-and-defend. But now, at least, they can see a way out of those hurtful arguments. And, even more important, they understand there are ways to prevent them from occurring in the first place.

"This is not something you can say you've taken care of once and for all," says Marilyn. "You've got to be aware of it all the time. It's an everyday thing."

THE ANTIDOTES TO CONTEMPT: FONDNESS AND ADMIRATION

The kind of criticism and contempt that Bob and Marilyn demonstrated in their first lab conversation is typically a bad omen for marriages. And yet, when we ask them how they met and fell in love, we see something that gives us hope. Marilyn's eyes still shine as she describes the young soldier who proposed to her as "wonderful." And Bob still gazes proudly at his wife when he remembers her as "very attractive, very jolly, and very talkative." Despite all the arguments and bad feelings that have accumulated in recent years, the two still hold an ember of warm feelings for each other, especially when they remember how they first fell in love.

One key to a happier marriage is to keep fanning such sparks of good feeling about your partner, and here's why: Our research has shown that feelings of fondness and admiration are the perfect antidotes to contempt. When couples make a full, conscious effort to notice things they like about each other's personalities and character, and to express that fondness right out loud, their relationships typically improve.

So be on the lookout. Constantly scan your environment and observe your interactions. Rather than finding fault, look for evidence that your partner is getting it right. Catch your partner doing something right. Then express appreciation. Find excuses to offer compliments and praise. Examples might be the way she's fixed her hair, or the fact that he cleaned the snow off your car windshield. Maybe she went out of her way to find your favorite brand of ice cream. Maybe he offered to watch your favorite TV show when you both know he would have rather watched the baseball game. Try to notice all the small things that each of you contributes to your life together, and when you see them, let your partner know you've noticed and that you're grateful.

Quiz: Is There More Room for Fondness and Admiration in Your Marriage?

To assess the current state of fondness and admiration in your marriage, read the following statements and answer each "true" or "false."

PARTNER A		PARTNER B
T/F		T/F

_____ 1. I can easily list three things I most admire about my partner. _____

_____ 2. When we are apart, I think fondly of my partner. _____

_____ 3. I often find some way to tell my partner "I love you." _____

_____ 4. I often touch or kiss my partner affectionately. _____

_____ 5. My partner really respects me. _____

_____ 6. I feel loved and cared for in this relationship. _____

_____ 7. I feel accepted and liked by my partner. _____

_____ 8. My partner finds me sexy and attractive. _____

_____ 9. My partner turns me on sexually. _____

_____ 10. There is fire and passion in this relationship. _____

_____ 11. Romance is definitely still part of our relationship. _____

_____ 12. I am really proud of my partner. _____

_____ 13. My partner really enjoys my achievements and accomplishments. _____

_____ 14. I can easily tell you why I married my partner. _____

_____ 15. If I had it all to do over again, I would marry the same person. _____

_____ 16. We rarely go to sleep without some show of love or affection. _____

_____ 17. When I come into a room, my partner is glad to see me. _____

_____ 18. My partner appreciates the things I do in this marriage. _____

_____ 19. My spouse generally likes my personality. _____

_____ 20. Our sex life is generally satisfying. _____

TO SCORE: Give yourself one point for each true (T) answer.

IF YOU SCORE 10 OR ABOVE: This is an area of strength for you. Your feelings of fondness and admiration will protect your marriage from the bad feelings that may come up between you.

IF YOU SCORE BELOW 10: Your marriage needs improvement in this area. You may need to take steps to revive positive feelings that were more obvious to you when your relationship began, or to build new feelings of fondness and admiration.

Exercise: Three Things I Like About You

Each of you chooses three characteristics from the list below that describe your partner. (If you see more than three, save the others to repeat the exercise another time.)

Loving	Funny	Vulnerable	Lusty
Sensitive	Considerate	Committed	Witty
Brave	Affectionate	Involved	Relaxed
Intelligent	Organized	Expressive	Beautiful
Thoughtful	Resourceful	Active	Handsome
Generous	Athletic	Careful	Rich
Loyal	Cheerful	Reserved	Calm
Truthful	Coordinated	Adventurous	Lively
Strong	Graceful	Receptive	A great partner
Energetic	Elegant	Reliable	A great parent
Sexy	Gracious	Responsible	Assertive
Decisive	Playful	Dependable	Protective
Creative	Caring	Nurturing	Sweet
Imaginative	A great friend	Warm	Tender
Fun	Exciting	Virile	Powerful
Attractive	Thrifty	Kind	Flexible
Interesting	Full of plans	Gentle	Understanding
Supportive	Shy	Practical	Totally silly

For each item you choose, think about an incident when your partner displayed this characteristic and it pleased you. Jot down some notes about this incident. Take turns sharing the traits and incidents with each other. Describe why this characteristic in him or her pleases you so much.

1. CHARACTERISTIC:_____

    INCIDENT:

2. CHARACTERISTIC:_____

    INCIDENT:

3. CHARACTERISTIC:_____

    INCIDENT:

Exercise: Nurturing Fondness in Your Relationship—A Seven-Week Plan

Have you ever had a gripe or an angry thought about your partner that you just couldn't release? Perhaps you had an argument and afterward you just kept playing that same negative thought over and over again in your mind. Or maybe you were feeling sad or angry for some other reason, but negative thoughts about your relationship kept coming up as well.

Our research shows that continually replaying negative thoughts about your partner can contribute to a downward spiral of distance and isolation in a marriage.

One solution is to train your mind to replace what we call "distress-maintaining" thoughts about your partner with "relationship-enhancing" thoughts. Doing so takes time and practice, but it's worth it because it can build feelings of fondness and admiration in your marriage.

Here's a seven-week plan for making this change. The plan provides five positive thoughts per week, and suggests an extra step or activity to make this thought stick. Many of these steps involve writing a few notes or journal entries, so you may want to keep a separate notebook or blank book for this purpose. If you don't like to write, just spend some time thinking about these topics and visualizing your ideas.

Think	*Do*
WEEK 1	
1. I genuinely like my partner.	List the one characteristic you find most endearing and lovable. Write about the time your partner showed this side best.
2. I can easily remember the joyful times in our marriage.	Pick one joyful time and write a short description of it.
3. I can easily remember romantic times in our marriage.	Pick one such time and describe the details about that time. Do you remember the setting, the mood, the feelings you had?
4. I am physically attracted to my partner.	Think of a physical attribute that pleases you. Spend some time fantasizing about this aspect of your partner.

Think	*Do*
5. My partner has specific qualities that make me feel proud.	Write down at least one characteristic. Under what circumstances do you usually feel this way?

WEEK 2

Think	*Do*
1. I feel a genuine sense of "we" rather than just "I" in this marriage.	Think of one thing that you have in common with your partner. Write about it or start a conversation with your partner about that issue.
2. We have some of the same general beliefs and values.	Describe one belief or value that you share. Think about how it feels to know that you and your partner provide a united front.
3. My spouse is my best friend.	What secrets have you and your spouse shared?
4. I can easily recall the time my spouse and I first met.	Write down the details you remember about your first romantic encounter with your spouse.
5. I get lots of support in this marriage.	Think of a time when you felt your spouse was really there for you.

continued

Think	Do
WEEK 3	
1. Our home is a place where I feel relaxed and not stressed.	Think about an instance when your spouse helped you to relax after a stressful time.
2. We have common goals.	List two such goals. Think about how it will feel to achieve them together.
3. I remember many details about deciding to get married.	Describe them in a paragraph.
4. There are some things about my partner that I don't like, but I can live with them.	List one of your spouse's minor faults that you feel you have learned to tolerate.
5. We share responsibilities for our life together.	Consider the way that you divide up chores on a regular basis.
WEEK 4	
1. We have a sense of control over our lives together.	Think of something important that you planned together that worked out well.
2. I am proud of this marriage.	Describe the aspect of your marriage that you're most proud of.
3. I am proud of my family.	Describe a specific time when you experienced this feeling.

Think	Do
4. I can recall happy memories about our wedding and honeymoon.	Describe at least one thing about these events that you enjoyed.
5. This marriage is a lot better than most I've seen.	Think of a marriage you know that's awful. Think about the way you've gotten past problems like these.

WEEK 5

Think	Do
1. I was really lucky to meet my spouse.	Write one benefit of being married to your spouse.
2. Marriage is sometimes a struggle, but it's worth it.	Write about a difficult incident or period of your lives that you weathered together.
3. There is a lot of affection between us.	Plan a surprise for your mate for tonight.
4. We are genuinely interested in each other.	Think of something to do or talk to your spouse about that you both find really interesting. Have that conversation.
5. We find each other to be good companions.	Plan an outing or trip together.

continued

Think	*Do*
WEEK 6	
1. My spouse is my confidant.	Think of times your spouse really listened and then gave you helpful advice.
2. My partner is an interesting person.	Think of a topic that interests both you and your spouse. Bring it up the next time you can just talk.
3. We respond well to each other.	Write a love letter to your spouse and mail it.
4. If I had it to do over again, I would marry the same person.	Plan a romantic getaway for your anniversary or other upcoming occasion.
5. There is lots of mutual respect in our marriage.	Plan to take a class together (sailing, cooking, ballroom dancing, etc.).
WEEK 7	
1. Sex is usually quite satisfying in this marriage.	Plan a romantic evening alone together.
2. We have come a long way together.	Make a list of all you have accomplished as a team.
3. I think we can weather any storm together.	Reminisce about having made it through a hard time.

Think	*Do*
4. We enjoy each other's sense of humor.	Rent a comedy film. Watch it together.
5. My mate can be very cute.	Get dressed up for an evening out.

CHAPTER 5

"You Don't Care About My Dreams"

Whatever architects Steve and Denise first met, they were thrilled to discover they shared so many interests—a love of nature, hiking, and travel. Coworkers at the same firm, they even liked the same books—especially those that inspire people to pursue their passions. Add to this mix a mutual attraction: Steve distinctly remembers first noticing "the freckles under Denise's eyes," and Denise was impressed by the way Steve's smile "could light up a room."

"This is going to be my first *real* relationship," thought Denise, who had recently left an unhappy marriage. For Steve, "being in a relationship with Denise seemed effortless."

But as even the most devoted couples learn, marriage can require lots of effort—especially when life tosses obstacles in the way of your dreams. That's certainly how it felt for Steve and Denise when, after a year of marriage, they learned they might not be able to have children.

Years of expensive fertility treatments, along with a series of miscarriages, put a serious strain on their marriage. Grief counseling and marital therapy taught them a great deal about communicating their feelings and supporting each other through difficult times. And eventually they conceived a baby whom Denise carried to term.

Logan was two years old when Steve and Denise visited our lab. And Denise, now a stay-at-home mom, was four months pregnant with their second child.

Despite their trials in eight years of marriage, Steve, thirty-eight, has remained an idealist who's not afraid to say what he wants—and doesn't want—from life. He loves backcountry adventure, playing the piano, and volunteering in his community, and he would like to have more time for these things in his life. But lately he feels trapped by the never-ending demands of his job and family life.

Steve's restlessness disturbs Denise, thirty-four, whose mom was recently diagnosed with a serious illness. Denise sometimes feels overwhelmed by the day-to-day responsibilities of caring for her mom and Logan, and she's worried that she may lose her current pregnancy. She says she wants to know that Steve is there for her, physically and

What's the Problem?

- *Steve and Denise don't address the dreams within their conflict—his dream of a more balanced life, her yearning for more security and support in times of crisis.*

- *Steve's failure to address her needs upsets Denise.*

- *Flooded with emotion, Denise can't hear and respond to Steve's attempts to take responsibility.*

- *Conversations get stalled.*

What's the Solution?

- *Postpone problem solving.*

- *Take turns talking about the dreams within the conflict.*

- *Look for areas of flexibility.*

- *Find ways to support the spirit of each other's dreams.*

emotionally. But these days she's not quite sure. This tension has led to some serious arguments, and that has them both concerned.

"Our fights come out of nowhere, with lots of passion behind them," says Steve. "It's especially bad when we're feeling stressed—like when we're paying the bills or when we were waiting for the results of a pregnancy test."

Denise agrees. "Our arguments can be pretty explosive," she says. To learn more about their conflicts, we ask them to rehash a recent disagreement. Denise recalls the day she unexpectedly had to take her mom to the doctor. Meanwhile, she wanted Steve to pick up Logan at the babysitter's house. But Steve had other plans. He was supposed to volunteer for a cancer support group that afternoon, caring for a child whose brother was getting chemotherapy.

What They Say	What We Notice
Denise: I was actually kind of angry with you. I felt frustrated because you were helping this family in crisis. But your own wife is going through a crisis, too—hoping to hold on to this pregnancy, helping my mom, and we've got our own son to take care of.	+ Expresses her frustration. − Attempts to make Steve feel guilty. − Doesn't say what she needs.
Steve: I think everything you're saying is legitimate in the short term. My concern is our long-term goals. We've talked about our ideals—things like volunteering and playing piano and having time to play with Logan. And volunteering is a real big part of it. If I give up volunteering, it just sends me into this funk of "All I do is work." I realize that the day-to-day demands have snared me. I have these passions and I just get slapped down every time.	+/− Starts by validating her, but doesn't really respond to her complaint. + Expresses his needs. − Blaming. − Criticizes her.

What They Say	What We Notice
Denise: When you say "the day-to-day snares," I wonder, am I a day-to-day snare? That's number one. And number two is, you could have let this little boy's mother know that you might not be there. I mean, the weekend I found out my mom was sick again, I was supposed to be doing my volunteer work. But I just immediately called the person and canceled. I said, "I'm sorry, I can't deal with this. My mom is seriously ill." So I'm really frustrated. I know about your dreams, and I know it's really been hard for both of us to makes our dreams meet. But where am I in this? Am I hindering you from your dreams? Or am I part of them?	+ Expresses her fear. – Blaming, one-upping him. + Expresses her insecurity, her needs.
Steve: I agree. We could sit down and decide, does my volunteering fit in? And we could really talk about that.	+ Responds without becoming defensive. – Doesn't respond to her need for reassurance.
Denise: But throughout life, these kinds of things are going to come up. You're not going have enough time to . . .	– Ignores his response.
Steve *(interrupting)*: I think . . . I'm sorry, go ahead.	+ Stops himself from interrupting.
Denise: No, I'm sorry, you go ahead.	+ Shows willingness to listen to him.

continued

127

What They Say	What We Notice
Steve: I think we need to bring a little closure to this, and maybe I have some thoughts you might want to hear.	− Tries to close the conversation before hearing her out.
Denise: Yeah, we need to keep the conversation more to the issue of volunteering.	+/− Shows willingness to work with him, but she gives up trying to be heard.
Steve: I think, long-term, we need to ask, "Do these volunteer opportunities work?" But as far as the immediate need, I probably wasn't clear with you. I didn't tell you that I was prepared to pick Logan up that afternoon. My problem is I didn't communicate that.	+ Takes responsibility for the problem.
Denise: Yeah, I agree. Because inside, I was thinking, this is *my mom*! And I realize that this other family is in a crisis, but this is like, you know . . .	+/− Expresses more feelings, but slips into blaming again.
Steve: I wasn't picking up the slack with Logan.	+ Validates her feelings. + Takes responsibility.
Denise: I think I was so emotional, and it was just so hard for me to say, "I just don't feel OK with what you're doing."	+ Takes responsibility. + Expresses insight into her own feelings.

What They Say	What We Notice
Steve: I think when these things happen, we need to come together and identify the problem. Say, "Steve, there's going to be a problem in how we deal with Logan at dinnertime. I don't have an answer for that problem and then the two of us need to sit down."	– Moving into problem solving before they've explored all their feelings. – Puts the responsibility on her.
Denise: I agree. But what gets me anxious is I know your mind doesn't work the same way my mind does, so I'm afraid that there won't be enough time . . .	+ Expresses her fear.
Steve *(interrupting)*: There is nothing wrong with you saying, "Steve, there's a problem here." I'm not going to say, "I'll get back to you in three days." Once again, the problem is I was perfectly willing to deal with Logan, and I just never mentioned it.	– Interrupts her. – Tries again to put most of the responsibility on her. – Defensive.
Denise: I can't read your mind.	– Defensive. – Slightly blaming.
Steve: Right. I need to verbalize what my intentions are. I'm just not very good about bringing them out.	+ Takes responsibility. – Trying again to close the issue before they've really expressed their feelings.

continued

What They Say	What We Notice
Denise: For me, it's more than that. I feel like your volunteering is just creeping in to take more and more of your time. It's creating more resentment, and I just feel overwhelmed by that. Because I am trying to keep everything else going.	+ Keeps trying to express her feelings, even though the process isn't working.

Our Analysis: Ignoring Dreams Beneath the Conflict Stalls Communication

Unlike the "explosive" arguments they describe having at home, Steve and Denise have done a good job of avoiding hostility in this discussion. They're talking about some very difficult issues, and yet their tone remains civil. They don't attack each other, and they express surprisingly little defensiveness. That's a real plus.

But they're not making much progress. Much like Mike and Maria in chapter 3, Steve is so focused on solving their immediate problem (his volunteer schedule) that they miss the chance to talk about issues beneath the conflict. That is, Denise needs Steve's reassurance that she has his support—especially during hard times like this one. And Steve wants to know that Denise respects his dream that he can still have a life of joy and adventure, even with their mounting responsibilities. Although both partners are expressing their own needs in this conversation, they are not doing a very good job of responding to each other.

Upset that her feelings are ignored, Denise becomes flooded with emotion. The trouble peaks when Denise hears Steve refer to their life together as a "snare." In the seconds following that remark, the heart monitor Denise is wearing indicates that her heart rate jumps from 95 beats per minute to 115.

"Any heart rate above 100 is going to interfere with your ability to focus and to concentrate," John explains. Consequently, Denise doesn't respond to Steve's attempts to take responsibility for the problem. In fact, Steve tries three times to tell Denise that he made a mistake that day by not conveying that he planned to pick up Logan. But Denise never acknowledges these attempts to repair the relationship. She's so frustrated by his failure to respond to her feelings that she can't get on board with his efforts to move on.

As the conversation continues to go nowhere fast, it's easy to see how tension could build and tempers might flare—especially if they were having this conversation at home amid the stress of caring for their toddler or rushing to doctors' appointments.

Our Advice

"It's important to recognize and honor the dreams and feelings within your conflict," John tells Steve and Denise. Couples may try to brush aside such issues in order to deal with the crisis of the day, but that doesn't make the conflict go away. And until dreams and feelings are recognized and honored, the conflict is going to keep resurfacing in ways that are often frustrating and sometimes painful.

What is the best way to uncover hidden dreams? By taking a step back from conflict, and exploring each person's position on a deeper level. The conversation can include questions like "Why is this issue so important to you?" and "Is there some story behind this that I should understand? Is it related to something important from your past?" (See the exercise "Responding to the Dreams Within Your Conflict" on page 145 for more questions.)

Once both partners get a chance to express their dreams and each feels understood, then they look for areas of flexibility and compromise. The idea is for each partner to come away from the conversation feeling as if his or her dream was respected and honored in some way.

It's not the kind of conversation you can have on the run. That's why it's so important for couples to have time alone together on a weekly basis at least—time to talk uninterrupted for an hour or two about what's happening in their lives, time to share their thoughts, feelings, and dreams about their life together.

We suggest that Steve and Denise try an exercise we developed for just this kind of conversation. The topic will be the same as last time— their conflict over his volunteer schedule. But this time we encourage them to try to uncover their individual dreams within that conflict.

As with many of our exercises, we suggest that Steve and Denise take turns as the speaker and listener. When one is talking, the other simply tries to draw that person out. Neither person should try to defend what they did that day. Nor should they try to debate the issues or persuade one another.

"Think of this as a fact-finding mission," says John, "not a problem-solving session." And yet, once partners try this exercise and start talking about the meaning beneath their conflicts, they may find it much easier to solve near-term problems in the future. "Sometimes when couples do this exercise, we literally see their fists open up," says John. "And once they relax, their dreams emerge, leading to better understanding and compromise."

What They Say	*What We Notice*
Steve: What part of my volunteering has really created the most concern for you?	+ Asking about her feelings is a great way to start.
Denise: It seemed like you were more wrapped up in how this other family was coping with their crisis than what was happening in our own home—the challenges we were facing with my pregnancy and my mom.	+/− Starting to express her needs, but still doing it in a blaming way.

What They Say	*What We Notice*
Steve: So it sounds like you were sensitive to how I was prioritizing things in our family below my volunteering.	+ Reflects back her feelings.
Denise: Yeah. I had a sense that our family would accommodate whatever other obligations you have in your life. Telling that other family, "I'm sorry, I can't do it," didn't seem like an option for you. And yet it is an option for you to tell me or Logan that. Sometimes I wonder, is it ever flipped? Does your family ever become the obligation that *always* gets met?	+/− Trying to express her own needs, but still too focused on blaming Steve.
Steve: How does it make you feel when I prioritize the family that way?	+ Great nondefensive response.
Denise: I certainly understand that it's easier to do this to the people you're closest to. Because you know we love you and we try to be there for each other. But I also wonder, what if I really needed it to be different? Most of the time I can really handle things, but when I get into these emotional crises, I panic.	+ Expresses understanding for Steve's position. + Expresses love for him. + Finally says what she needs.
Steve: Was it just this instance, or are you worried about what might happen in a future, more serious time?	+ Good question to explore her feelings.

continued

What They Say	What We Notice
Denise: Well, I'm not worried about you leaving the relationship. I just wonder whether I'm lumped into all of the things you have to fend off. You spoke of your dreams. Well, what about the day-to-day living with me, just the ordinary stuff that we have to do? Is our life together as important to you as your dreams of traveling, or kayaking more, or volunteering more? Or am I really just one of those things that has to happen? Because I like to be at the top of your priorities, but sometimes I'm not sure.	+ Good, honest questions. + Reveals her feelings of insecurity and her need for reassurance.
Steve: So it sounds like you're scared that I associate you with the mundane obligations of life. Are there ways that I can help you understand that you are part of my passion? That being with you is part of my dream?	+ Shows he's really listening. + Strong reassurance. + Asks her what she needs.
Denise: Well, we've talked about the idea of really making time for each other. I like the way you always take Logan on Friday afternoons. And I know this really isn't about me, but it's a really neat feeling to know that I can look in your calendar and there it is. From twelve to five o'clock on Friday, you're going to be with Logan.	+ Now that she feels reassured, she can begin to move into problem solving. + Tells him what she wants and needs. + Expresses appreciation for him.
Steve: OK. I'll try to think of more ways I can do that for you, too.	+ Acknowledges her needs. + Takes responsibility.

What They Say	What We Notice

(Time is up, so they switch sides. Steve starts by talking about the way volunteering fits into his dreams of how he'd like his life to be.)

Steve: I'm the guy who always wonders why we have to work so hard, or why there is so much pain and anger in life. That's why I use that term "the daily grind." I know the joy I've felt when I've been on a hike with you and we're standing up on the side of the mountain. Or when we're in the kayak, or I'm playing some tunes on the piano. That joy is just so profound that I wonder, why can't I always experience that? My volunteering is a part of that. And it's a very impractical, very ideal way of looking at it. But when I see threats to my volunteering, it feels like I'm missing out, and that feels like a big loss.

+ Expresses his dreams, his desires.

+ Reassures her by including her in his dream.

Denise: If one of those items isn't there, do you somehow feel that you've been cheated?

+ Good questions; nondefensive.

continued

What They Say	*What We Notice*
Steve: I just have this sense that I've let things get out of balance. When was the last time we were in the mountains together? I think that I've neglected that part of my life for so long that I react to any little thing you ask for as "Wow, one more person that needs something." That's why I want to talk more about the way I've been equating you with the person that needs things versus what I want in my dreams. It really works both ways. I want you to be part of my dreams. I'd rather have you on a train with me in India or in a kayak on the Sound than sitting at home making sure there are no stains on the kitchen floor. When I'm talking about that train in India, I forget to tell you, "You're by my side. And if you're not, I don't want to be on that train." I just haven't been clear about that. I want to take you and Logan away. I want to go to India. I want to play piano and have all three of us downstairs playing drums and piano and dancing. I just want all three of us to be joyful. But it's amazing how the mortgage just keeps coming in every month.	+ Honestly expressing his needs. + Expresses insight about his feelings. + Expresses his desire to be close to her and to have her be part of his dream. + Reassures her that he wants to be with her. + Expresses his frustration with day-to-day demands.
Denise: I'm just wondering, if diapers have to be changed, and bills have to be paid, and floors have to be scrubbed, do you wish that all these mundane things would just go away?	+ Expressing her worries. + Asking about his thoughts and feelings.

What They Say	What We Notice
Steve: I just get this sense that I've neglected my dreams for so long that I'm saturated with the mundane things. I think if we just got a dose of regular walks in Magnuson Park, or a short trip to Mexico now and then, things would be better. I could bring myself back to center where washing dishes is no big deal.	+ Expresses his feelings. + Takes responsibility for those feelings. + Expresses willingness to compromise.
Denise: Right.	+ Communicates understanding.
Steve: It's not that washing the dishes is so bad. It's just I can't remember the last time I was on a train. Just a train ride to Portland! I've just neglected that for too long.	+ Expresses his feelings.

At the end of this conversation, we're impressed by the affection and interest Steve and Denise have displayed. It's great that Steve was willing to express his dreams *and* listen to Denise's feelings.

Steve says he found the talk "freeing" because he didn't feel obligated to find the perfect solution right at that moment. "I didn't feel like I had to make it go somewhere, so I was able to build my thoughts as I went along," he explains. "I could say, 'Maybe this is what's going on inside.'"

Both partners are more responsive and more open to each other's influence this time. This allows them to take the conversation in a positive direction instead of a negative one.

Still, Denise feels a bit worried. She hears Steve's affection for her, but she's going to need lots of reassurance that he's not staying in the relationship because he feels trapped; he's there because he wants to be. "I'm still afraid I'll keep him from those dreams and he'll reach a point where he goes, 'This just isn't good for me,' " she says. "We have trouble even finding time for little walks in Magnuson Park."

It's true. With a two-year-old and an infant, packing an afternoon picnic can feel like a major troop movement. But we remind them that this is just a stage their family is going through while their children are small. During this time, it's important to honor the *spirit* of each other's dreams—even if you're not in the position to make those dreams come true right now.

"If adventure is something that you both value, then perhaps it's something that you do in little pieces today—while continuing to dream of big adventures later on," says Julie. "Kayaking in Puget Sound may not be a trip to India, but both adventures have that same dreamlike quality for Steve. And he wants to share that with you, Denise. He's not about to give that up."

Steve's suggestion of a train trip to Portland is a great idea. It keeps his dreams of travel alive while they're dealing with diapers and nap schedules. And if Steve can show Denise—with his actions as well as his words—that he's there to share the responsibilities of raising the kids and caring for her mom, she'll be reassured that he's honoring her feelings as well.

Another key is to take the time needed to fully explore the dreams within the conflict. "You may not be able to do it the very moment a conflict happens—especially if your heart rate is 115 beats a minute," John reminds them. "When that's happening, you may be too flooded to think and to communicate clearly." So take a "time out" and promise to revisit the issue when you can talk calmly about it without interruption, he advises. The exercise on page 62 ("Calm Down to Avoid Flooding") may be useful. And the exercises at the end of this chapter can help you explore the dreams within your conflicts.

One Year Later

It's been a great year for Steve and Denise. Their new baby boy arrived on time, healthy and strong. Denise's mom recovered from her illness. And they bought a new home near the beaches of Puget Sound. They purposely chose a house with a big garage so they could keep the kayaks handy for spontaneous day trips.

Both Steve and Denise have quit their volunteer jobs—although Denise says she'd like to do more when the boys are older. "It may be something like distributing groceries for a food bank—something that Logan could get involved in."

The idea of taking the boys along is catching on. At age three, Logan has already been kayaking, snowshoeing, and hiking in the mountains. "We're not going off to India for a while, but I can see that we'll be doing a lot of wandering with the boys," says Steve.

The couple is also making a conscious effort to improve communication around day-to-day family needs. They now set aside time each Sunday night to discuss their schedule for the week ahead—a ritual Denise finds reassuring. "It helps us to see things down the pike that might create turmoil. Like if I have a doctor's appointment that's going to throw dinner off schedule, Steve might say, 'How can I help? What can I do to make things easier?'"

Denise says she still feels harried sometimes, which can lead to worries about her marriage. "But then the kids will go over to Mom's so Steve and I can get some time alone together. And I'm always amazed at how immediately we're able to connect again."

YOUR HIDDEN DREAMS AND ASPIRATIONS: THE "PRAIRIE DOGS" OF MARITAL CONFLICT

Our research shows that all marriages experience a certain number of perpetual conflicts—differences that don't go away, no matter what. Conflicts may differ from couple to couple; while one pair may constantly disagree over money and housework, another may continually clash over religion and parenting.

Since perpetual conflicts don't disappear, the goal is to live with them in ways that allow understanding, dialogue, and compromise. Failure to do so can lead to gridlocked conflict—a condition where partners are so entrenched in their own positions that there's no give-and-take. Putting up with gridlocked conflict is a bad idea because it leads to the kind of frustration, resentment, and anger that can be very harmful to a marriage.

So how do you avoid—or break out of—such gridlock? One of the best ways is to explore the dreams within your disagreements. By dreams, we mean the individual hopes and aspirations within each position on the issue that each person has—the dreams that are attached to your life history and that hold a lot of meaning in your life. Those dreams may be linked to your sense of identity—for example, what it means to be a member of your family, your race, or your religion. They may be connected to deep philosophical beliefs you hold about issues like power or love or loyalty. When you talk about those dreams, you may say things like, "That's just the way I am," or "I've always felt this way."

The trouble is, the connection between a couple's gridlocked conflict and their dreams is not always apparent. That's because we hold our dreams so close to our hearts that talking about them can make us feel quite vulnerable. In fact, we have referred to dreams as "the prairie dogs of marital conflict." Prairie dogs are elusive little creatures that live in complex tunnels beneath the surface of the earth, only popping up when they can be sure there are no predators about to attack. If they sense an enemy in their midst, they're gone in a flash. In the same way, our dreams only come to the surface of our interactions when we feel that it's safe to share them. Otherwise, the only thing our partners see is our position in the conflict.

Just because a dream is hidden, however, doesn't mean it's not driving the conversation. Here's a common example: A couple with a joint checking account discovers that one partner has failed to track all expenditures. The argument that results is about more than writing down numbers in a checkbook. It has to do with each partner's closely held dreams about issues of power, loyalty, honesty, security, freedom, and so on.

Partners may have a hard time revealing and hearing each other's deepest feelings about these dreams as long as they're arguing about the checkbook, however. To make the environment secure enough for dreams to emerge, you have to stop debating the issue and start creating an environment that's safe enough for dreams within each position to emerge. Once you get all your dreams out on the table, you may see each other's positions from a surprising new perspective. You may even find yourself saying things like "I had no idea this was so important to you. No wonder you couldn't yield on that. Now I understand why you've had to stand your ground." And as a consequence, you may be in a better position to start talking about areas of flexibility and compromise. The following exercises will give you some guidance for doing just that. Help is also available at the end of chapter 10, in the section called "Don't Get Gridlocked over Perpetual Issues."

Quiz: What Are the Dreams Within Your Conflicts?

With your partner, scan the list of dreams on the next page. In the second column, indicate which partner feels strongly about that dream. Now think about a recent disagreement. Can you see how this dream might be related to that disagreement? If so, have the partner who feels strongly about that dream jot down some notes about that conflict. Then share the exercise on page 145, which may help you discuss the dreams beneath your conflict and find some common ground.

Dream	This dream is important to:	How the dream relates to your conflict
Examples:		
A sense of freedom	<u>Jack</u>	Our summer vacation (I really want to run away with you to Hawaii instead of going to Nebraska.)
Knowing my family	<u>Jill</u>	Our summer vacation (Having you beside me at my family reunion in Nebraska means so much to me.)
A sense of freedom	___	
The experience of peace	___	
Unity with nature	___	
Exploring who I am	___	
Adventure	___	
A spiritual journey	___	
Justice	___	
Honor	___	
Unity with my past	___	
Healing	___	
Knowing my family	___	

Dream	This dream is important to:	How the dream relates to your conflict
Becoming all I can be	____	
Having a sense of power	____	
Dealing with my aging	____	
Exploring a creative side of myself	____	
Becoming more powerful	____	
Getting over past hurts	____	
Becoming more competent	____	
Asking God for forgiveness	____	
Exploring an old part of myself I have lost	____	
Getting over a personal hangup	____	
Having a sense of order	____	
Being able to be productive	____	
A place and a time to just "be"	____	
Being able to truly relax	____	

Dream	This dream is important to:	How the dream relates to your conflict
Reflecting on my life	_____	
Getting my priorities in order	_____	
Finishing something important	_____	
Exploring the physical side of myself	_____	
Being able to compete and win	_____	
Travel	_____	
Quiet	_____	
Atonement	_____	
Building something important	_____	
Ending a chapter of my life	_____	
Saying good-bye to something	_____	
Finding love	_____	
Other:_____	_____	
Other:_____	_____	

Exercise: Responding to the Dreams Within Your Conflict

1. When a conflict comes up, use the chart on pages 142–144 to iden-tify the dreams that each of you has within that conflict.

2. Designate one person as the speaker and the other as the listener.

3. The speaker tells the listener all about his or her dream. The lis-tener's job is to draw the information out of the speaker using ques-tions like these:

- What's important to you about this dream?

- What's the most important part?

- Why is this part important?

- Is there a story behind this for you? Tell me that story.

- Is there something from your life history that relates to that story?

- Tell me all the feelings that you have about this dream.

- Are there any feelings you left out? What do you wish for here?

- What would be your ideal dream here?

- How do you imagine things would be if you got what you wanted?

- Is there a deeper purpose or goal in this for you?

- Does this relate to some belief or value for you?

- Do you have some fear about not having this dream honored? Do you imagine some disaster?

The listener should not try to debate the issue or express opinions about the speaker's dream. In fact, neither partner should use this exer-cise to try to convince the other that his or her position in the conflict is the "right" position.

4. When the speaker is done, switch roles and explore the other partner's dreams.

5. Once your dreams are out in the open, look for ways that *each partner* can be flexible in order to honor the other partner's dreams.

6. If you find it hard to support your partner's dream, try this:

• Visualize your partner's dream as two concentric circles.

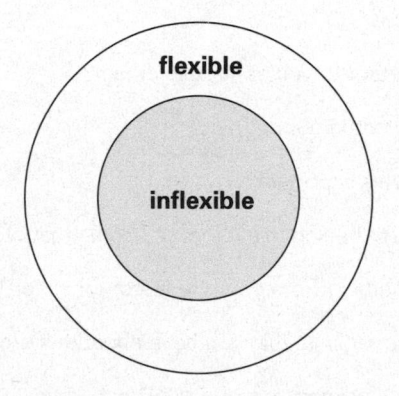

• The "inflexible" middle circle holds the part of your dream that you must have honored. (Example: Steve needs some sense of adventure, even if his dream of traveling to India can't be honored right now, when they have small children.)

• The outside "flexible" circle holds the part of your own dream that you *can* be flexible about. (Example: Denise can support the spirit of Steve's dreams by going along with smaller adventures for now—i.e., by kayaking close to home and by daydreaming with him of bigger adventures once the kids are older.) Try to make that outer circle as big as possible by searching for common ground and honoring your partner's dream.

- If you're having trouble filling the outside circle, consider the various levels of support you might offer and ask, how far am I willing to go? Examples:

  LEVEL 1. I can respect your dream.

  LEVEL 2. I can respect your dream and agree to learn more about it.

  LEVEL 3. I can financially support your dream to some degree.

  LEVEL 4. I can join you in your dream to some degree.

  LEVEL 5. I'm on board. Let's go for it.

- Realize that this is an issue of compromise, and compromise never feels perfect. Each person has to be willing to give something away in order to receive something in return. The important thing is that each person feels his or her dreams are understood, respected, and honored.

CHAPTER 6

"You're So Distant and Irritable All the Time"

Kevin was new to Boston and working part-time as a jani-tor the first time he met Suzanne. He remembers her sassy haircut, the flannel shirt she wore, and the casual chat they shared as he cleaned her office. Her "sparkly smile" made such an impression that when he spotted her two years later, he made the connection.

"I was at this friend's art opening and he walked into the gallery and said, 'Suzanne! Suzanne! It's me, Kevin!' And I was like, 'Hi! Who are you?' " Suzanne tells us, laughing. "But I thought he was a nice guy!"

Two years later still, they met again at that same friend's holiday party. This time it was Kevin who made the impression. "He just radi-ated warmth," Suzanne says. "I remember looking in his eyes and feel-ing very drawn in, very comfortable. I was intrigued."

The next day, Suzanne sent him a box of chocolate-covered cherries with a note that read, "Kevin, I'm really enjoying getting to know you."

"I didn't open the box for twenty-four hours," says Kevin. "I just kept looking at it, saying, 'My goodness! My goodness!' "

Looking back, Suzanne believes it was Kevin's persistent friendli-ness and optimism that allowed their romance to take flight. And after seven years of marriage, they say they'd like to recapture the affection and passion they once shared. "When we do connect, it's just wonderful," says Suzanne, thirty-five. "There's so much humor and fun."

But these days that sense of connection eludes them. They're feeling isolated from each other emotionally and physically—and that distresses them both.

"It's like we're not a team anymore," says Kevin, forty-two.

"So what is it that's coming between you?" John asks.

"The bills," Kevin answers immediately, as though it were a reflex.

"I don't think it's that," adds Suzanne quietly.

"OK, so it's taking the dog out every morning and every night," Kevin says, using sarcasm to drive home his point. For him, even the simplest routines have become a source of irritation.

Childless by choice, Kevin and Suzanne make a decent living—he

What's the Problem?

- *Kevin is depressed and withdraws.*
- *Both feel isolated, lonely.*
- *Suzanne gets critical and controlling in efforts to connect with Kevin.*
- *Kevin resists talking about his sadness.*
- *When Kevin finally talks about his feelings, Suzanne gets uncomfortable and sidetracks.*

What's the Solution?

- *Seek treatment for Kevin's depression.*
- *Be willing to listen to each other's feelings.*
- *Ask questions that encourage emotional sharing.*
- *Don't lose sight of Suzanne's needs.*

as a paralegal and she as a speech therapist. Still, Kevin worries a lot about money. For years he's been trying to convince himself—and Suzanne—that if they could just make more and spend less, maybe he wouldn't feel so hopeless and tired all the time.

"When Kevin feels that he's not making enough money, he retreats," Suzanne explains. He stops talking, spends a lot of time alone, and becomes increasingly irritable.

Kevin explains that solitude makes him feel better in the short term. "But quickly things start to back up on me," he adds. "My productivity goes down. And I get angry—at the dog, the cats, and at Suzanne."

Suzanne has her own problems with productivity because of a rare blood disorder that causes occasional bouts of fatigue. When she's not feeling well, she'd like to rely on Kevin for comfort. But his moodiness makes that difficult. She admits that she sometimes reacts to Kevin's withdrawal by picking a fight. She criticizes the way he's driving or cooking, for example, because an argument feels less lonely than no connection at all. But in the end, it always backfires. Rather than drawing Kevin closer, poking at him makes him even more irritable, more withdrawn.

Although they can still connect, talk, and share deep feelings at times, these occasions are becoming less frequent. Meanwhile, both are feeling increasingly sad and lonely, and neither knows the way out of their predicament. After evaluating their questionnaires and hearing them talk about their interactions, however, we begin to suspect that Kevin's dark moods are one source of the problem.

"Can I be frank?" Julie asks, turning to Kevin. "I think you're depressed. And it's really crippling you in some way. It's causing you to withdraw, to shut down. It's making you feel like a failure."

It may also damage your marriage, Julie continues. "I can see, Suzanne, that you love this man so much, but you feel stumped. You try to reach out with affection and talking, but you don't get much back. So then you try to reach out with criticism, and that doesn't work, either. You're stymied."

Depression can be like a third party coming between partners and creating a sense of hopelessness, Julie adds. And unless the partners are willing to talk about it, improving the marriage may be impossible.

Kevin protests at first, pointing to the "stigma" of admitting he's depressed. But we assure him that the depression is not his fault. Often it's caused by a chemical imbalance that can be treated with counseling and medication.

We also emphasize that talking to Suzanne about the problem is essential to healing their relationship. If they can learn to connect with each other during the dark times, both partners will feel less isolated from each other. They'll view each other as allies in their efforts to battle Kevin's depression, to cope with Suzanne's illness, and to win back more loving feelings for each other.

Here's what happens when Kevin and Suzanne agree to talk about these issues:

What They Say	*What We Notice*
Kevin: You know, Suzanne, I *am* depressed. I'm sorry, because it puts this wall between us. It keeps me from moving on.	+ Good honest expression of feeling. + Acknowledges how it affects her.
Suzanne: Well, honey, do you think your dad was depressed?	+/− Shows interest, but backs away by shifting the attention to Kevin's father.
Kevin: Yeah, I think my father was depressed.	−/+ Responds.
Suzanne: What do you think that was about?	− Continues to sidetrack.
Kevin: About his history. *(He sighs and then falls silent.)*	− Appears discouraged, but he's not telling her why.

continued

151

What They Say	What We Notice
Suzanne: You know, I think so many people feel that way. I feel that way a lot, too.	− Minimizes at first, as though it's "no big deal." + Supportive statement that she understands how he feels.
Kevin: I just feel like a fake.	+ More feeling.
Suzanne: How come?	+ Shows interest.
Kevin: Because I don't do anything. You know that I want to write. But it's like, "You want to write about life? You don't even want to live it."	+ More feeling.
Suzanne: You're being so hard on yourself! How come?	+/− Question shows she's listening, but "How come?" may lead them into intellectualizing rather than sharing feelings.
Kevin: I don't know. I feel kind of flat. There's definitely something missing in my life. And this past week has been really tough because I have been so tired. Fatigued.	+ Doesn't try to analyze; continues to share feelings.
Suzanne: Yeah, I worry about you.	+ Shares her own feelings; acknowledges that she cares.
Kevin: And I've already told you, I just feel old.	+ Reveals more.

What They Say	What We Notice
Suzanne: Oh, you! Honey, you know what I was thinking? We haven't really been exercising. You used to be so athletic. I think we should do something together. I really think we should look into the tandem bike. I know it's expensive, but . . .	– Minimizes; looking for a quick fix.
Kevin: There are a lot of tandems out there that don't get used.	– Resistant because It's too early for problem solving.
Suzanne: Well, yeah, but we can just rent one for a while.	– Ignores his resistance; keeps trying to problem solve.
Kevin: I feel like I'm depressed. There is now an eight-hundred-pound gorilla in the room.	+ States his feelings once more, this time telling her how big the problem is.
Suzanne: I'm totally—I'm acknowledging that. So tell me more about it. What does it feel like to be depressed? Do things feel dark and heavy?	+ Great response, asking him to describe how it feels.
Kevin: Heavy. Heavy. I look at my brother. And he seems to have so much energy.	+ Responds; shares feelings about himself in relation to his brother.
Suzanne: You think? What does your brother talk about when you call him?	– Backs away by asking him about his brother rather than his own feelings.

continued

What They Say	*What We Notice*
Kevin: Everything that's not him. I don't know. I have had a hard time doing anything. I make endless lists.	+ Gets the conversation back on track.
Suzanne: Do you feel like your work is challenging for you?	+/− Asking a question is great, but again it's analytical—taking him away from his feelings.
Kevin: It's challenging. But nothing I'm incapable of. I just don't think I have any passion for life right now.	+/− Subtly lets her know he doesn't want to go there, but he's not telling her what he needs from her—empathy. + Opens up further.
Suzanne: So really anything you'd do right now, you don't feel like you could be passionate about.	+ Reflecting back his feelings, shows she's listening.
Kevin: I just feel like I don't have any tools to do anything. I feel like I am dark and in that fetal position.	+ More feelings.
Suzanne: How long has this been going on?	+ Good question.
Kevin: Well, I would say since the Cuban Missile Crisis.	−/+ A bit sarcastic, but he really wants her to get how important this is.
Suzanne: Before I was born! Was there ever a time when you felt alive and not depressed?	+ She shows she gets it. +/− Question shows interest, but takes the focus off here and now.

What They Say	What We Notice
Kevin: Certainly when I first moved here. That was an incredibly alive time for me.	+ Responds.
Suzanne: How come?	+/− Again, good to ask questions, but still too analytical.
Kevin: It felt like I had taken ankle weights off. I was floating, I don't know. Now I feel like I'm in a perpetually overcast mood. But until I just got fingered, I could keep fooling myself. But now we both know and I can't.	+ Shares feelings. + Tells her what he needs: for both of them to face the issue.

Our Analysis: Avoiding Emotional Intensity Postpones Healing

When the conversation ends, Suzanne says she's relieved to understand finally why Kevin has been so distant. At the same time, Kevin tells us he's amazed that Suzanne isn't angry: "Why doesn't she say, 'You bastard! *You've* been the problem all this time!'?"

The reason, of course, is Suzanne's deep concern for Kevin, which she demonstrates in this conversation. In turn, she finally gets what she needs—some honest, open communication from him about his feelings. She also demonstrates her love with interested questions and compassionate responses, John observes. Still, we spot ways that these questions and responses could be even better. For instance, Suzanne has a tendency to avoid the intensity of Kevin's emotions by introducing side topics to the conversation. She brings up issues such as Kevin's dad's depression and Kevin's need for exercise. While these topics are related, talking about them in this moment takes Kevin away from sharing his feelings with her and therefore interferes with their process of building intimacy.

Suzanne also makes the common error of rushing into a problem-solving mode too early. Suggesting they purchase a tandem bike could be helpful later on, but as Kevin's reaction shows, he's not ready to start this kind of brainstorming yet. First, he needs Suzanne to spend more time listening to him express his feelings. He won't be ready to talk about solutions with her until he feels reassured that she can understand and accept what he's saying. We suspect Suzanne may not feel completely comfortable with the depth of emotion that Kevin is sharing. Perhaps she, too, is scared of the uncertain implications. But if she can learn to hang in there with him as he processes his feelings, she'll be helping to reestablish a connection that's been missing from their relationship and that may even help him to recover.

In addition, Suzanne's open-ended questions show sincere interest in Kevin's problems. She's doing her best to draw him out. The ways she's phrasing some of her questions could be a problem, however. Questions like "Why?" or "How come?" draw answers that come from the head instead of the heart. Kevin and Suzanne don't need the intellectual exercise of analyzing Kevin's problems right now. Rather, they need to share their feelings about those problems. Her question "What does it feel like to be depressed?" is more likely to draw a helpful response. We advise her to avoid "why" questions.

And, finally, we notice that Kevin and Suzanne never get around to discussing Suzanne's needs and feelings. That's not surprising, considering that Kevin's revelations about his depression are so new to them. Still, we want them to be aware that, even in a crisis, both partners' needs must be recognized and considered.

Our Advice

Kevin's willingness to talk about his depression, and Suzanne's willingness to listen, is a great sign that they can grow closer. To help this process along, we offer this advice:

1. BE A CARING WITNESS TO EACH OTHER'S STRONG, NEGATIVE FEELINGS

"It's hard for partners to believe that they're doing anything for each other when they're just sitting there, considering the other person's sadness or frustration," John explains. "But usually it's enough to just be present and to empathize. Think of yourselves as two birds sitting on the same perch, viewing the world, and chirping together. That sense of togetherness can be sufficient." In fact, trying to problem-solve too soon can interfere with intimacy. "Remember, your goal isn't to fix the feelings; it's to help each other feel less alone," John advises.

2. ASK QUESTIONS THAT LEAD TO THE HEART INSTEAD OF THE HEAD

Instead of asking "why" or "how come" questions—which lead to analysis—we encourage Suzanne and Kevin to ask each other questions that require them to consider their feelings. Examples: "How are you feeling about this right now?" or "What is the most difficult part of this experience for you?" (For more ideas, see the exercise called "Establish a Ritual for Stress-Reducing Conversation" on page 167.)

3. DON'T LOSE TRACK OF SUZANNE'S NEEDS

With so much focus on Kevin's depression, it would be easy for Suzanne to fall into the role of a caretaker who never expresses her own needs. This would not be good for either partner, or for their marriage. During our session, Kevin tells Suzanne that he feels most "involved" in their relationship *when she needs him* emotionally. So, in addition to talking about *his* internal world, the pair needs to make room in their conversations for Suzanne's concerns. What are her worries, her goals, her desires? What can Kevin do to offer her reassurance and comfort?

4. GET TREATMENT FOR DEPRESSION

We urge Kevin to talk to his doctor or a mental health professional about treatment for depression. This could include counseling, antidepressant medication, or both. We reiterate that depression is often caused by a biochemical imbalance, and that there's no shame in asking for help.

In this next dialogue we ask Kevin and Suzanne simply to continue their conversation about Kevin's depression, keeping our advice in mind.

What They Say	What We Notice
Kevin: On the one hand I'm thinking, geez, how much is this going to cost?	+ Expresses worry.
Suzanne: *(smiles and rolls her eyes)*	+ Teases him nonverbally, letting him know she supports him.
Kevin *(smiling)*: What? Come on. I've got to think it!	+ Accepts her support, joins in the teasing.
Suzanne *(still smiling)*: Of course.	+ Shows she accepts him, even though he's tight with money.
Kevin: On the other hand, it makes me hopeful, because what is life all about? Is it about paying off my debts? Hell, no. It should be about you and me, standing in the backyard wondering where to plant the zucchini.	+ Breakthrough statement of optimism. + Lets her know that enjoying life together is what really matters to him.
Suzanne: You know, naming things always is the first step. Now we know there's a problem and we can work on it together. It explains what's been going on, and that's a relief.	+ Expresses her support for him; her willingness to work as a team. + Validates his optimism. + Expresses her relief.

What They Say	What We Notice
Kevin: Well, it gives us a kind of a backdrop to look at things with different eyes.	+ Acknowledges they're on the same side.
Suzanne: Yeah, that's right. And you know, I also want to go on to talk about my own health issues, OK?	+ Validates his statement. + Brings up her own needs.
Kevin: Sure. I was thinking about how I feel about your blood disorder. Quite honestly, it scares me. And the scary thing about that is that I won't be there for you. Or that I'm *not* there for you.	+ Responds to her request to talk about her needs. + Expresses his worries about her health and his ability to support her. − Turns his attention back to himself and his own problem rather than focusing on her feelings.
Suzanne: What do you mean?	+ Asks for clarification.
Kevin: That I can't—that I won't rise to that challenge. Whatever that challenge is.	+ He gives her the clarification.
Suzanne: And I was wondering, what if it was the other way around? What if you were sick? I think I'd be scared a lot. I get terrified just when you tell me you're fatigued.	+ Shows she understands and empathizes. + Shares her feelings.
Kevin: Right.	+ Hears her.
Suzanne: Because . . .	+ This interruption looks like a problem, but he seems to finish her sentence just as she would have. Shows they're on the same page.

continued

What They Say	What We Notice
Kevin: What could it be?	
Suzanne: Yeah. But, you know, you never show that you worry about me. But sometimes I do wonder. I kind of want to poke you and say, "Is it just me? Or are you worrying here, too?"	+ Expresses her loneliness. + Expresses her need for him to be concerned about her and to express that.
Kevin: I'm worrying.	+ Responds to her need, lets her know he cares.
Suzanne: Because when we answered the questionnaires, I wasn't able to put down anything about the future. Every day I wonder, how long? Am I facing death? Were you thinking the same?	+ Goes further, telling him her deepest fears. + Asks about his feelings.
Kevin: No, but I think my life is sort of a living purgatory. I'm not so much worried about dying prematurely—I'm more worried about living too long.	− Doesn't respond to her fears. + Honest response, telling her the difference between being depressed and worrying about his own health.
Suzanne: Hmm.	+ Hears him.

Suzanne does just what we've advised her to do in this conversation: She makes a brave attempt to address her own needs by talking about her illness. Afterward, she tells us that she feels "a little frustrated" by the outcome; she isn't sure that Kevin really listened and understood.

Her response makes sense, we tell her. Kevin does seem to have a hard time shifting his focus to her experience. That's why they both need to pay attention to the balance of concern in their relationship.

At the same time, they also need to be patient with each other and their process. After seven years of sidestepping important issues, "you both have so much you need to say," explains Julie.

"It's like you've opened up whole new territories of conversation— your fears, your regrets, your values, your dreams," adds John. "It's going to take some time to fully explore all these areas."

We see lots of reasons to be optimistic about their future, we tell them. Some couples, after years of avoiding difficult issues, feel they have nothing to share with each other. That's not true for Kevin and Suzanne, who both express a desire to know each other at a deeper level. "There's so much going on for you," John marvels. "There's so much for you to talk about."

One Year Later

After our session, Kevin made an appointment with a therapist and started getting treatment for his depression, including antidepressants. As the clouds of sadness and lethargy started to lift, he felt motivated to become more physically active, so he joined a gym and started exercising daily. After about six months, he found he no longer needed the medication to keep his spirits up. Now he's off the antidepressants and he feels he has more energy than he's had in years. He's enjoying his job. He has taken up guitar—a pastime he'd set aside years ago. He's even changing his attitude about money. He recently bought himself a new guitar—a purchase that seemed far too frivolous a year ago. And as a result of his new, more liberal attitude toward spending, he and Suzanne are having fewer arguments about finances.

Because Kevin is less withdrawn, he and Suzanne are finding it easier to get along. Still, the couple has challenges ahead—including Suzanne's chronic illness. "I go through rough periods when I'm not feeling well and I get real controlling and grouchy," she explains. Both partners say they'd like to get better at sharing their feelings and comforting each other at times like this. And now that Kevin's depression has improved, they feel optimistic that they could benefit from couple's therapy. They've made an appointment with a marriage therapist to start sessions soon. "We're hoping that going to therapy will make us talk and hear each other better," says Suzanne. "And I think that's going to help immensely."

HELPING YOUR PARTNER THROUGH DEPRESSION

In their first dialogue, Kevin uses the common metaphor of an "eight-hundred-pound gorilla" to describe his depression. Suzanne, who had been subtly avoiding the topic, suddenly gets it. The depression is a third party in their marriage that must be acknowledged. If they keep trying to ignore it, things will only get worse.

Seeing depression as a third party is valuable because it allows partners to quit blaming themselves or each other for problems depression can cause. It compels them to face those problems, to empathize with each other, and to start working together for solutions.

Unfortunately, many people have a hard time admitting, or even recognizing, when they're depressed. This can be especially true for men, who are often raised to deny their feelings. When they experience the emotional emptiness or numbness that can be part of depression, they may not realize anything's wrong. On the other hand, a man may feel ashamed to admit that he *is* feeling down—that anxiety, sadness, or fatigue are keeping him from being productive at work, from enjoying leisure-time activities, or from getting excited about sex. Such feelings can conflict with a man's desire to see himself as a good provider, a good husband, and a good lover. Consequently, he may try to keep his negative emotions hidden. Meanwhile, his wife is in the dark, left to wonder why he's becoming increasingly irritable or withdrawn. Under these circumstances, it's common for wives to react as Suzanne did—to start criticizing and trying to control their husbands' behaviors. She may be thinking he's stubborn, lazy, or antisocial. But depressed? This may not occur to her.

In contrast, women are often more willing to admit to feeling sad or anxious. Still, many are reluctant to seek help because they're taught to believe that women are just naturally more emotional than men—that feeling "blue" or "bitchy" is just a normal part of a woman's life experience. They may blame their sadness on premenstrual syndrome (PMS), menopause, or other hormonal fluctuations that can cause normal changes in mood.

But depression—an unrelenting sadness or anxiety that continually blocks your ability to feel happiness and satisfaction with everyday life—is *not* normal for men or women. It's a mood disorder that can be caused by a chemical imbalance and made worse by stress or grief. The good news is that depression often can be treated successfully with counseling or medication, or both. Changes in lifestyle—such as exercising more and learning to manage daily stress—can also help.

Symptoms of Depression

- *A persistently sad, anxious, or "empty" mood.*

- *Feelings of hopelessness.*

- *Feelings of guilt, worthlessness, helplessness.*

- *Loss of interest or pleasure in hobbies and activities that you once enjoyed, including sex.*

- *Decreased energy, fatigue (like wearing concrete shoes).*

- *Difficulty concentrating, remembering, making decisions.*

- *Sleeping too much, or not being able to sleep.*

- *Loss of appetite or weight loss.*

- *Overeating and weight gain.*

- *Thoughts of death or suicide; suicide attempts.*

- *Restlessness.*

- *Irritability, grouchiness, being overly critical.*

- *Persistent physical symptoms that don't respond to treatment, such as headaches, digestive disorders, and chronic pain.*

If you suspect that your partner is depressed, here are some steps you can take together to prevent the condition from harming your marriage:

Encourage your partner to talk to a doctor or mental health professional.

Increasingly more health-care professionals are prepared to help their patients with depression. Tell your partner there's no shame in asking for help, and there's a lot to gain from feeling better.

Once diagnosed, encourage your partner to stick with treatment.

While there are many effective ways to treat depression, not all medications or therapies are effective for all people. In addition, some of the most common therapies—such as antidepressants—often take several weeks to start working. On top of this, people with depression can be easily discouraged. So you may need to give your spouse extra encouragement to continue treatment, or be willing to try new therapies if one approach doesn't seem to be working.

Learn to recognize and talk about the way depression affects your relationship.

There may be times when your spouse seems especially irritable or withdrawn. If you can understand these behaviors as symptoms of depression, it may prevent you from feeling rejected or hurt.

Help your partner stay safe.

Be aware that severe depression can lead to suicide. Check in with your partner about his or her feelings of hope or hopelessness. If you sense that your spouse is thinking about suicide, seek help from a therapist or crisis line right away.

Make sure the kids' needs are met.

Children shouldn't be burdened by a parent's depression. So take a close look at the kids' needs—especially if the depressed parent is their primary caretaker. Does that parent have enough energy, emotionally and physically, to respond to the children in kind, positive ways? Do you get the sense that the kids are caring for the parent instead of the other way around? If so, you may need to make other arrangements—such as having another adult care for the children while the depressed mom or dad gets treatment.

Respond to your spouse with empathy, while stating your own needs.
If your partner becomes harsh and critical, for example, you might reply, "It feels like your depression is talking now. Can you be a little gentler with me?" Or, if your spouse seems withdrawn, you might say, "I know you don't feel like connecting right now, but I need to tell you that I'm feeling lonely." Stating your needs in this way gives your spouse an opportunity to reassure you that, yes, he or she does care, and no, the issue is not personal. At the same time, you're letting your spouse know that you understand and care about what he or she is going through, as well.

Connect by touching.
Sometimes couples can connect through the emotional fog of depression via touch. Try hugging, cuddling, or massage as a way to comfort your spouse when he or she is feeling down. Avoid making sexual demands if your spouse isn't interested. Just focus on providing comfort and support.

Quiz: Are You Depressed?

Below is a list of problems and complaints that most people have from time to time. Read the list and rate each item based on how much discomfort that problem has caused for you in the past week, including today. Use this following scale of 0 to 4. **0** = Not at all, **1** = A little bit, **2** = Moderately, **3** = Quite a bit, **4** = Extremely

- Loss of sexual interest or pleasure   ____

- Feeling low in energy or slowed down   ____

- Thoughts of ending your life   ____

- Crying easily   ____

- Feelings of being trapped or caught   ____

- Blaming yourself for things   ____

- Feeling lonely   ____

- Feeling blue   ____

- Worrying too much about things   ____

- Feeling no interest in things   ____

- Feeling hopeless about the future   ____

- Feeling everything is an effort   ____

- Feeling worthless   ____

Total: ____

Find your score by dividing the total by 13:   ____

If your score is higher than 1.5, you may be depressed. If you find this mood persists for more than two weeks or so, talk to your doctor or a mental health counselor about your symptoms. (*Source: Symptom Checklist 90*, by Leonard R. Derogatis.)

Quiz: Are You Anxious?

Here's another list of problems and complaints that most people have occasionally. Read the list and rate each item based on how much discomfort that problem has caused for you in the past week, including today.

Use the following scale of 0 to 4. **0** = Not at all, **1** = A little bit, **2** = Moderately, **3** = Quite a bit, **4** = Extremely

- Nervousness or shakiness   ____

- Trembling   ____

- Suddenly scared for no reason   ____

- Feeling fearful   ____

- Heart pounding or racing   ____

- Feeling tense or keyed up   ____

- Spells of terror or panic   ____

- Feeling so restless you can't sit still   ____

- Feeling that something bad is going to happen to you   ____

- Frightening thoughts and images   ____

Total: ____

Find your score by dividing the total by 10:   ____

If your score is higher than 1.24, you may be anxious. If you find this mood persists for more than two weeks or so, talk to your doctor or a mental health counselor about your symptoms. (*Source: Symptom Checklist 90,* by Leonard R. Derogatis.)

Exercise: Establish a Ritual for Stress-Reducing Conversation

Research shows that one of the best things a couple can do for their marriage is to establish a ritual of regular conversation for coping with everyday stress and occasional sadness. This is the time—ideally each day—when you catch up, focus on each other, swap stories, and show support.

Such conversations can help you to manage pressure, anxiety, and sadness due to problems at your job or in difficult relationships with relatives and friends. These talks can be especially helpful if one or both of you struggle with depression as Kevin did. And even if your mood is generally upbeat, meaningful conversations can help you to handle life's challenges while staying emotionally connected. Think of it as being like a regular trip to the bank; your goal here is to make deposits in your "emotional bank account."

Use the following instructions and questions to design a conversation ritual for you and your partner. Try it a few times and then evaluate how it's going. Make adjustments as needed to design a ritual that works for you.

1. Designate fifteen to thirty minutes each day to talk about your day.

You may already do this to some extent. But we suggest that you make it intentional. You may want to attach the conversation to some other activity that you do day in and day out—something like eating breakfast together, commuting, taking a walk, or sharing coffee after dinner. The idea is to commit to making the conversation a *significant part* of that experience.

What is the best time of day for you to have a stress-reducing conversation with your partner? _____

Where is the best place to have it? _____

2. Do it the same way every time.

Examples: Sit at the same table, light a candle, use the same two matching coffee mugs. The idea is to make it feel like "a ritual," something you do together every day to feel connected to each other.

What elements will you use in your conversation ritual? _____
_____

3. Eliminate distractions.

Turn off the television. Let the phone ring. If you have small children, arrange for them to be involved in some other activity (sleeping is nice) so Mom and Dad can talk.

How will you make sure you've got each other's full attention? _____
_____

4. Take turns talking and listening.

Discuss the most important things that have happened to you since the last time you talked. What transpired at work? What did the doctor say? How was your class? Did you talk to your mom? Make sure that each partner gets equal time to talk about his or her day. At first, you can use a clock to time it. Later on, sharing the floor will come naturally.

What are likely topics for each of you in these conversations? _____
_____

5. Show support for your partner as you listen.

- Demonstrate genuine interest by asking questions: "How did it go?" "What was the most important part?" "How do you feel about that?" "What did that mean to you?" "Tell me everything that happened."

- Communicate understanding: "I can understand why you feel that way." "I'd be stressed out, too." "So it sounds like you're worried."

- Listen for emotion and respond in kind: "That's really sad." "I can see why you're angry." "Wow, that's exciting!" "I'd be tense in that situation, too."

- Celebrate your partner's success: "That's wonderful!" "I'm so proud of you!" "I'll bet you're so relieved."

- Take your partner's side in conflicts: "That guy is a total jerk." "How could she treat you like that?" (Remember, this is not the time for the listener to complain or criticize the speaker. And don't side with the enemy!)

- Show solidarity: "This is our problem and we will face it together." "I can understand because something similar happened to me."

- Be affectionate: "Come here and let me hold you." "I'm totally on your side."

- Offer help with problem solving: "Let's figure this out." But remember, understanding must come before advice. Don't rush to problem solve. Listening is the most important part.

6. Evaluate your experience.

After practicing a few days, analyze how the conversation is working. Ask these questions:

- Is the time and place working out for you?

- If not, do you need to make adjustments to your schedule so you can make it work?

- Are you able to avoid distractions?

- Are there any elements you'd like to add to make it more satisfying?

- Do you feel that your partner is sharing his or her experiences?

- Do you feel that your partner is listening to you?

What changes, if any, would you like to make in your ritual? _____

_____

CHAPTER 7

"I Shouldn't Have
to Nag!"

Growing up, Craig dreamed of marrying a woman like Beth—somebody he described as fiery, demonstrative, passionate. "I always believed a woman like that could awaken those qualities in me," the thirty-four-year-old machinist from Milwaukee explains. "So when I saw Beth, she excited me."

The two had met nine years earlier in Miami, where Beth was waiting tables to put herself through graduate school. Craig had escaped the winter weather to vacation in Florida with friends.

Beth, now thirty-nine, was instantly attracted to Craig as well. "I couldn't believe I met this guy who was not only handsome and smart—he was also extremely funny!" she remembers.

Their romance flourished through letters, short visits, and long telephone calls. Intense, time-limited conversations heightened the experience. "We felt as if we were looking into each other's essence," Craig recalls.

They got married just six months later, even though Craig's job and Beth's schooling kept them living in separate states. Then, after nearly a year of long-distance marriage, Beth moved to Wisconsin.

"It was immediate culture shock!" says Craig. Both fiercely

independent, the two faced off over issues of finances and where to live—conflicts that are still unresolved. Beth believes Craig is careless with money, while Craig feels Beth holds the purse strings too tight. Beth dislikes the harsh Wisconsin winters, and would like to move back to Florida. But Craig can't imagine leaving his family, his friends, and his job at the auto plant, where he revels in his role as union steward.

But the couple's most serious disputes center on household chores—an area of conflict that's grown increasingly contentious since their son Skylar was born five years ago. Because Beth usually works part-time as a fund-raiser for a charitable organization, the couple has agreed that she should do most of the housework and child care. But her workload at the office is often unpredictable, and sometimes she needs Craig's help with chores like laundry, cooking, and cleaning. Craig says he doesn't mind pitching in, but he needs reminders.

What's the Problem?

- Beth opens conversations with criticism, sarcasm, or contempt—i.e., "harsh start-up."

- Craig reacts defensively.

- He is unwilling to accept her influence.

- Her self-critical thoughts and feelings of unworthiness block her ability to accept his appreciation and help.

What's the Solution?

- For Beth: "Soften start-up."

- For Craig: Be open to her influence.

- Express more appreciation.

- For Beth: Accept the compliments he offers.

This irritates Beth because she feels Craig should be more attuned to their life together and what she needs. "I shouldn't have to nag!" she insists.

Lately their quarrels over housework have become so frequent and so painful that it's harming their marriage.

"The way we argue is disgusting!" laments Beth. "Whenever we get a moment to talk, something always blows up. So we end up wondering, 'Why do we even try to spend time together?' "

Craig recalls times when he and Beth felt much closer—when they bought their new house, for instance, or when his union went out on strike and Beth was so supportive. "We kind of rallied and worked together," he says. "It felt like we were on the same team, and that permeated everything—how we communicated and how we accepted each other. We felt fond of each other."

It hasn't been that way lately, though. These days he says he often views Beth as "hard" or "lashing out," rarely vulnerable. She's his adversary—"the person who is trying to make me spend less money, who is criticizing me because I don't work enough around the house," he says.

Even the humor has dissipated from their relationship, says Beth, sadly. Craig rarely laughs at her jokes anymore.

The couple also worries about the way their arguments may affect their son. Both say they'd like Skylar to see his parents respecting each other, discussing tough issues, and getting along. "But a lot of time he sees me as angry because I feel like I'm doing it all," says Beth.

Providing a better example for Skylar is important to both Craig and Beth, so we suggest that they try discussing their conflicts over housework with Skylar in mind.

Here's what happened:

What They Say	What We Notice
Beth: I want Skylar to grow up seeing teamwork. I want him to see us as the adults and himself the child—rather than seeing that I'm picking up after two kids. *(Pauses.)* You're smiling.	– Spoils a positive beginning with criticism and mild insult.

continued

What They Say	What We Notice
Craig: You've already referred to me as a kid.	+ Notices insult and gently tells her so.
Beth: Well, I sometimes feel that way—like I am cleaning up after two kids.	− Softens her complaint, but continues criticism; ends up defensive.
Craig: And I think we've got to work this stuff out so that it's not played out in front of Skylar.	+ States his complaint. + Takes some responsibility by saying "we."
Beth: I'd like to be able to say, "Can you vacuum?" without having you continue to type on the computer. We got into a fight about this on Saturday because I didn't say, "Can you vacuum *now*?"	− Ignores his complaint. + Expresses her need, her complaint.
Craig: You asked if I could vacuum, and the vacuuming got done.	− Defensive.
Beth: Right. And by the time I asked you to vacuum, I was totally frustrated because I had already scrubbed two tubs, three sinks, and two toilets—and I had to go to work. You want me to ask you to do things. But it's beyond me why I need to ask you to participate in cleaning up messes that we both make.	− Doesn't give him credit for vacuuming. − States complaint in a critical way, which escalates the argument. − Sarcasm (a form of contempt).
Craig: Well, I do participate. You describe feeling fed up, but I think you should ask for help before it gets that far.	− Defensive. +/− States his need, but uses "you should" rather than a request.

What They Say	What We Notice
Beth: I feel like it's going to start a fight.	+ Expresses her fear.
Craig: Give me an example of a time.	+ Asks for more information.
Beth: When I was carrying the dresser upstairs, you sat on the computer. And I said, "Can you help me?" We're talking about a dresser! Not like a little jewelry box. It was a *dresser!*	+ Expresses her feelings. – Harsh, accusing tone.
Craig: OK. Then what happened?	+ Asks for more information.
Beth: I said, "Can you help me carry this dresser upstairs?" Not a common request. And you said, "I'm in the middle of something." So I took the damned drawers out, and then carried this freaking dresser upstairs by myself. And you sat there. I felt like, "I cannot believe this man will not move and help me carry this dresser!" And then I saw that you were playing a baseball game on the computer! I thought you were doing something important for work!	+/– Expresses her complaint and her feelings about it, but does it in a harsh, accusing way.
Craig: Well, there's the issue of "I need you to do this" versus "I need you to do this *now.*"	– Doesn't acknowledge her frustration. +/– Stays calm, but defensive.
Beth: I get the feeling you hate the word *now.*	+ Probes for information about his feelings.

continued

What They Say	What We Notice
Craig: No, I've actually requested that you use the word *now* so that I understand. So that if I am in the middle of something, I can say, "I really can't help you now. I can help you in ten minutes."	− Defensive at first. + Clarifies his need.
Beth: Right. And I thought, "OK, it's hard for me to ask, but I'm going to ask." And then when you said, "I'm busy right now and I'll help you later," I took it as a slap in the face—like I'm not important enough for you to put down what you're doing.	− Doesn't respond to his stated need. + Reminds him how hard it is for her to ask for his help. + Clearly communicates how his refusal to help makes her feel.
Craig: But you *are* important. And I do want to help you. That's why I'm trying to identify if something needs to be done *now*.	+ Reassures her that she is important. + Tells her what he needs.
Beth: Can we just assume that I mean now? If I'm asking you, I mean *now!*	− Ignores his statement that he cares. − Ignores his stated need again. − Harsh tone escalates the conflict.
Craig: But do you understand that I have a flow in my life? You could have said, "Is now a good time to carry a dresser up the stairs?"	− Defensive.
Beth: And so what if it's not a perfect time?	− Ignoring his need. − Contemptuous.

What They Say	What We Notice
Craig: Well, I'm not asking for a perfect time.	– Defensive.
Beth: It feels like you are.	– Continues conflict.
Craig: No. I want communication and understanding. I want to be able to say, "Excuse me, I'm right in the middle of this thing"— even if it's just a game. "I've played it for seven innings and I really don't want to walk out in the middle of it. Is two and a half minutes going to cause a big deal?"	– Defensive. + Clearly states his needs. – Won't budge toward her position; shows he won't be influenced by her.
Beth: And I could ask you the same question: "Is it really 'a big deal' if you miss these two innings?"	– Ignores his statement of need; restates her own instead. – Won't budge on his needs, either; they've reached an impasse.

Our Analysis: Harsh Words and Defensiveness Trump Good Intentions

Despite their anger and frustration, we see strengths in Beth and Craig's relationship. One is their sense of urgency; they're trying hard to make a connection—a sign that there's still a lot of love between them. Also, they both want to improve their marriage for Skylar's sake. This shows they believe the stakes are high, which may motivate them to make positive changes.

But where to begin? The top of their conversation holds some clues. Notice how Beth is barely out of the gate before she criticizes Craig by calling him a child. We call this tendency "harsh start-up," which is the habit of beginning your interactions with criticism or contempt. Our research shows that conversations that begin this way are doomed to failure. In fact, we found that we could predict the outcome of a fifteen-minute conversation 96 percent of the time based on what happened in the first three minutes. Consequently, it may not matter how much Beth wants to improve her marriage. If she starts a lot of her conversations with Craig by insulting him or hurting his feelings, they won't make much progress. And, indeed, Craig shows his discouragement early on. His smile is a gentle warning that things aren't going well. He tries a few times to turn the conversation around by refocusing on Skylar, stating his needs, and asking Beth questions. But as Beth's criticism continues and intensifies, he becomes more and more resistant to anything Beth says. From this defensive position, he offers no indication that he's open to Beth's perspective. In other words, he's not about to agree that he should help with the housework without being asked. And his refusal to accept Beth's influence on this issue makes Beth even more frustrated and critical, sending them into an escalating spiral of attack-and-defend.

Another complicating factor is that Beth has a hard time accepting Craig's attempts at kindness. When he says, "You *are* important," for instance, it goes right by her. We suspect she's clinging to so much left-over resentment from years of arguing that it's drowning out Craig's positive words. Also, we learn in our interview with Beth and Craig that she carries lots of self-criticism and feelings of unworthiness because of childhood experiences.

"It sounds like you were raised to believe that you don't deserve praise," Julie observes. "So even when Craig compliments you, you don't accept those words. No matter what he says, you still feel crummy."

"It's a form of self-protection," John explains. "If you were raised with lots of criticism, you may feel vulnerable when somebody says something nice to you. You feel afraid that if you open yourself up to that kindness, you might also be opening yourself up to get slammed. So you try not to expect much."

Those same feelings of low self-regard have led Beth to believe she doesn't really deserve to ask for Craig's help, we discover. She equates asking for help with negative behavior on her part—-in other words, "nagging."

The trouble is, she really does feel overwhelmed with work at times. When that happens, she wishes Craig would just offer his help and save her from turning into a nag. (Remember, "nag" is her perception, not his.) When he doesn't offer help, she becomes resentful and angry toward Craig— feelings she expresses just as she learned as a child— through criticism and contempt.

Beth tells us she's aware of her critical nature and its origin, and she often makes resolutions to be kinder toward Craig.

"That usually lasts four or five days," Craig explains.

"Then I go back to being a witch," adds Beth.

In his defense, Craig responds quickly, *"I'm* not calling you that."

Meanwhile, Julie sees the opportunity for insight: "Is that how you see yourself?" she asks Beth.

"I think I do," says Beth sadly. Then she adds, "I'm a good person with a good heart, and I really do care. And I start off trying to be positive, but we just . . ." Her voice trails off as she makes a big, sweeping downhill gesture with her right hand.

"I get to feeling so hopeless," Beth adds, turning to Craig. "And I have this fear that one day you'll get so fed up with me, you'll just up and leave."

This confession takes Craig by surprise. "I don't feel that way. Even in tough times, I feel that we're going to hang in there," he says. "And I hope that the day will come when you feel that way, too."

Our Advice

To help Beth and Craig build more hope and confidence in their marriage, we suggest some basic changes in the way they interact.

1. PRACTICE "SOFTENED START-UP"

First, we advise Beth to use "softened start-up" rather than "harsh start-up" when she talks to Craig about their conflicts. That is, she needs to bring up her complaints to Craig in a more neutral, less accusing way. There's nothing wrong with saying, "I felt angry when you sat at the computer while I carried the dresser up the stairs." Indeed, Beth needs to let Craig know when his behavior upsets her. But her intensely critical, sarcastic tone is getting in the way of her message.

2. BE OPEN TO YOUR PARTNER'S INFLUENCE

Craig, on the other hand, needs to be more open to Beth's influence. Many people have trouble accepting their partner's ideas, suggestions, or requests because they believe that doing so will cause them to lose power in the relationship. However, our research has shown that just the opposite is true—especially for men. Husbands who allow themselves to be influenced by their wives actually have more power in their marriages than men who don't. That's because wives who feel empowered and respected in their marriages are more likely to go along with their husband's ideas and suggestions as well.

People who allow themselves to be influenced by their partners stop creating obstacles for each other and learn to compromise. We refer to this attitude as "the Aikido principle" because it's based on the same rule that's used in this modern Japanese martial art—that you must yield to your opponent in order to win. As paradoxical as it may seem, you become more powerful by sharing your power with others.

Craig's willingness to accept Beth's influence may also help her to become less frustrated and angry with Craig, so that she would be less likely to use harsh start-up when she's upset. In fact, our research also shows that when men share power in their marriages, their wives are far less likely to be critical and contemptuous toward their husbands.

So, what would this look like for Craig and Beth? It might mean that Craig would actually agree to some of the conditions that Beth is asking for. He might, for example, commit to vacuuming on weekends *even if she doesn't remind him to do so.*

3. TELL YOUR PARTNER WHAT YOU NEED

We also suggest that Beth be very explicit with Craig when she feels she needs him to be more open to her ideas and requests. She might say things like these:

- *"I really need you to listen to me right now."*

- *"I need to feel that what I say to you matters."*

- *"I need you to accept my influence in this situation."*

4. EXPRESS AND ACCEPT APPRECIATION

In addition, we suggest that both Craig and Beth show much more appreciation for each other. Our session revealed that they harbor a lot of resentment toward each other for past arguments and disappointments. The best way to move beyond such pain is to express gratitude for all the positive things you see in your partner. Your compliments don't have to be elaborate. They can be simple, frequent statements of positive things you notice in the moment. Examples might be:

- *"I like that color on you."*

- *"You were so patient when Skylar needed help with his math."*

- *"You had the oil changed in the car today? That's great that you remembered."*

Of course, expressing gratitude is just one part of the equation. The other is to hear and accept your partner's appreciation—rather than deny or ignore it, which Beth so often does. To help her change this pattern, we suggest that Craig keep offering his appreciation even when she pushes it away. And when she does so, he might remind her to stop, listen to his words, and "take it in." The goal is for Beth to learn to feel and believe all the good things about herself that Craig sees in her.

"It's hard to listen with new ears, to censor the self-criticism, and open yourself up to more positive messages," John explains. "But, over time, we believe the practice of offering and accepting positive, caring messages will make a difference. Your fondness for each other will grow, and your anger and criticism will diminish."

Here's what happens when Craig and Beth try the conversation again, using our suggestions:

What They Say	What We Notice
Beth: I've been working twice as many hours as I'm used to working. And I've been feeling overwhelmed with housework. I need some help to figure out how I can get more help from you without feeling like I'm nagging.	+ Good "softened start-up." + Great statement of feelings, describing the situation and her needs. + Makes request without blaming.
Craig: OK. I've seen that you're doing a lot more with your job. And I know how it feels to be overwhelmed. I think it would be really great if we could talk about both getting what we need. So tell me what you need.	+ Acknowledges her contribution. + Expresses understanding of her behavior and her feelings. + Expresses willingness to listen and work on the problem.
Beth (laughs, exasperated): I just told you. I want to figure out a way to split the housework in a more equal fashion without my having to continually ask for help. Can we just set up a list of chores and commit to what we'll do? Would that work for you?	− Slightly critical, impatient response. − Doesn't give him credit for willingness. + Clarifies her request. + Makes a suggestion. + Asks him a question about his needs.

What They Say	What We Notice
Craig: Well, I think a list can be a good idea. And I think it's important for you to be willing to ask for help as well. Because I'm concerned that I'm not going to be able to give you everything you need without some reminders from you.	+ Gives her credit for asking for help. + Shows some willingness to accept her idea. + Expresses honest fear that he's going to let her down.
Beth: Well, how about if we just make a list and put a copy on the refrigerator where we can both see the load that we're supposed to be carrying?	− Doesn't respond directly to his concern about her suggestion. + She makes the proposal more concrete.
Craig: OK. I think a list is a good idea.	+ He finally agrees, accepting her influence. + He compliments her idea.
Beth: Thank you. *(She smiles sweetly, playfully.)*	+ Expresses pleasure that he's responded to her suggestion. (Playful attitude helps a lot.) + She accepts his appreciation.
Craig *(smiling, too)*: You're welcome. I also want it to be OK for you to ask for help. So if the list isn't totally working the way that you'd like it to work, it's OK for you to remind me. I don't view it as nagging. I want you to understand that I care. I see all the work that you do around the house and I think it's awesome.	+ Shows even more willingness to support her. + Repeats his need for verbal reminders. + Expresses that he cares. + Expresses more appreciation.

continued

What They Say	*What We Notice*
Beth: It feels really good to hear you say that right now. And I think I need to hear it periodically. I know you can't do that all the time—like, "Wow, that toilet is really sparkling today!" But if I hear it, I feel like my effort is not a waste of my time.	+ She "takes in" his appreciation. + Expresses her need to hear it. + Her humor continues to help.
Craig: Right. And I think that's reasonable. And for all the work that you do around the house, I think that you deserve that.	+ Responds to her expressed need. + Continues appreciation.
Beth: Should I ask for it?	+ Asks for information.
Craig *(hesitantly)*: No.	+ Honest response.
Beth: Because you hate it when I ask for a compliment.	+ Probes for more understanding of his feelings.
Craig: No, I'm going to give you my best pledge that it's going to come without your having to try to remind me. Because I feel that prompted appreciation seems somewhat hollow.	+ Responds by clarifying his commitment and feelings. + Promises to meet her need.
Beth: So you want to be reminded about the chores.	+ Validates his need and shows she understands.

What They Say	What We Notice
Craig: Yes, and I want you to understand that you deserve the right to ask for help. I want you to understand that I want to help.	+ Responds. + Tells her he values her. + Expresses willingness to help.
Beth: Do you swear?	+ Asking for reassurance.
Craig: I swear.	+ He gives it.
Beth: And I'm going to work on feeling more worthy of asking and not worrying that you're going to get mad.	+ Shows that she took in his healing words. + Expresses willingness to do her part.
Craig: This conversation makes me hopeful. I think this will also feed into what Skylar sees.	+ Expresses optimism. + Reminds her of their shared goal (to be better role models for their son).
Beth: Right.	+ Expresses agreement.

At the end of our session, Craig and Beth feel optimistic—especially when it comes to Skylar.

"I think of standing in the kitchen and you coming up behind me and giving me a hug," Beth tells Craig. "That would be nice for Skylar to see."

"What a great way to state your needs," John points out. "You could have said it this way: 'You'd never think of just coming up to me in the kitchen and giving me a hug, would you?' The way you just stated it was so much better!"

Beth accepts the compliment. But then she worries that it won't be easy to change. "That last conversation felt contrived. I had to keep telling myself, 'I am *not* going to be negative.' "

"It will feel like that for a while because your instincts tell you that the negative statements are 'the truth' and therefore you should state it," Julie explains.

"But it's not necessary, is it?" says Beth.

"It's really not," says Julie. "And it's not helpful."

"There will always be times when either of you are negative, harsh, or defensive," warns John. "These are well-worn grooves. But when it happens, don't feel like it's a lost cause. You can turn it around. And over time, if you find that it's happening in just 30 percent of your conversations instead of 90 percent of your conversations, that's a huge improvement!"

One Year Later

Our follow-up interview reveals that Craig and Beth's marriage has improved in much the way John predicted it would. The couple reports that their efforts to share more appreciation have made a big difference.

"We're getting better at saying, 'Thanks for doing this,' or 'Hey, I noticed that,' " says Craig. "We still have our meltdowns, but they're less severe and they last for a shorter duration. And we used to hold grudges afterward, which creates a kind of funk over the house. Now there's less damage being done when we tend to recover quicker."

"We're making more deposits in our emotional bank account," Craig adds, referring to a concept they learned about at one of our workshops. The idea is to keep a tally of all the specific steps you take to connect in positive ways throughout the day. These might include phone calls, favors, compliments, signs of physical affection. You don't track them in order to compete. Rather, you do it to make sure that you're creating an ample supply of fondness and good feelings toward each other. This surplus of positive regard can really come in handy when it's time to face the conflicts that inevitably come up.

Beth says Craig is slowly getting better at accepting her ideas and suggestions. For example, she's the thrifty one in their partnership, so she has tried for years to persuade Craig to save his expensive dress shoes for special occasions. "It just doesn't make sense to me that you'd need to wear $150 shoes to take out the trash," she explains. So it was great for her to look out the window recently and see Craig mowing the lawn in his well-worn work shoes. With no prompting from her, he pointed to his shoes and yelled, "See? I'm accepting influence!"

Both Beth and Craig say they've still got lots of conflict in their marriage, and they've come to accept that many of their differences will always be there. This acceptance makes it feel like less of a struggle.

"We celebrated our tenth anniversary this summer, which was significant for both of us," Beth explains. "After a decade together, we know each other so much better. He does this stupid thing and I do that dumb thing. And you know what? It doesn't matter! We're still together!"

Quiz: Harsh Start-up: A Problem in Your Marriage?

Beth and Craig often got off to a bad start in discussing their conflicts because Beth had a habit of starting conversations with a statement of criticism or contempt. This "harsh start-up" made Craig feel so defensive that he wouldn't listen to Beth, which made her even more frustrated and angry—increasing the chance that she'd introduce her next complaint with criticism and contempt as well. This vicious cycle was making it nearly impossible for them to solve their problems.

The following questionnaire may help you determine if harsh start-up is harming your marriage:

PARTNER A		PARTNER B
T/F		T/F
_____	1. My partner is often very critical of me.	_____
_____	2. I hate the way my partner raises an issue.	_____
_____	3. Arguments often seem to come out of nowhere.	_____
_____	4. Before I know it, we're in a fight.	_____
_____	5. When my partner complains, I feel picked on.	_____
_____	6. I seem always to get blamed for problems.	_____
_____	7. My partner is negative all out of proportion.	_____
_____	8. I feel I have to ward off personal attacks.	_____
_____	9. I often have to deny charges leveled against me.	_____
_____	10. My partner's feelings are too easily hurt.	_____
_____	11. What goes wrong is often not my responsibility.	_____
_____	12. My spouse criticizes my personality.	_____
_____	13. Issues get raised in an insulting manner.	_____
_____	14. At times my partner complains in a smug or superior way.	_____
_____	15. I have just about had it with all this negativity between us.	_____
_____	16. I feel basically disrespected when my partner complains.	_____
_____	17. I just want to leave the scene when complaints arise.	_____
_____	18. Our calm is suddenly shattered.	_____
_____	19. I find my partner's negativity unnerving and unsettling.	_____
_____	20. I think my partner can be totally irrational.	_____

SCORING

Give yourself one point for each "true" answer.

If you score under five, harsh start-up is probably not a big problem in your marriage. You and your spouse initiate difficult discussions with little criticism or contempt. As a result, your chances for handling conflict are good.

If you scored over five, you're probably using too much criticism and contempt when you talk about problems. Taking a more gentle approach will improve your ability to handle conflict together. The following exercise may help.

Exercise: Turning Harsh Start-up to Softened Start-up

Our research shows that the way you start your conversations makes a big difference in the overall quality of your marriage. Harsh start-up—that is, beginning with criticism or contempt—causes the interaction to go downhill fast. Partners become defensive and withdraw, leading to emotional distance and loneliness. The opposite is softened start-up, which is free of criticism and contempt.

Below are five examples of common marital conflicts, followed by examples of harsh start-up and softened start up.

1. The holidays are approaching and you're worried because your partner often spends more on her family than the two of you can afford.

HARSH START-UP: "I hate the holidays! Your shopping always drives us into debt."

SOFTENED START-UP: "I really want to enjoy the holidays with you this year. But I'm worried about the bills. Can we talk about a budget?"

2. Your partner likes to go to clubs with friends each weekend, but you like to spend more evenings at home together.

HARSH START-UP: "I'm sick of going out with your friends all the time."

SOFTENED START-UP: "I feel like spending time alone together. How about if I cook a nice dinner on Saturday and we stay home for a change?"

3. After a bad day at work, you come home to a headache, a messy house, and two quarreling kids. Your partner arrives, turns on the baseball game, and asks, "What's for dinner?"

HARSH START-UP: "How the hell should I know? And why do I always have to cook?!"

SOFTENED START-UP: "I don't know, and I don't feel very well. It would be great if you'd take care of dinner."

4. You'd like to make love tonight, but your partner's been distant. You wonder whether he even finds you attractive anymore.

HARSH START-UP: "What's wrong with your sex drive lately? You sure don't seem like the guy I married."

SOFTENED START-UP: "I've really been missing you. Remember how we made love at the cabin last summer? Tell me what I can do to get you interested."

Now, draft a list of conflicts that are common in your marriage. Then think of ways you might start a conversation with your partner about these issues, using softened start-up.

Here are few simple rules to remember as you begin:

- *Complain, don't criticize or blame.*

- *Start your sentences with "I" instead of "you."* (Example: I feel anxious when we're running late," versus "You never seem to get ready on time.")

- *Talk clearly about what you need.* (Example: "I need for us to agree on our budget" versus "I wish you'd quit wasting money.")

- *Be polite.*

- *Express appreciation.*

THE COMMON CONFLICT:_____

_____

SOFTENED START-UP: _____

THE COMMON CONFLICT:_____

_____

SOFTENED START-UP: _____

THE COMMON CONFLICT:_____

_____

SOFTENED START-UP: _____

THE COMMON CONFLICT:_____

_____

SOFTENED START-UP: _____

THE COMMON CONFLICT:_____

_____

SOFTENED START-UP: _____

Quiz: Are You Open to Your Partner's Influence?

Another problem we perceived in Beth and Craig's marriage was Craig's unwillingness to accept influence from Beth. Our research shows that this problem—which is most common among husbands—can be harmful to a relationship. That's because it leads wives to become frustrated and angry, increasing the chances that they'll become highly critical and contemptuous—behaviors proven to be quite destructive in a marriage.

To find out if accepting influence is a challenge in your marriage, answer the following questions:

PARTNER A		PARTNER B
T/F		T/F
_____	1. I am really interested in my partner's opinions on our basic conflicts.	_____
_____	2. I usually learn a lot from my partner, even when we disagree.	_____

PARTNER A		PARTNER B
T/F		T/F

_____ 3. I want my partner to feel that what he or she says really matters to me. _____

_____ 4. I generally want my partner to feel influential in this marriage. _____

_____ 5. I can listen to my partner. _____

_____ 6. My partner has a lot of basic common sense. _____

_____ 7. I try to communicate respect, even during our disagreements. _____

_____ 8. If I keep trying to convince my partner, I will eventually succeed. _____

_____ 9. I don't reject my partner's opinions out of hand. _____

_____ 10. My partner is not rational enough to take seriously when we discuss our conflicts. _____

_____ 11. I believe in lots of give and take in our discussions. _____

_____ 12. I am very persuasive, and usually can win arguments with my partner. _____

_____ 13. I feel I have an important say when we make decisions. _____

_____ 14. My partner usually has good ideas. _____

_____ 15. My partner is basically a great help as a problem solver. _____

_____ 16. I try to listen respectfully, even when I disagree. _____

_____ 17. My ideas for solutions are usually much better than my partner's ideas. _____

_____ 18. I can usually find something to agree with in my partner's position. _____

_____ 19. My partner is usually too emotional. _____

_____ 20. I am the one who needs to make the major decisions in this relationship. _____

SCORING: Give yourself one point for each "true" answer, except for items 8, 10, 12, 17, 19, 20. Then subtract one point for each "true" answer to items 8, 10, 12, 17, 19, 20. If you scored 6 or above, accepting influence is an area of strength in your marriage. If you scored below 6, you and your partner need to make improvements in your willingness to accept influence from each other.

Exercise: Using the Aikido Principle to Accept Influence

Couples who have trouble accepting influence from each other often argue and feel defensive. One partner makes a complaint or suggestion and the other responds with a statement of denial or refusal. In these situations, neither partner wants to admit he or she is wrong. Neither one wants to be in the shameful position of being "the loser." But the trouble is, the arguments that ensue can be harmful to your marriage.

An alternative to this deadlocked position is to accept influence. We refer to this as "the Aikido principle" because it involves a concept crucial to this Japanese form of martial art—that you must "yield to win." In other words, you don't go head-to-head with the person who is attacking you; you fall in line beside your partner instead. This can be done simply by asking your partner questions about his or her point of view and expressing willingness to look at the problem from a new perspective. Responses might be:

- Explain your thinking to me.

- What are all your feelings about this issue?

- Tell me why this is so important to you.

- Tell me how you would solve the problem if you were going to solve it alone.

- I may not be looking at it the same way you do. Tell me how you would approach this.

- What are you afraid of in this situation?

- What disasters are you trying to avoid?

- What are your goals around this issue?

- This seems to be important to you. Tell me why.

- Help me understand why you feel so strongly about this.

Responding in this way can be totally disarming—especially if your partner is poised for a fight. It changes the energy of the conversation, allowing the two of you to approach the conflict from the same perspective and build understanding. You may even find a compromise.

One reason the Aikido principle is so successful is that it restores dignity to the conversation and allows both partners to maintain their self-respect. There are no winners and losers in this kind of exchange. Partners can have different points of view, and that's OK.

The following chart shows a few examples of alternative responses to complaints and attacks. As you read them, imagine the different tracks the conversations might take, based on whether you choose to go head-to-head or to yield and be influenced. Which response do you think might lead to a closer relationship?

Your partner complains or attacks you.	You go head-to-head; you don't accept influence.	You yield to win; you accept influence.
I don't like you going out for drinks after work all the time.	I don't do it "all the time." I only go out on Fridays.	This seems to worry you. Tell me what you're afraid of.

Your partner complains or attacks you.	You go head-to-head; you don't accept influence.	You yield to win; you accept influence.
You told your mother we'd have Thanksgiving with her before you asked me what I wanted to do.	I'm sorry but you know how important Thanksgiving is to my mother.	I'm sorry. That was probably the wrong thing to do. What do you think we should do now?
You're spending way too much on clothes.	What do you know about fashion?	Maybe I don't think about spending money on clothes the same way you do. Let's talk about it.
They passed you over for a promotion again? I can't believe you put up with this!	Look, there's nothing I can do about it, so forget it!	It makes me unhappy, too. Do you have any suggestions?
Look at the mess you left in this bathroom. It drives me nuts!	You're upset because I left the towels on the floor? You're a lunatic!	Tell me why this bothers you so much.

Think about an argument you and your partner recently had or are likely to have in the future. Imagine how the conversation might go if one of you were to respond to the other's complaint or attack with a statement that accepts influence. Write down your imagined complaint/attack and your imagined response.

COMPLAINT OR ATTACK:_____

_____

Response that accepts influence:_____

COMPLAINT OR ATTACK:_____
_____

Response that accepts influence:_____

COMPLAINT OR ATTACK:_____
_____

Response that accepts influence:_____

COMPLAINT OR ATTACK:_____
_____

Response that accepts influence:_____

COMPLAINT OR ATTACK:_____
_____

Response that accepts influence:_____

COMPLAINT OR ATTACK:_____
_____

Response that accepts influence:_____

COMPLAINT OR ATTACK:_____
_____

Response that accepts influence:_____

Using the Aikido principle to accept influence may not come naturally at first. Most of us are much more conditioned to respond to complaints or attacks in a defensive way. But if you can stay calm and think creatively in the moment, a nondefensive response is possible. You may find the result so positive that you'll decide to make it a habit in the future.

CHAPTER 8

"There's No Passion, There's No Fun"

In fifty-one years of marriage, Jack and Maureen have tried to follow the old advice: "Accentuate the positive, eliminate the negative." So when Jack remembers meeting his sweet-natured bride at college in 1950, he focuses on his good fortune. "I always felt lucky that you agreed to marry me," he tells her.

But Maureen insists he's being too modest. "You were the plum in that year's senior class," she reminds him. "You could have had any girl on campus. I was the lucky one."

Such appreciation continues as they talk about all they've shared over the years. Both former social workers, they're grateful for their home, the three children they raised, their church community, and their good sense in saving for a comfortable retirement.

And yet, when pressed to describe the entire picture of their marriage, it's clear that both partners feel something's missing—and it has been for a long time.

"We have a warm affection for each other, but we're not very adventurous or fun loving," says Maureen, seventy-four. "We don't have a lot of passion or fun in our marriage."

"We're both quite shy in the bedroom," adds Jack, seventy-six.

What's the Problem?

- *Maureen hides her anger.*
- *When she does talk about being mad, she focuses largely on the needs of others, not on her own.*
- *Jack often withdraws when Maureen gets angry.*
- *Ignoring Maureen's anger makes both feel emotionally distant—interferes with passion, fun, sexual response.*

What's the Solution?

- *For Maureen:*
  - *Identify and express what's making you angry.*
  - *Express anger in a more constructive way.*
  - *Express more appreciation of Jack.*
- *For Jack: Listen and respond to Maureen's anger.*

"Maybe we were more uninhibited when we were younger."

"I don't think I ever felt uninhibited," Maureen says sadly. "I used to feel very sorry for myself about it, but I don't so much anymore."

Still, she longs for more emotional intimacy with Jack—a dream she still believes is possible. "I would like to reach a point where we're sharing feelings that we don't share now," she explains. "I think there are whole areas that we're afraid to express."

For example, when Maureen gets angry, she always tries to hide it from Jack. She's afraid that it would hurt their relationship, she explains. And, in fact, Jack has revealed in our questionnaire that he usually responds to Maureen's anger by withdrawing. He doesn't see any point in discussing difficult feelings.

"I think one of my big fears has been that if I looked at my anger honestly, it would result in a separation and that's not what we want," Maureen says as Jack nods in agreement.

But lately it's been getting harder for Maureen to keep her anger under wraps. They point to a recent incident in a church discussion group as an example. Maureen noticed that the men were monopolizing the conversation while all the women in this characteristically polite crowd passively listened. She had a sense that some of the women in the group wanted to share ideas, but they felt intimidated by a few domineering men in the group. This whole idea that her women friends were being silenced against their will started to eat at Maureen. So, after fuming silently for quite some time, she made a sudden angry comment, letting the whole group know how mad she was about the way they were behaving. "If we women were to break off and go somewhere else to meet, we'd be talking our heads off!" Maureen snapped at the man leading the discussion. Meanwhile, the rest of the group—including Jack—sat stunned and bewildered.

Maureen's outburst had repercussions. On the way home that night, Jack told her she had behaved inappropriately and it embarrassed him. And the next day the discussion leader sent Maureen an e-mail message saying she had hurt his feelings. As a result, Maureen made the difficult choice to quit attending the group.

At the same time, she noticed that acting out caused some positive ripples in her life. "Expressing myself in that painful situation, rather than just stuffing it down, made a difference in my physical response to Jack," Maureen explains. In other words, it somehow allowed her to feel sexier.

This doesn't surprise us, we tell her. Keeping a lid on your anger creates distance in a relationship, and that makes it hard to have fun together, to take risks emotionally and physically, and to enjoy sex. But if you use your anger to stand up for what you need, you gain self-respect, which is an important part of feeling free to express sexual feelings.

This makes sense to Maureen. "Sometimes I think that if Jack and I would fight more passionately, there would be more passion in our whole relationship, but I haven't been sure," she says.

Another good thing happened, says Maureen. After several weeks of absence, she got a note from a male friend in the group asking her to return. When she called to thank him, he told her he knew what she was

199

going through. "It was the most wonderful conversation," She recalls. "Nobody has ever understood the kind of pain I was in the way that this man did."

"What if you could have a conversation with Jack that would make you feel that well understood?" John asks. "What if Jack could help you to open up in that way?"

"That's the kind of progress I was hoping we could make with your help," Maureen replies as Jack nods in agreement.

Because this incident seemed like such a turning point for Maureen and Jack, we suggested they discuss their feelings about it with each other. Here's an excerpt of that talk:

What They Say	*What We Notice*
Maureen: Do you have any understanding of what I've been trying to express?	+ Reaching out to him.
Jack: Well, I know that we've talked about men having both a masculine and feminine side and you said my feminine is kind of submerged or something.	+ Nice attempt to express understanding, even though it reveals his confusion.
Maureen: No, Caroline said that in that dream class.	− Correction with a hint of criticism, resentment.
Jack: So I guess I need to get a clearer understanding.	+ Admits he doesn't understand; still trying.

What They Say	What We Notice
Maureen: Well, when you and the other men get to talking, it seems to me that all awareness of what the other people are feeling is gone. I feel the speaker has a responsibility to be aware of the people in his or her audience.	+ Expresses her anger.
Jack: I suppose I could practice that.	+ Amazingly accepting.
Maureen: I'm going to risk something here, and I hope I don't pay for it later on. We were at the Smiths' Tuesday night, and the men spent all evening talking about experiences in World War II. On the way home, you said what a great time you had had. But I felt like my head was going to explode!	+ Takes a risk to tell him how strongly she feels about this. + Clearly complaining without criticizing.
Jack: Well, do you deny that some people have more to say than others? Take our book group, for example. We have a retired professor in the group. He has spent his whole career drawing from the literature, and . . .	− Defensive response.
Maureen: And therefore I'm supposed to be quiet because he has so much more to say?	+/− Expresses anger, but with slight sarcasm.
Jack: Well, yeah. That's what I'm asking.	+ Asking for clarification.

continued

What They Say	What We Notice
Maureen: Well, I don't see it that way. In fact, it even occurred to me that some people may feel too intimidated to speak up because we've got this expert in the room. If we're going to have a class and somebody's going to teach it, let's call it a class. But if we're going to have a club to discuss a book that everyone has a reaction to, let's make sure it's a conversation. Let's make sure that everybody has a chance to talk.	+ Continues expressing her feelings. – Distances herself from her anger by talking about the group instead of her own personal experience; relies on "we" instead of "I."
Jack: Well, it's a little mind-boggling to me that these women have remained passive and silent. I just have to assume—	+ Expresses his confusion honestly. – Somewhat defensive.
Maureen: It's because—*(she catches herself for interrupting him and covers her mouth with her hand).*	+ Stops herself from interrupting, a good repair.
Jack: It's because they're more interested in what one of the other speakers has to say than in expressing themselves. You're saying that's not the case and maybe they're just being passive out of habit.	+ Shows he's getting her point; does not take her criticism personally.
Maureen: I look around at these discussion groups and I see women my age who are of a certain kind. We're what I call "nice ladies." We don't want to be told we're "not nice." That would be pretty threatening. But I think there has got to be a different way of being in these groups other than just being a passive "nice lady."	+/– Taking more responsibility for her feelings, but still creating distance by talking about "we."

Our Analysis: Failure to Express Anger Leads to Emotional Distance

We see some very good things happening in this conversation. Although Jack shows a bit of defensiveness, he seems quite willing to hear Maureen's complaint and to accept her suggestions for fixing the problem. That's a tremendous advantage for this marriage.

Also, Maureen does a good job of describing her anger. But it would be better if she'd talk more about her *own* feelings in this situation rather than the needs of all the women in their group. We suspect that talking about the group's needs makes the conversation feel safer for both her and Jack. But it also puts some distance between them—and that may be the distance that she's most longing to cross.

Our Advice

We invite Jack and Maureen to think about how they can support each other to become more emotionally engaged.

For Jack, this means continuing to do what he's done in this first conversation—to keep talking and listening and responding—despite the fact that he may feel like withdrawing from the conversation when Maureen is angry.

To help Maureen go deeper in expressing her own personal feelings, we suggest that she take a closer look at what's happening in those moments when her anger first comes to the surface. She might ask, "What's my goal in this situation?" and "What's getting in my way of accomplishing that goal?"

This advice strikes a chord with her. "I have always been led to believe that anger is wrong and that I have no right to be angry, but I think that my anger has enabled me to get through things," she says.

"Do you believe that getting angry is a matter of preserving your dignity?" John guesses.

"That's correct, and I think I learned that as a child," she says, referring to a time when she was sexually abused by an older relative. "I simply got angry and closed everybody off. I decided, 'I'll make my own way, thank you very much, and I'm not ever telling you how I feel again.'"

"So being angry became a matter of self-respect for you," says John.

"I think so," Maureen answers.

"And you don't respect being a compliant, 'nice lady' anymore?"

"No, I don't," she says.

"Would it mean a lot to you if Jack could support you in expressing your feelings in an open, honest way?"

"Yes, it would," she replies. "And when I say that something makes me angry, it doesn't mean that anybody's right or wrong. It's just what I'm feeling in the moment."

Jack, who's been listening intently, nods in agreement. He's taking in everything she says. In fact, he's been doing this throughout the session, demonstrating an extraordinary willingness to listen to her and to be influenced by her. In addition, he often offers her compliments.

What is Maureen's response to all this positive attention? While she's certainly respectful to Jack, we notice that she doesn't seem to acknowledge or appreciate his kind attention as much as she could. While Maureen tells *us* she really appreciates how Jack responds to her, we think it would do wonders for their relationship if she would tell *him*—moment by moment—that she notices the good things he says and does.

The pair agrees to take our advice as they return to the topic of the church discussion group.

What They Say	What We Notice
Maureen: I would like to see the person who is running the group check in with each person occasionally to see how they are feeling about the discussion.	+ Begins with constructive suggestion.

What They Say	What We Notice
Jack: So you would feel better if you had some positive support from me for that sort of thing. And I don't have any problem with that. I guess some of my problem is . . . *(He pauses to collect his thoughts.)* You know that when we got married fifty years ago, you may have been an angry person, but it was sure hidden underneath. Do you remember what my father said? "You've introduced us to a very sweet, gentle girl."	+ Expresses support. + Accepts influence. + Takes the conversation to a deeper, more personal level. + Expresses his confusion about the changes he's seen in her.
Maureen: In those days I wasn't in touch with my feelings.	+ Reframes his statement to clarify.
Jack: But now it's almost as if I'm married to a different person.	+ Expresses his feelings and confusion.
Maureen: That's right. It *is* almost as though you're married to a different person. And the more I try to be genuinely who I am, rather than what I think—or somebody else thinks—I *ought* to be, I run the risk of becoming somebody you don't like. And I think there are times that you don't like me.	+ Validates his feelings. + Talks about her own feelings rather than the group. + Expresses her fears and worries. + Great honesty.
Jack *(nodding, thoughtfully)*: Yeah. *(Long pause.)* To be perfectly candid, when you have an outburst of anger with a group of people who have gotten together to discuss religion—people we hardly know—I am nonplussed.	+ Honesty in return. + Validates her feelings. + Expresses his anger, embarrassment, fear.

continued

What They Say	What We Notice
Maureen: And that's why I need to learn a different way of expressing myself in those situations. I was attempting to be honest and I didn't do it very well. I've got to find a different way of expressing my anger. Through the years, it was always OK for *you* to be angry in the marriage.	+ Takes responsibility for the problem. +/− Expresses her feeling that their double standard about anger has been unfair; a bit critical, defensive, sarcastic.
Jack: Umhmmm.	+ Taking it in.
Maureen: You frequently were angry and expressed it in a male fashion.	− Still critical.
Jack: Ummhmm. Well. Yeah. There is that different cultural expectation. But I personally think I should avoid getting angry and I do to the greatest degree that I can. When I'm angry, I just head out for a walk and walk it off.	+ Shows he's listening. − A bit defensive.
Maureen: I suspect that that doesn't help us to get closer.	+ Clarifies what she wants from him—emotional intimacy.
Jack: No. Well, I told you after the meeting that I was upset. I made that pretty clear. I didn't just sit around and avoid talking about it.	+ Validates her need. − Still a little defensive.
Maureen: And that's why we were able to talk about it.	+ Points out their strength, their progress.

What They Say	What We Notice
Jack: So is there anything else I could do to be more positive and supportive of your needs with regard to . . . *(He pauses again.)* Well, I guess there's this whole business of the dining table, how you feel that with me always sitting at the head of the table, that you feel diminished.	+ Asking her what she needs. + Shows support for her goal of getting more respect.
Maureen: Yeah, it was never my intention of having that table. I wanted a round one.	+ Validating his thought; accepting his suggestion.
Jack: So would it be a move in the right direction to just get rid of that table? To sell it in a yard sale and get a round table?	+ Very supportive, showing he accepts her influence.
Maureen: *(Pauses and looks at him intently, with one eyebrow raised.)* Ummhmm. For me it would.	+ Expresses her amazement, and validates that he's on the right track.
Jack: Well, that's one indication of support. And I could do something about the book club on Sunday. But I don't want to move in and say, "From now on, we're going to do it this way."	+ Still supportive, while being realistic.
Maureen: No, that would be awkward. But I think it would be good to go around and give everybody a chance to talk.	+ Validates his realism. + Accepts his support.
Jack: Yeah. OK.	+ Reassures her that he means it.

In this second conversation, Jack and Maureen show great progress in their willingness to share deep feelings openly and honestly. They both reveal a little bit of defensiveness in this conversation, but they're talking about some very difficult issues here, so that's to be expected.

What truly impressed us was Jack's demonstration that he's paying attention to Maureen's feelings. When he suggests getting a new dining room table, he's showing Maureen, in a really concrete way, that he supports her goal of attaining more dignity and more respect. Maureen is also showing that she cares about Jack's feelings, especially when she admits that she should learn to express her anger in more constructive ways.

Although Maureen's appreciation for Jack doesn't surface in this conversation, it does appear later on as we're wrapping up our session.

"This really is what Jack is like," she tells us. "If I can just work up my courage to get across what I'm feeling—and if I can do that without making him feel like he's under attack—then he really comes through for me."

With that in mind, we encourage Maureen to keep being emotionally honest with Jack. And we encourage Jack to keep paying attention to Maureen—especially when she's angry.

"As surprising as this may sound, a wife's anger can be a real resource—particularly in a marriage like yours," says John. "It's a sign that Maureen's no longer deadening her responses. It's a sign that she's coming alive. And that can be the key to having much more passion and fun in this relationship."

One Year Later

Seated at their new, round dining room table, Maureen and Jack describe the shifts in their marriage over the past year as "a 180-degree change."

"Maureen has become more cheerful, more positive, and much more assertive," says Jack.

"And I think Jack is beginning to enjoy himself more. That's been very nice to see," says Maureen.

They both attribute much of the change to Maureen's conscious effort to tell Jack when she feels angry and why. Jack is grateful for Maureen's honesty because he's no longer in the dark about what's bothering her, and they can usually find solutions.

Here's just one of many examples: Jack recently rearranged a kitchen cupboard, moving some of his medication into a space Maureen was using for her pills. "Months ago, I would have stewed about how thoughtless he had been, but I wouldn't have said anything," says Maureen. "This time I told him how I felt. I said, 'This area is mine and I don't like it that you invaded my space.'" Then she got a chopstick and used it to divide the space, designating one area for her and one for him.

Jack's reaction? "I felt a little surprised, because I thought that part of the cupboard was just sort of a general area. But if she feels that way, that's OK. It seemed like a good, practical way to make sure that we didn't get into a snit."

"I'm learning that if I make myself clear, Jack is so willing to accommodate me," Maureen adds, smiling warmly at her husband. "And, lo, these fifty years, I missed all those opportunities to teach him!"

Maureen's also aware that she missed many opportunities to appreciate Jack. So now, "Instead of only seeing negative things about him, I have begun to see all the positive things," she reports. In fact, she's made a list of his attributes, which she shares with us. It includes words like *supportive, affectionate, accepting,* and *trusting.* Turning to him, she sees him beaming. "And when you're relaxed and smiling, you're quite handsome," she adds.

More affection and less resentment are helping Maureen and Jack relax into new levels of sexual pleasure, as well.

"At the tender age of seventy-four and seventy-six, we're finally getting there," says Maureen, "and it's so much fun!"

HOW ANGER CAN ENHANCE
A MARRIAGE

Jack and Maureen's experience shows the good changes that can happen when couples learn to accept anger and use it as a catalyst for improving their marriage.

One key is to recognize anger as a positive emotion. In fact, images from brain scans show that we experience anger on the left side of the brain, along with feelings of amusement and intense interest. Unlike sadness or fear—which are experienced on the right side of the brain and cause us to withdraw from the world—anger can stir us to engage with others, to take action, and to get involved.

Like all emotions, there's a logic and purpose to anger. We typically get angry when we see injustice, believe we've been treated unfairly, or encounter an obstacle to achieving our goals. If we can learn to use anger constructively, it can inspire us to make positive changes on our own behalf—to try harder, to fight for what's fair, and to communicate more passionately. We can use anger to *italicize* our language so that other people can hear and understand how strongly we feel about an issue. And, as Jack and Maureen learned, we can use anger to improve our relationships.

For anger to be useful, however, you must be willing to express it and respond to it openly. And that can be a real challenge, especially if you experience anger as frightening, destructive, or out of control. From this perspective, anger may seem like a snowball of thoughts and feelings that gathers more strength and power as it goes downhill. (Example: "How could he treat me that way? He must think I'm some kind of loser, an idiot . . . That makes me so furious I could just fly off the handle . . . Who knows what might happen? I'll show him who's a loser . . .") A cascade of angry thoughts like this gives way to feelings of more shame, more fear, and more intense anger, until the emotions feel like an avalanche, threatening to destroy everything in its path.

If you typically lose control of your anger in this way—or fear that you might—you may benefit from counseling that can help you to rewrite the script. With assistance, you may learn to perceive anger as a logical, legitimate experience that can be managed and that can lead to improved conditions in your life. (Example: "I feel angry because of the way he treated me . . . I have a right to feel this way . . . It makes sense to have these feelings . . . I really need to be heard here . . . I can handle this feeling . . . If I speak up now, I can fix this situation and make it better . . . ") When you can experience anger as a positive, constructive force in your life, you may no longer feel as if you have to keep your anger hidden all the time. You learn to express it, so that others can better understand your experience, which leads to less resentment and a better chance at problem solving.

In marriage, couples may improve their relationship by reacting to each other's anger with this same kind of respect. If you approach your partner's anger with the idea that there's a logical, legitimate reason behind his or her feelings, then you may be able to use that anger as a resource for improving your marriage.

The secret is to help your partner understand the source of his or her anger. Asking simple, open-ended questions without trying to change your partner's feelings may be useful. Such questions might be "Why are you angry?" "You seem so frustrated right now. Tell me what's going on." "What do you need right now?" "What do you wish would happen in this situation?" (See more questions in the exercise on pages 216–17.)

But what if you feel that your spouse's anger is aimed directly at you? Well, that's a challenge, for sure. The angry partner needs to do his or her part by expressing feelings in ways that avoid contempt, hostility, or blaming. They need to focus on their own needs rather than their partner's faults or deficiencies. This allows the partner who's listening to feel less defensive, more willing to be influenced. The two of you will be less likely to fall into patterns of attack/defend/counterattack.

The importance of having somebody listen to you when you're angry can't be overstated. Years ago, psychologists believed that if people would just express their anger—"get it off their chests," so to speak—they could "get over" being angry and their lives would improve. This idea of being able to banish anger as though it were as simple as relieving a pressure valve has since been proven wrong. In fact, psychologists have found that simply venting your anger—i.e., ranting or raging without the benefit of an understanding listener—just makes you *angrier*. What you need when you're angry is empathy. You need somebody to listen and to say, "I care about what you're going through, and I want to understand." Having a receptive listener helps you to accept your angry feelings, work through them, and calm down.

Of course, it's hard for people to listen and to be understanding and caring when they're under attack. So take care to express anger in ways that are constructive and respectful—especially when the person you're most angry with is your spouse. The section titled "Healthy Complaining Versus Harmful Complaining" in chapter 1 may help.

A SPECIAL MESSAGE FOR HUSBANDS: "EMBRACE HER ANGER"

We believe that either partner's anger—expressed and understood—can be a resource for improvement in marriage. But our research shows this is especially true for women's anger. That's why one of the most powerful messages we give to husbands is this: "Embrace your wife's anger." Pay attention to it and follow it to its source. That's where you're likely to find the keys to making your marriage better.

We believe this message is especially pertinent today because women are now being educated and empowered to achieve more economically, politically, and socially. But our culture still teaches that women who assert themselves to get what they want are being "pushy" or obnoxious. Women who get angry when their goals are blocked are labeled "bitchy" or rude.

"Nice ladies," as Maureen told Jack, may feel angry, but many don't express their anger—especially not in the company of men. Consequently, these same "nice ladies" are often frustrated and misunderstood. They feel disrespected and resentful toward the men in their lives, and that resentment snuffs out feelings of appreciation, affection, passion, and romance. Meanwhile, their anger "leaks out" at inopportune moments—in the middle of a church discussion group, for instance.

Where does this leave a man like Jack, who would like to have a more loving relationship with his wife, but feels bewildered or upset by her chilly responses or angry outbursts? We believe he can make tremendous progress toward greater intimacy in his marriage by tapping into his wife's anger and helping her to say what's on her mind. This can be done by asking her questions when she's angry, and showing concern about the things that make her mad. To do so shows that he cares about what she's feeling, what her goals and aspirations are, and what's getting in the way of those desires. By doing so, he proves that her perspective really matters to him. He becomes her confidant and her ally.

Aretha Franklin had it right when she sang, "R-E-S-P-E-C-T—*find out what it means to me.*" Embracing your wife's anger means showing her your respect. And, as Aretha demonstrates, "just a little bit" can go a long way toward unleashing feelings of appreciation, affection, passion, and romance.

Quiz: How Do You Feel About Anger?

The following quiz can help you and your spouse compare your attitudes about expressing anger.

As you read each question, think about recent episodes when you or your spouse felt angry. If you're not absolutely sure how to answer, that's OK. Just indicate the answer toward which you more or less lean.

PARTNER A		PARTNER B
T/F		T/F

<table>
<tr><td>_____</td><td>1. I am either calm or I blow up in anger; there's not much in between.</td><td>_____</td></tr>
<tr><td>_____</td><td>2. I can tell when I'm starting to get angry because I feel a little grumpy or irritated.</td><td>_____</td></tr>
<tr><td>_____</td><td>3. I think it's best to keep my angry feelings to myself.</td><td>_____</td></tr>
<tr><td>_____</td><td>4. My view is that if you suppress anger, you're courting disaster.</td><td>_____</td></tr>
<tr><td>_____</td><td>5. Anger is usually inappropriate.</td><td>_____</td></tr>
<tr><td>_____</td><td>6. Getting angry makes me feel more powerful, as if I'm standing up for myself.</td><td>_____</td></tr>
<tr><td>_____</td><td>7. For me, anger is a time bomb waiting to explode.</td><td>_____</td></tr>
<tr><td>_____</td><td>8. Anger gives you drive.</td><td>_____</td></tr>
<tr><td>_____</td><td>9. I think getting angry is uncivilized.</td><td>_____</td></tr>
<tr><td>_____</td><td>10. For me, anger and getting hurt go together; when I'm angry, it's usually because I've been hurt.</td><td>_____</td></tr>
<tr><td>_____</td><td>11. I don't see the difference between anger and aggression.</td><td>_____</td></tr>
<tr><td>_____</td><td>12. It's hard for me to sit still when I'm angry.</td><td>_____</td></tr>
<tr><td>_____</td><td>13. I think people should pay the consequences for angry outbursts.</td><td>_____</td></tr>
<tr><td>_____</td><td>14. When I get angry, people know they can't just push me around.</td><td>_____</td></tr>
<tr><td>_____</td><td>15. I cope with my anger by letting time pass.</td><td>_____</td></tr>
<tr><td>_____</td><td>16. Getting angry feels like blowing off steam, letting go of pressure.</td><td>_____</td></tr>
<tr><td>_____</td><td>17. Anger is OK as long as it's controlled.</td><td>_____</td></tr>
<tr><td>_____</td><td>18. For me, anger is a natural reaction, like clearing your throat.</td><td>_____</td></tr>
<tr><td>_____</td><td>19. When people get angry, it's as if they're dumping their garbage on other people.</td><td>_____</td></tr>
</table>

214

PARTNER A	PARTNER B
T/F	T/F

_____ 20. I think that if you always try to hide your anger, it will make _____
you sick.

_____ 21. Anger is like fire; you've got to stop it right away, or it will _____
consume you.

_____ 22. Anger gives me energy; it motivates me to tackle problems _____
and not be defeated by them.

SCORING: Add one point for each even-numbered item (2, 4, 6, 8, etc.) that you answered "true." Subtract one point for each odd-numbered (1, 3, 5, 7, etc.) item that you answered "true." The higher your score, the more comfortable you are with anger.

If you and your spouse have substantially different scores, you may have lots of conflict about the way anger is expressed in your marriage. The following exercise may help you to reconcile some of that conflict.

Exercise: When You and Your Partner Have Different Ideas About Anger

Partners' attitudes about expressing anger may differ widely based on their experiences with anger as a child or experiences that may have occurred in their adult lives when they let their anger show. If you and your spouse find yourselves at odds over this issue, it's usually best to discuss your feelings about anger directly. The following steps can help:

1. Take the quiz on the previous pages and discuss how each of you answered each item.

2. Take turns answering the following questions about your individual histories with the emotion of anger:

- How did you feel as a child when your father became angry with you? With your mother?

- How did you feel as a child when your mother became angry with you? With your father?

- What significant things have happened in your life when you have become angry at some person, situation, or thing?

3. As you and your partner answer these questions, try to understand how your life experiences with anger may differ. Despite those differences, express understanding toward your partner if you can.

4. See if you can arrive at an agreement about expressing anger in your marriage that honors both of your points of view. Some compromise may be necessary. The following exercise may help.

Exercise: Responding to Anger in a Helpful Way

Anger often comes up when somebody's got a goal, but they're feeling blocked or frustrated in their attempts to achieve it. Sometimes that person might not even know what their goal is. They just know they're angry and they'd like to feel better. The first step may be to figure out what the goal is. Then you can figure out what's getting in the way and what to do about it.

On page 217 are some questions to help with that process. You can use them by yourself when you're feeling angry. Or you can use them as a starting point for a conversation with your spouse when he or she is mad.

If you decide to use them with an angry spouse, remember this rule: *Understanding must come before advice.* In other words, it's better to let your partner get all his or her feelings out and for you to try to understand those feelings, before you begin problem solving or exploring what to do.

Also, if the conversation gets so intense that one or both of you start to flood (that is, your heart rate soars and you can't think clearly), you may need to take a break and set a time to come back to the conversation. (See the exercise in chapter 2, "Calm Down to Avoid Flooding.")

- What are you angry about?

- What are your goals in this situation?

- What are your needs here?

- What do you want to see happen?

- What are you trying to accomplish?

- What does this issue mean to you?

- What are all your feelings about this situation?

- What is so frustrating for you in this situation?

- What do you see as the obstacles to getting what you want?

- What's standing in your way?

- What's painful about this situation?

- Is there something about this that seems unfair?

- Is there something about this that seems immoral or wrong?

- What have you tried to do in the past?

- Has that worked before?

- If so, can you do it again? If not, why not?

- What could you do differently this time?

- What are some other things that you can think of doing to accomplish this same goal?

- How can I help you?

CHAPTER 9

"We Only Have Time for the Kids Now"

Like many parents of small children, Ron and Melissa look back at their childless years together and marvel at all the time they once had to just relax. As newlyweds living near Cincinnati, Ron was in business school while Melissa taught art classes at a community college. At the end of the day, they would meet in their kitchen and swap stories.

"Ron loves to cook," Melissa explains. "So I would watch and we would yak while he made the meal."

"We always ate dinner late because it took a long time to prepare," he remembers. "Then, afterwards, we would just sit for the longest time and just talk."

All that changed when Ron and Melissa became parents after eight years of marriage. Now, when Ron comes home from his job as a manager at a software company, he's greeted at the door by their two sons, Alex, age four, and Collin, ten months. Melissa, now a stay-at-home mom, is often exhausted by 6:00 p.m., and she's ready for Ron to take the kids off her hands.

"I feel like it's crunch time as soon as I walk in the door," Ron complains. "There are too many things happening all at once. Alex wants my attention.

I need to change my clothes. I need to get dinner made . . ."

"I usually cook these days," Melissa responds, and Ron nods in agreement, falling silent, looking sad. It's obvious that their long, intimate dinners are a thing of the past.

All told, Ron and Melissa say they're a "great team" when it comes to meeting their kids' needs. "But sometimes I feel like that's all we are," says Ron, forty-two.

Take bedtime, for example. Melissa, thirty-six, feels strongly that babies should not sleep alone. So, for the time being, Collin has a place in his parents' bed. The trouble is, the baby often doesn't rest well near Melissa; he keeps trying to nurse throughout the night. So, lately, Melissa's been leaving him in the bed with Ron and going off to the guest room to sleep by herself. Consequently, the couple finds very little time for cuddling with each other. Sex at night is out of the question.

As for the rest of the day, Melissa says there's never enough time or energy to relate to each other as lovers. "We want to be connected that way, but I'm always afraid that if I tell Ron, 'I

What's the Problem?

- *Ron and Melissa focus totally on their kids' needs, while ignoring their emotional and sexual needs as a couple.*

- *Melissa feels lonely, isolated from Ron, so she pursues his attention.*

- *Ron feels criticized, incompetent in Melissa's eyes, so he withdraws.*

- *Neither partner clearly states needs.*

- *Neither partner has a blueprint for handling conflict.*

What's the Solution?

- *Express your needs to each other in more specific ways.*

- *Turn toward each other's needs.*

- *Learn to use a blueprint for handling conflict.*

- *Make your marriage the top priority, recognizing how this will benefit the kids.*

feel lonely,' or suggest that we do something together, he'll respond with, 'Sure, Melissa. But when are we going to find the time?' "

Ron and Melissa describe their relationship as a kind of pursuit: Melissa's always pressing Ron for more attention and more help, and Ron is perpetually pulling away. Our research shows that this dynamic— where the wife persistently seeks help and attention from a retreating husband—is common among couples adjusting to parenthood.

"He communicates with me, but it's almost grudgingly," she says. "He'll complain, 'You're so intense, Melissa!' And I'm like, 'Yeah, that's because you're not here!' I don't like being intense. But I want you to notice me!"

"What does 'intense' mean to you?" John asks.

"It means she's always getting in my space with some immediate demand," says Ron.

"Yeah, I *want* to be 'in your space!' " says Melissa, exasperated. "That's the problem."

"But I always end up feeling like I've failed you before I even get the chance to respond," says Ron.

To hear more, we ask Ron and Melissa to discuss a recent conflict. They zero in on a tense moment that happened while preparing dinner the night before.

What They Say	*What We Notice*
Ron: I think I make assumptions when I read your body language. It's this vibe that you're impatient with me—disapproving. Like last night, when we were getting ready for dinner, I was crouched down at the refrigerator and you tried to give me the baby.	+ Takes responsibility as he describes the problem. +/− Tries to avoid blaming, but slightly critical.

What They Say	What We Notice
Melissa: Oh, right.	+ Shows she's listening, nondefensive.
Ron: I was putting stuff into the back of the fridge, and all of a sudden there's this baby hovering over my head. And I'm thinking to myself, "Would you give me five seconds to do this before I have to grab the baby? Just back off that much!" I get this feeling that I've done something wrong. I feel like I'm being slow or stupid.	+/− Describes his frustration, but slipping into accusation. + Good description of feelings.
Melissa: The feeling of impatience is hard for you?	+ Good question.
Ron: Yeah, because it seems very disapproving. And I don't . . .	− Blaming.
Melissa: I think it's that I'm desperate. I have less patience now than I would like to have. And I feel that I talk more than you want me to. It's like you're thinking, "I've heard it all. You're repeating yourself." So now I try to talk less. I don't talk when I probably should. Like I should say, "Ron, I can't carry a crying baby around and do what I need to do. Would you hold him, please?"	− Interrupts. + Expresses her feelings. − Assumes she knows what he's thinking ("mind reading"). + Takes responsibility for her part of the conflict.
Ron: Right.	+ Shows he's listening.

continued

What They Say	What We Notice
Melissa: And if I said that, then you wouldn't be so surprised. *Maybe. (Sarcastic tone.)* You wouldn't feel like I was so impatient because there would be warning with words.	+/− Takes responsibility, but her sarcasm shows contempt.
Ron: Ummhmm. The problem is the way I read you. It just gets me into trouble all the time.	+ Still listening, admits that his "mind reading" is a problem.
Melissa: Well, yeah. Because you think I'm angry and I'm not. And then you get angry because you think I'm angry.	+ Good insight.
Ron: I'm thinking, "Why is she pissed at me?"	+ He validates her insight.
Melissa: See, we're misinterpreting each other! It doesn't come across to me as "Why is she pissed at me?" It comes across as "She's pissed, so now I'm pissed!" And then I *am* pissed. I get upset because you're angry at me and I don't know *why* you're angry at me. You're angry at me because you think I'm angry at you.	+ More good insight about how their fights escalate when they make assumptions, don't state their feelings. + Expresses feelings.
Ron: Right.	+ Validates.
Melissa: It's a lose-lose situation. And being stuck about sex—it feels the same way. I don't know how to get out of the loop we're in.	+/− More good insight, but could say more about how she feels.

What They Say	What We Notice
Ron: I don't, either.	+ Validates.
Melissa: I fantasize. I wrote on the anniversary card I gave you, "Let's practice falling in love again." That's really what I'd like. I'd like us to both go, "OK. We're going to have an attitude change for a week." To just have a test period where you would think, "Now, I'm going to think that Melissa thinks I'm brilliant and sexy and prepared."	+ Starts to share her feelings. + States what she needs.
Ron: Until the next time I'm not.	+ Reveals his feelings of inadequacy in her eyes.
Melissa *(impatiently)*: No! No! No, not until the next time you're not. Just to try that attitude.	+/− Clarifies her need, but tone is critical.
Ron: Ummhmm. *(Long silence.)*	+/− Indicates he's listening, but doesn't tell her how he feels.
Melissa: So when did it change between us? Why did it change?	+/− Question shows willingness to go deeper; but "why" may result in intellectualizing, when what they really need is to share immediate feelings.
Ron: I don't know. That's a good question.	+ Shows responsiveness.
Melissa: Because if it had been like this fifteen years ago, we wouldn't be together now.	− Critical.
Ron: I guess it's a result of having had the same arguments a number of times. Having that same feeling of "Here we go again."	+ Good insight.

Our Analysis: Focus on the Kids Disguises the Real Trouble—Failure at Expressing Needs

Ron is right. Recurring dead-end arguments can lead to a sense of hopelessness, and that's not good for a marriage. Still, we see embers of hope in Ron and Melissa's relationship. We notice, for example, that both partners listen carefully to each other and respond in ways that are nondefensive. They're proud of the "teamwork" they share in caring for their children, and their devotion to their kids motivates them to look for solutions to the difficulties they're facing as a couple.

At the same time, they're quite frustrated. Like many couples adjusting to life with children, they tend to attribute many of their problems to their role as parents. They tell themselves that they're so busy meeting the kids' needs, there's no room to think about their needs as a couple. But as we've learned in our research, meeting your kids' needs and meeting your spouse's needs are not mutually exclusive goals. In fact, the best thing you can do for your child is to take good care of your marriage—and that's where we find Ron and Melissa struggling.

One problem is the way they express their needs to each other. For example, Melissa tells Ron that she wants to "practice falling in love again." But it's not clear to him how they're supposed to do this. Meanwhile, he seems quite anxious at the prospect of letting Melissa down. Exploring his family history, we learn that when Ron was a young teenager, his parents divorced and his mother left the family. It's not unusual for children of divorce to experience a sense of grief and helplessness at their inability to keep their families intact. In fact, Ron tells us he feels he was "always disappointing" his mother.

"This childhood experience may contribute to a sense of discomfort with Melissa's emotional intensity," John tells Ron. "It leaves you feeling no matter what you do, it won't be good enough," says John.

So when Melissa complains that she's "lonely" or "desperate" for his help—but then doesn't communicate what would make her feel better—Ron feels destined for failure. Faced with the prospect of disappointing Melissa, he withdraws. Poised to believe that he can't do right by his wife, he often reads more into her irritation or frustration than is warranted. Meanwhile, Melissa becomes frustrated by Ron's reaction and complains more intensely, causing Ron to become even more discouraged, to retreat even further.

Our Advice

Ron and Melissa need to do a better job of identifying and expressing their needs to each other. When Melissa feels she needs Ron's help, attention, or affection, she should tell him, *in precise ways,* what she's looking for. By using specific words or actions, she gives Ron a chance to help her feel understood, comforted, nurtured, attractive, and loved. (Examples: "I need you to hold me." "I need to set a date for dinner—just the two of us." "I need you to tell me I'm pretty." See the exercise "Give Me a Clue" on pages 235–36 for more.)

In addition, Ron needs to tell Melissa how she can help him to feel more accepted and competent in her eyes. Would it help, for example, for Melissa to acknowledge when Ron responds to her requests? What would it mean to him for Melissa to say that she appreciates how he paid attention, made the effort, and got it right?

We also suggest that Ron try some new responses when he feels uncomfortable with Melissa's demands. For example, rather than retreating from her intensity, he might say, "I'm afraid I'm going to let you down again, and that's not acceptable to me. I want to meet your needs. So tell me specifically: What do you want in this situation? What do you need right now?"

"Couples don't do this very much," John tells them. Instead, they simply engage in a kind of competition of self-sacrifice. "One partner will say, 'You don't get your needs met in this relationship? Well, I don't get my needs met, either!' But imagine what would happen if partners responded, 'You don't get your needs met? That's wrong! Both of us should be satisfied in this relationship, so let's figure out how to make that happen.' "

And finally, we suggest that Ron and Melissa use the "Blueprint for

Handling Conflict" that's described on pages 241–42. We believe this exercise can be especially helpful for them because of Ron's tendency to withdraw when Melissa's complaints become emotionally intense. The blueprint provides a way to stick with the discussion, build understanding, and arrive at compromise.

In this next conversation, we suggest that Ron and Melissa try to clearly tell each other what they need from this relationship.

What They Say	What We Notice
Melissa: I'm trying to figure out how to make our relationship a priority—along with meeting the parenting needs and work needs. Because I often hear, "There's no time for being physically close." But there *is* time for reading a book or working on a project, or something else.	+/− Boldly addresses the issues, but doesn't tell him how she feels about it.
Ron: Ummhmm.	+ Shows he's listening.
Melissa: And I think it would be good to spend some time being physically closer to each other. If I were to say, "I need to feel attractive to you," or "I need you to feel like I am attracted to you," what do we do about that? How do we . . . ?	+/− Gets close to addressing her needs, but focuses on how to "solve the problem" rather than how she feels about it.
Ron: I think we have to do a lot more things in passing. Like having a phone conversation. Or just squeezing it in between cooking and sitting down to dinner. Maybe some of the touching will happen if we just try to do things in little instants.	+/− Shows willingness to work with her, but he, too, is focused on the "how-to" rather than on his feelings.

What They Say	What We Notice
Melissa: OK.	+ Validates, accepts what he's saying.
Ron: Like if I just come by and give you a hug and keep on going. If we can make that more of a habit, I think that would be really nice.	+ Starts to address his feelings, what he feels would be "nice."
Melissa: I think we could have held hands when we were walking during lunch today. *(Long silence.)* I guess it's scary. I'm scared of jumping off this bridge after not being physically in touch for a while.	+ Expresses her disappointment. + Expresses her fear.
Ron: Ummhmm.	+/– Listening, but not really drawing her out with questions.
Melissa: And I'm thinking that you perceive being physically in touch as being sexually in touch.	+/– Expresses her fears, although in an analytical way, which can take her away from feelings.
Ron: OK.	+ Listening.
Melissa: You say that I don't like it when you touch me. And, yeah, when you grab my butt when Alex is there, that doesn't feel appropriate to me. But holding hands or a hug or something—that feels more like it. Then we could be in touch without it being intimidating.	+ Starts describing her feelings. + Expresses her needs for affection.
Ron: Sure.	+ Accepts what she's saying.

continued

What They Say	What We Notice
Melissa: When we're not in touch that way, having you grab my butt feels sort of crass.	+/− More feelings, starting to criticize.
Ron: OK.	+ Accepts.
Melissa: Like it's not coming from someplace loving.	− More criticism.
Ron: So you don't want me to do that when Alex is in the room. And you don't want me to do that when we're feeling out of touch.	+ Shows he understands.
Melissa: I need to start more gently than that.	+ Clarifies.
Ron: I agree.	+ Accepts.
Melissa: What do you need? Or what are you feeling right now?	+ Good questions.
Ron: Well, I think I need to feel comfortable touching you.	+ States his need.
Melissa: I'd like you to feel comfortable touching me. When you don't touch me, I feel pretty bad.	+ Validates his needs. + Expresses her feelings.
Ron: Ummhmm.	+ Listening.

What They Say	What We Notice
Melissa: And you're distancing yourself for some reason. I don't know why you're not comfortable.	− Criticizes him.
Ron: Often when I kiss you, you don't look in my eyes and I'm not sure why.	+ Gives information.
Melissa: I didn't know that.	+ Takes it in.
Ron: And last night before we went to bed you were in the middle room . . .	+ Gives her a specific example.
Melissa: Oh yeah, I was sort of looking around.	+ Goes along with him.
Ron: You were looking at a catalog. Then you got up to brush your teeth and I was kind of following you around and I really just wanted to kiss you. And I think I finally caught up with you on your way back into the room. And you just sort of said, "Good night." And I really felt brushed off.	+ Expresses specific need. + Expresses feeling.
Melissa: And I felt really sad.	+ Expresses feeling.
Ron: Huh.	+ Takes it in.
Melissa: I felt really sad and really lonely. The whole time.	+ Expresses feeling.

continued

What They Say	What We Notice
Ron: Hmm. Interesting.	+ Listening.
Melissa: And I would have loved to hear, "I want to kiss you good night." Or, "Can we snuggle?" That would have felt great for me.	+ Expresses specific need and longing.
Ron: OK. I just need to tell you more.	+ Accepts what she's saying.
Melissa: Or you could say, "What do you need?" or "How are you feeling?" That would be great.	+ Working it out, telling him what she needs.
Ron: Good. I can do that.	+ Accepting her influence.
Melissa: Yeah. We could figure out a way to not feel lonely. I could figure out a way to feel close to you.	+ Expressing approval, acceptance, hope.

This conversation has taken Ron and Melissa into new territory—a place where they're bravely talking about feelings and needs that were previously cloaked in tension and silence. This is not an easy conversation for them, but as they demonstrate, it gives them a sense of hope that their marriage can improve.

Before closing, we encourage both partners—but Ron especially—to keep asking questions and reflecting back the answers they hear. This may encourage Melissa to be more specific in stating her needs. Then he'll have the information he needs to prove to her that he's listening and willing to meet her needs.

We also encourage them to make their relationship the number-one priority in their lives for at least the next year. This sounds challenging, especially considering their commitment to being great parents. But we remind them that improving their marriage is probably the best thing they can do for their children's well-being.

And finally we remind them that putting their marriage first means that each spouse is willing to do more than his or her fair share. "Don't worry if things seem out of balance—if it feels like you're giving more than fifty percent to this partnership," says John. "That's the way it has to be for a while." If Melissa says she needs help with the kids, Ron needs to drop everything and be there, John advises. If Ron needs reassurance that he's appreciated, Melissa should provide that reassurance without condition. Acting this way could build a new foundation of trust, appreciation, and affection. If that happens, they'll be reaping the rewards for many years to come.

Two Months Later

Ron and Melissa say they accepted our advice about communicating their needs—and it's had good results. They've agreed, for example, that when one person wants something, all they have to do is say so. "We can just say, 'This is what I need, and I need it now,'" Ron explains. "And the other person will respond without a lot of questions or delay."

This agreement has taken much of the tension out of their day-to-day lives together, the couple reports. Each partner is spending less emotional energy wondering, "Is it OK to ask?" or "Do I deserve this?" Whether the request involves help with a crying child, a hug when feeling lonely, or time to sit down and hash out a problem, the answer is the same: "Here I am." The results are warmer feelings and more spontaneity. And with less tension and hesitation in their interactions, they've having sex more often.

In addition, Ron and Melissa are making more time for guilt-free, individual pleasures. For example, Melissa is taking a yoga class twice a week. Ron is planning a week-long hiking trip with a friend. These activities require lots of cooperation around child care and household chores. But they're also a way for the partners to say, "I really care about you and your happiness—so go. Do something nice for yourself. I've got it covered."

WHAT'S WRONG WITH A CHILD-CENTERED MARRIAGE?

For couples intensely committed to being good parents, having a "child-centered marriage" may not sound like such a bad thing. After all, kids need and deserve an enormous amount of attention from their moms and dads. Problems arise, however, when couples use their parenting obligations as an excuse for neglecting their relationship with each other.

In a child-centered marriage, kids can become the great distraction—a convenient way to ignore your need for adult conversation or romance, or to sidestep marital problems that ought to be addressed. Examples of child-centered couples might include:

- *the pair who points to a child's sleep patterns as the reason they've stopped having sex*

- *the partners who say that between Little League, Scouts, and science projects, there's absolutely no time for that weekend getaway*

- *the couple that claims that the husband's job must be the primary focus of his life because the family needs a substantial income to send the kids to the best colleges*

Do you see the pattern? The couple's needs are always trumped in favor of the kids'. But in the long run, the children's needs aren't really being served at all. Parents who feel they missed important experiences or necessities in their own upbringing may be at special risk for having a child-centered marriage. These parents may be so focused on "getting it right" for their own offspring that *everything* else—including their marriage—takes a backseat to their children's needs. The sad irony is that in striving to create the perfect life for their children, these parents fail to provide what kids need most—a happy home. Spouses who neglect the health of their marriage may inadvertently create an environment that's rife with tension and susceptible to downward spirals of defensiveness, criticism, contempt, and stonewalling.

Our research has shown that growing up in a strife-filled environment can have a strong negative impact on children's attitudes and achievements. Children who live with unspoken tension in the family may become anxious, depressed, introverted, and withdrawn. Children who live with hostility and contempt become aggressive with their peers.

On the other hand, parents who take good care of the marriage—who listen and respond to each other's needs—provide their kids with great role models for healthy relationships. They also create a relaxed, happy environment where kids can thrive physically, emotionally, and intellectually. In our workshops with new parents, we often encourage couples to think of their marriage as they would a cradle. It's here in the safety of your stable, loving relationship that your child's heart can rest. Keeping that cradle strong and peaceful is the best thing you can do to ensure your child's long-term well-being.

To determine whether yours is a child-centered marriage, take the following quiz. For more advice on prioritizing family needs, see the section in chapter 3 "How a Little Selfishness Can Help Your Marriage."

Quiz: Is Your Marriage Child Centered?

Answer the following questions:

PARTNER A   PARTNER B
T/F   T/F

_____   1. I often find myself disappointed in this relationship.   _____

_____   2. I have learned to expect less from my partner.   _____

_____   3. It's hard for my deepest feelings to get much attention in this relationship.   _____

_____   4. I feel as though our life together is one long list of errands we have to do.   _____

_____   5. I feel as if I can't do anything right.   _____

_____   6. I often feel criticized by my partner.   _____

_____   7. There is not much intimacy in this relationship right now.   _____

_____   8. Our great conversations have somehow vanished.   _____

_____   9. Sometimes our relationship feels empty to me.   _____

_____   10. I don't feel very important to my partner anymore.   _____

_____   11. We are now separate and unconnected emotionally.   _____

_____   12. We don't really talk very deeply with each other.   _____

_____   13. There's not enough closeness between us.   _____

_____   14. The children take up all of our energy.   _____

_____   15. My partner seems to have lost interest in me.   _____

_____   16. I don't feel that my partner is very attracted to me these days.   _____

_____   17. There's certainly not much romance or passion in this relationship.   _____

_____   18. I can't really say that we are very good friends right now.   _____

_____   19. I am lonely in this relationship.   _____

SCORING: If you answered "true" on six or more of the items above, you and your spouse need to put more focus on your relationship as a couple in order to recognize each other's needs and to turn toward bids for connection. The following exercises may help.

Exercise: Give Me a Clue

What would you say if your partner asked, "What do you need from me in this marriage?" Perhaps you'd answer, "I need to feel loved," or "I need to feel respected." But would your spouse know what to do in order to help you feel that way?

This exercise may help you and your partner determine specific actions each of you can take to meet the other's needs. The idea is to eliminate the need for guesswork or "mind reading." Partners no longer need to feel "clueless" when responding to each other as friends, confidants, and lovers.

The instructions are simple. Read the examples below. Then get two sheets of blank paper. Each of you should write down five things (feelings, values, ideals) that you need from the relationship. Then, for each need, give three examples of actions your partner could take to help you fulfill that need. Then take turns sharing what you've written.

Tip: Try to state your needs in positive ways rather than as complaints. For example, don't say, "You never tell me what happens at work." Say, "I'd like to hear more about your job."

Examples:

WHAT I NEED: I need to feel loved.

Three actions my partner can take that would help me feel this way:

1. Touch me in an affectionate way. (Hold my hand when we walk down the street, put your arm around me in a crowd, snuggle close when we're watching TV.)
2. Make a date to spend time alone with me.
3. Do small, thoughtful favors for me. (Pour me a cup of coffee, offer to run an errand for me, cook my breakfast once in a while.)

WHAT I NEED: I need to feel that you're my friend.

Three actions my partner can take that would help me feel this way:

1. Take my side in an argument.
2. Invite me to do things with you.
3. Agree to see the movie I want to see sometimes.

WHAT I NEED: I need to feel sexy.

Three actions my partner can take that would help me feel this way:

1. Touch me this way (then demonstrate).
2. Kiss me out of the blue.
3. Tell me when I do something that excites you.

WHAT I NEED: I need to feel appreciated.

Three actions my partner can take that would help me feel this way:

1. Say thank you when I do things for you. (Cook dinner, get the car washed, pay the bills.)
2. Say nice things about me in front of other people.
3. Plan a dinner for my birthday.

WHAT I NEED: I need to feel respected.

Three actions my partner can take that would help me feel this way:

1. Listen when I tell you my opinion of the news.
2. Be on time to pick me up.
3. Try my suggestion for fixing something.

Exercise: Turning Toward Your Partner's Bids for Connection

We believe Melissa and Ron can improve their marriage by clearly telling each other what they need in terms of acceptance, friendship, affection, and romance.

Imagine, for example, what might have happened on that lonely night they describe on page 229 if either one had made a clear bid for emotional connection. What if either Ron or Melissa had said, "I really want to kiss you right now"? And what if the other had responded, "That's what I really want, too"?

Our research has shown that such exchanges are the stuff that happy marriages are made of. Whether a partner wants sex, affection, conversation, or just some help with the yard work, the story is the same: One partner makes a bid in the form of a comment, a gesture, a question, a touch, or a facial expression. And the other partner "turns toward" that bid with interest, empathy, or support.

While turning toward your partner's bids leads to the growth and development of a loving, caring relationship, "turning away" by ignoring your partner's bids has just the opposite effect. Whether the slight is intentional or simply caused by mindlessness, continually disregarding your partner's bids leads to increased conflict, hurt feelings, and the deterioration of your relationship.

"Turning against" your partner's bids with arguments and hostility also has a negative impact. It can make the bidding partner feel hurt and fearful, so that bidding stops, feelings are suppressed, and the relationship begins to wither.

Below is a list of situations in which partners commonly bid for emotional connection. As you read each item, imagine your partner offering this bid to you. Then imagine ways that you might turn away, turn against, or turn toward the bid. Over the next several weeks, see what happens when you make an effort to habitually turn toward your partner.

Examples:

BID: My partner pours me a cup of coffee as I'm working at the computer.

Turning-away response: Silence. No acknowledgment.

Turning-against response: "Looks like you made it too weak again."

Turning-toward response: "Thanks. That's so thoughtful."

BID: My partner reads aloud a joke that he or she thinks is funny.

Turning-away response: "Have you seen my black shoes?"

Turning-against response: "I can't concentrate when you're reading like that."

Turning-toward response: "That's funny." Or "I don't get it. Tell me why it cracks you up."

BID: My partner tells me some bit of news about a relative.

Turning-away response: _____

Turning-against response: _____

Turning-toward response: _____

BID: My partner mentions something that needs to be done in the yard.

Turning-away response: _____

Turning-against response: _____

Turning-toward response: _____

BID: My partner tells me we're out of laundry detergent.

Turning-away response: _____

Turning-against response: _____

Turning-toward response: _____

BID: My partner admires the neighbor's new car.

Turning-away response: _____

Turning-against response: _____

Turning-toward response: _____

BID: My partner touches me in an affectionate way.

Turning-away response: _____

Turning-against response: _____

Turning-toward response: _____

BID: My partner complains about a chronic health problem.

Turning-away response: _____

Turning-against response: _____

Turning-toward response: _____

BID: My partner says he or she is worried about our child.

Turning-away response: _____

Turning-against response: _____

Turning-toward response: _____

BID: My partner touches me in a way that usually leads to sex.

Turning-away response: _____

Turning-against response: _____

Turning-toward response: _____

BID: My partner tells me he or she is very tired.

Turning-away response: _____

Turning-against response: _____

Turning-toward response: _____

BID: My partner recalls something from childhood that was very hurtful.

Turning-away response: _____

Turning-against response: _____

Turning-toward response: _____

BID: My partner tells me about an incident at work where he or she felt unfairly treated.

Turning-away response: _____

Turning-against response: _____

Turning-toward response: _____

Busting the Myth of Spontaneity in Romance

"No time for sex and romance" is one of the most common complaints we hear from parents. The problem, they say, stems from nonstop, immediate demands of caring for young children. Once the kids arrive, it feels as if your entire life is booked. When you're not at work, you're running errands, doing housework, or caring for the brood. You feel that you have no privacy. And if you get around to having sex at all, it's usually at the end of the day when both of you are exhausted. For many tired parents, making love often feels like "the last chore of the day."

That's why we heartily recommend that couples schedule regular "dates"—evenings or weekends when you get a babysitter so you can have time alone together to keep romance alive in your relationship.

"But scheduling sex and romance takes all the spontaneity out of it," we hear couples complain. "That's no fun." We contend that such thoughts are a big mistake. To understand why, think about the most romantic times in your relationship. If you're like most people, you'll be remembering those first few dates. Now think back to how you used to get ready for those times together. You may remember preparations that were anything but spontaneous. In fact, people in new romantic relationships are often thinking far ahead, with considerations such as, how will I dress? What perfume will I wear? Should I dim the lights? How will I make my moves? And, most of all, how will all this feel? Did all the preparation take the fun out the relationship? Hardly. Instead, it added fuel to the sense of anticipation and excitement for the evening ahead.

So we advise couples to get their calendars out and start planning. Set aside some time and then use your imaginations to plan for romance, plan for sensuality, and plan for sex.

If, for whatever reason, planning for sex causes one or both partners to suffer "performance anxiety"—that is, to fear that they won't fulfill their partner's needs or expectations for the date, that's OK. The key is to talk to each other about those fears and offer reassurance. Then together you can take your expectations down a notch and focus on simply experiencing relaxation and pleasure together. Plan time for activities like hot baths, back rubs, touching, holding, and simply making each other feel good physically and emotionally. If sex happens, that's fine. But if it doesn't, you'll still have met your expectation of enjoying time together.

Exercise: A Blueprint for Handling Conflict

Some people avoid conflict because they fear getting hurt or hurting their partners. In fact, some know from experience that arguments with their partners *always* end up that way; the two start to disagree, the disagreement escalates and then "blows up." Meanwhile, nothing gets resolved.

If that's your experience, the following exercise may help. Based on the ideas of social theorist Anatol Rappaport, we developed this exercise as a structure or "blueprint" for couples to use in talking about their differences.

Step 1. Set aside a quiet time to discuss one single conflict at length.

Step 2. Designate one person as the speaker and one person as the listener.

Step 3. The speaker begins talking about the conflict, saying everything they want to say about their point of view. The listener can ask questions and take notes. Writing things down gives the speaker the distinct feeling that what they're saying really matters to the listener—and that's the point of the exercise.

When the listener asks questions, those questions are simply to ensure understanding. *The listener must delay talking about solutions and postpone any attempt to try to persuade the speaker.* The listener can't use questions to imply he or she disagrees. The listener should not present his or her own views. The listener can't correct the partner's facts or express reactions to the speaker's view. The listener's job is simply *to listen*. The whole interaction should be civil and polite.

Step 4. When the speaker is completely finished, the listener restates the speaker's point of view. The speaker listens carefully and clarifies anything the listener didn't really seem to grasp. Then the listener restates the position. This process repeats until the speaker is satisfied that the listener really understands.

Step 5. Switch roles and start over with Step 1.

Once you've completed these steps, you or your partner have not yet persuaded each other to see things differently. You may still have conflicting points of view. The exercise postpones persuasion until each person can state the partner's entire point of view to the partner's satisfaction. Then, and only then, can persuasion begin. You may now discuss your differences and try to compromise, or you may still "agree to disagree." Either way, however, it's likely that each of you will feel heard and better understood. In that state, you feel more emotionally connected to your partner, and that makes for a stronger marriage.

CHAPTER 10

"You're Not Satisfied Unless There's Some Drama"

Terry was attracted to Amanda the first time he saw her entering the kitchen in the Austin restaurant where they both worked. But she let him know early on that she wasn't interested.

"I told him I didn't go out with coworkers," the former waitress remembers. "And besides, I was more inclined to date wild, long-haired drummers in rock bands."

This clean-cut law student, who was working part-time as a cook, didn't fit the mold. But a few weeks later, when he invited her to join him hiking in the Hill Country, she consented.

"He was taking his dog, and I just love dogs, so I decided to go," explains Amanda, now thirty-five. Soon she found herself sitting next to him on a rock, thinking, "Wow, I'd really like to kiss him!"

She resisted the impulse—for about six hours. But by the end of the day, she wasn't limiting herself to drummers anymore. And by the end of the year, they'd moved in together.

Nine years later, Terry looks back to those early days as "a real roller-coaster ride." He blames the turmoil on the old saw "opposites attract." That is, the qualities they found most attractive in each other were the very things that drove them apart. While Amanda was outgoing,

What's the Problem?

- *Terry and Amanda have many "perpetual issues"—ongoing conflicts based on differences in personality and preferred lifestyle.*

- *When Amanda states her feelings about a conflict, he backs away.*

- *To avoid conflict, Amanda backs away, too.*

- *Habitual retreat from feelings creates emotional distance.*

- *Emotional distance contributes to physical distance.*

What's the Solution?

- *Quit avoiding conflict.*

- *Seek dialogue over perpetual issues.*

- *Communicate acceptance of each other's personalities; appreciation that "opposites attract."*

- *Take time alone together to rebuild emotional and physical intimacy.*

Terry was more introverted. While Terry strived for stability, Amanda was looking for excitement, taking risks.

"Her friends would party all weekend long, doing all kinds of crazy stuff," Terry, now thirty-seven, remembers. "Amanda liked the chaos of that scene, but I wasn't comfortable with it."

Amanda was often unhappy because she wanted their lives to be "more glamorous," says Terry. But Amanda says their problems actually centered on her longing for autonomy. "Terry was the stronger, more solid person in our relationship and I always felt like I was being subsumed into him," she explains. "I really resisted that."

She moved out several times, but invariably she'd return. "I couldn't go for more than two or three days before I really missed him and felt like I just need to touch base," she says. "So then I'd come back. He was my best friend."

After four years of ups and downs, Amanda had a conversation with her mom that changed everything. "I was telling her, 'Terry's a nice guy, but I don't think I want to be with him forever.' And my mom nice guy, but I don't think I want to be with him forever.' And my mom said, 'OK, young lady—then you break up with him right now and leave him for good!' Her words just shocked me and I started to cry. I said, 'God, no. I can't imagine my life without him.' But she said, 'Well, that's where you'll end up if you keep doing what you're doing.' "

A year later, Terry and Amanda were wed.

By the time they visit the Love Lab, they've been married nearly four years, their daughter Danielle is two years old, and their second baby is on the way. Terry has a job with a prominent Austin law firm. Amanda is working part-time as a corporate trainer.

Although they've been generally happy, both complain that they don't feel as close emotionally or physically as they'd like to. In addition, they're continually struggling with a host of problems we call "perpetual issues"—that is, fundamental differences in personality or lifestyle preference that repeatedly create conflict.

"She's always dreaming up things for us to do that would be dramatic shifts in our life," says Terry. "Things like moving to Costa Rica or joining the Peace Corps. Last week she thought we should become organic farmers. And I'm thinking, 'Where does this stuff come from?' "

"I just have a certain level of adrenaline that needs to be channeled into something exciting," explains Amanda.

"And that tendency drives me crazy," Terry complains. "I very much want things to be comfortable. It's not that I'm totally averse to change . . ."

"But I'm totally averse to calm," Amanda laughs.

Conflicts over finances also continue. "I'm somewhat conservative financially," says Terry, "but I don't always communicate the plans that I have."

"So when he wants to spend money on something I think is frivolous, he says we have the money," Amanda explains. "But when I want to spend money on something, all of a sudden he says, 'We can't afford that right now.' "

Whatever the conflict (money, friends, lifestyle), if Amanda keeps pressing an issue, "Terry just tenses up and gets real quiet," she says.

"I don't like conflict very much," he admits. "I don't even want to talk about it."

Still, he and Amanda both know they've got to keep talking about important issues if they're going to bridge the gap that's growing in their relationship—a gap that's starting to affect their sexual relationship as well.

"It's impossible for me to be sexually aroused when I am not emotionally engaged," explains Amanda. "Foreplay for me is deep conversation."

To get a better picture of how they approach perpetually difficult issues, we ask them to try discussing a current hot topic. They decide to talk about money and how to manage it during Amanda's upcoming maternity leave. Here's an excerpt of that conversation:

What They Say	*What We Notice*
Amanda: We haven't had much time to sit and plan because we've had so much going on.	+ Shares responsibility for the problem of not planning.
Terry: Ummhmm.	+ Shows he's listening.
Amanda: Which is why I keep feeling so anxious, but then I feel sort of silly—like I'm making a big deal out of it when I know there are all these other things that . . .	+/− Describes her feelings, but then discounts them.
Terry: Right. I feel if I've got time to sit and talk, then I've got time to get other stuff done.	−/+ Interrupts, but validates what she's saying. + States his priorities.

What They Say	What We Notice
Amanda: Yeah. And we're getting to this place where we really do need to make the communication a priority. But I know there is all the landscaping stuff and the house stuff. I've tried on a couple of occasions to set up times for us to have to talk about things.	+ States her real need: to communicate. + Expresses frustration, without blaming.
Terry: Have you?	+ Shows he hears her; asking for a reminder.
Amanda: Well, that's why Mary took Danielle. That was supposedly what we were going to do.	+ Shares information.
Terry: I don't recall we got to that.	+ Shares responsibility.
Amanda: No, we didn't. *(She laughs nervously.)* I think you ended up having the softball game.	+/− Tries to keep it light, but slightly blaming.
Terry: That's right. And then I went out to the pub with the team.	+ Acknowledges responsibility for the problem.
Amanda: And I went out with Mary and Danielle for a while. I mean, it was my fault, too. But now I'm feeling that need to follow you around and say, "Hey, what's our plan here?" And I'm having a hard time.	+ Shares responsibility. + Expresses her need, worries.

continued

247

What They Say	What We Notice
Terry: And I'm concerned because I've got that case coming up in San Antonio. That's kind of a rush, rush, high-stress engagement for me.	+/− Expresses his need, but doesn't acknowledge hers.
Amanda: Yeah.	+ Validates, shows she's OK with his work.
Terry: I mean, I'll have three hours in the car each day.	− Slightly defensive.
Amanda (kidding): Maybe I should just go with you and we could talk in the car. (She laughs at her own joke.) That would be fun.	+ Makes a joke to keep it light.
Terry (smiling): Yeah.	+ Accepts the joke.
Amanda: I mean, I'm getting really kind of scared about the whole thing. Like last night when I thought I might be in labor, it was just kind of scary. Because we haven't really had a chance to talk about . . .	+ Expresses more feelings.
Terry: We need a couple more weeks.	− Avoids focusing on her feelings.
Amanda: And I'm starting to get that feeling of wanting to jump in front of your face and go, "We're going to have this baby very soon!" And it's like you don't have time to talk. That's not a priority.	+ Expresses feelings, but in a more intense way. − Slightly blaming.

What They Say	What We Notice
Terry: You said you were not going to go back to work until September. Is that right?	+/− Finally focuses on her, but zeroes in on her work schedule rather than her feelings.
Amanda: Well, I don't know. I feel really uncomfortable with the idea of leaving a newborn in day care.	+ More feelings.
Terry: Yeah, I'd just as soon you take as long as we can afford.	+ Shows support for her emotionally.
Amanda: I just wasn't sure if we could afford that. I don't want to end up with the same situation we had after Danielle was born. I felt that because I wasn't bringing in a paycheck, I didn't have any authority over any expenditures. Even though I was working harder than I'd ever worked in my life. And yet you get really tense about where we are financially and you make remarks when I need some money transferred into my account.	+ Expresses more fears, going deeper.
Terry: What for?	− Ignores her feelings, focusing on the spending instead.

continued

What They Say	What We Notice
Amanda: You'd say, "You figure out where the money's going to come from, because I don't know." And I don't know what the problem is. Because just a month ago, you were buying wine and fancy yard equipment. When you're making expenditures like that, I'm thinking, "Huh? Well, I guess we're doing pretty good!"	– Blames, attacks.
Terry: We were doing fine (nervous laughter).	– Tries to deflect her feelings.
Amanda: Until the stock market crashed (smile).	– Goes along with him, backing away from her own concerns and feelings.

Our Analysis: Perpetual Issues Lead to Conflict Avoidance, Lack of Connection

The smiles and laughter in this conversation point to a great strength in Terry and Amanda's marriage—their genuine feelings of warmth and affection for each other. This brings a sense of "we-ness" to the relationship. They both seem willing to share responsibility for their problems. And while there's a little bit of blaming going on, we don't see a lot of defensiveness. That's another strength. Also, when the conversation gets tense, Amanda is quick to offer repairs in the form of soothing remarks, punctuated with a joke or a smile, which Terry accepts. This kind of interaction keeps the tone of their conversation friendly and productive.

So why, if there's so much warmth and good humor in this relationship, are they feeling increasingly isolated from each other emotionally and physically? A closer look at the dialogue reveals some subtle clues.

Notice that each time Amanda talks about her feelings, Terry tends to back away. For example, when she says she's worried about their lack of planning around finances for her maternity leave, he responds by asking her for concrete information about her work schedule. And when she talks about her fear of having no money of her own after the baby arrives, he asks her why she needed money when their first child was small.

To his credit, Terry's questions probe issues related to the topics Amanda brings up. This shows he's interested in what she's saying. But he doesn't seem comfortable grappling with the emotions she's expressing. His words fall short of letting her know that he understands her fears and worries, empathizes with her, and would like to offer reassurance. In fact, if you were to look at his words alone, it would be hard to determine whether he and Amanda share anything more than a joint checking account and babysitting duties.

Terry is not alone in his avoidance. Each time he sidetracks the conversation, Amanda goes right along with him—perhaps out of fear of losing the connection altogether. In this way, they remind us of David and Candace in chapter 2—the couple who were so afraid of trouble after recovering from David's extramarital affair that they sidestepped every conflict that came their way. And perhaps the turmoil in Terry and Amanda's early relationship has had the same effect on them.

The trouble with avoiding conflict, of course, is that it can cause a gulf in the relationship to grow. This may be particularly hazardous for couples like Terry and Amanda, who have such basic personality differences—and therefore so many perpetual conflicts. Habitually trying to sidestep all these issues leads to emotional distance. And for Amanda, especially, that lack of emotional connection leads to a lack of interest in sex, romance, and passion.

Our Advice

Rather than avoiding conflict, Terry and Amanda should take a careful look at their goals around their differences. We're not suggesting that they try to find the perfect solution to their disagreements over money, friends, lifestyle, and so on. Obviously there's no single true answer to the kinds of perpetual differences this couple faces. Amanda is a planner, Terry is not. Terry likes solitude, Amanda would rather party. Amanda likes lots of change, Terry likes things to stay stable. Neither partner is "right" or "wrong" in these desires. So the best approach is to simply *establish a dialogue* about the conflict—to be able to talk about your disagreements on an ongoing basis and still feel good about each other. The idea is to "make peace" with your differences, realizing that a happy coexistence will require lots of compromise, lots of give-and-take ahead.

It also helps to realize that your perspective on your partner's personality is just that—one person's perspective. In fact, Terry and Amanda tell us that in their own families of origin, Terry was considered quite "wild" compared to his brothers. And Amanda was "the stable, practical one" among her siblings.

We advise Terry and Amanda to try viewing their conflict as they would a third party outside the relationship—a project that the two of them are going to keep working at in a collaborative way. "The problem is *not* your partner," John says. "The problem isn't this 'money thing' or this 'planning thing' over which you disagree. That problem is like a soccer ball that the two of you are kicking around. You work together, looking at it together from different angles, figuring out how to get it down the field. Sometimes you make progress in your discussions and sometimes you don't. But you learn to live with it and don't let it harm your relationship."

The most important thing is to avoid getting "gridlocked" in your positions, he adds. To become gridlocked is like being in a bumper-to-bumper traffic jam; there is no movement, no compromise. You feel stuck and eventually you begin to see each other as enemies on either side of the issue. Remember, you don't have to be adversaries just because you hold opposite points of view. As Terry stated early on, "opposites attract"—and for good reason. When opposites are willing to see the world from the other person's perspective, they get to see the whole picture, and that can be a terrific advantage for couples.

Recognizing that you can talk about your conflicts without harming the relationship is also a great advantage in terms of building emotional intimacy—which is just what Terry and Amanda need to do. So in their next conversation, we advise them to go further into their feelings about a perpetual issue, focusing this time on *accepting* each other's differences. This time they discuss another long-standing conflict—their disagreement over the best place to live.

What They Say	What We Notice
Amanda: I think I'm fearful sometimes that, left up to you, we would just never . . .	+ States her fear.
Terry: We'd stay in the same house.	+ Shows he understands.
Amanda *(laughing)*: We'd be in the same house. And it's not that I'm unhappy there, but I feel like there's much that I want to do and experience.	+ Softens her complaint with laughter. + Goes deeper into feelings, needs.
Terry: Well, I agree that we need to do as much as we can, but you know how I feel about throwing everything out of the window and starting over. I'm well down the road in my career and I'm afraid of changing the course too much.	+ Validates her need. + Expresses his own fear.
Amanda: Ummhmm.	+ Shows she's listening.

continued

What They Say	What We Notice
Terry: I wish I could be more like you. I wish I could embrace change, because it would make our life more interesting, I'm sure.	+ Expresses appreciation for her personality.
Amanda: I'd like to be more like you, because it would make me a little more comfortable, but . . .	+ Expresses appreciation back.
Terry: But we're not going to change each other.	+ States acceptance of their differences.
Amanda: No.	+ She agrees.
Terry: So we have to be happy living together.	+ States shared goal of happiness.
Amanda (laughing): Or split up.	+ Keeps it light with humor.
Terry laughs.	+ Accepts her joke.
Amanda: My worst fear is that I'm ultimately going to have to make a decision between . . .	+ Goes further into feelings.
Terry: Well, let's talk specifics. We've always had this idea that we're going to move on to a different house after a few more years.	− Interrupts her at a crucial point to avoid going deeper.

What They Say	What We Notice
Amanda: And I was thinking three years . . .	− Goes with his train of thought, allowing him to take her away from expressing her feelings.
Terry: Why would we have ever bought a house if we were thinking of moving in just three years?	− Interrupts her again; domineering.
Amanda: Because that's the amount of time it takes before you would consider . . .	+ Responds with information.
Terry: Yeah, but I don't like to think about that.	− Interrupts her again; domineering.
Amanda: Don't you see how I have compromised in this situation to better fit your lifestyle? And for the most part, I'm fine with that. I certainly wouldn't go back and do it any differently if it meant not having our children.	+ Expresses her frustration, resentment. +/− Reassures him that she values the relationship, but holds back a bit.
Terry: But what if it just meant not having me?	+ Reveals fear of losing her; asks for reassurance.
Amanda: Oh, that's all part of the package.	+ Offers some reassurance.
Terry: But it's separate.	+ Keeps pressing for the reassurance he needs.
Amanda: No, I wouldn't do it differently if it meant not having you.	+ Gives him the complete reassurance he needs.

continued

255

What They Say	*What We Notice*
Terry: Good. That's nice to hear.	+ Expresses his relief, gratitude.
(They pause as Amanda laughs. Then they sit for a moment, just smiling at each other.)	+ Express warmth and affection.
Terry: When we do move, where do we go?	+ Now he's ready to go along with her; asks for her ideas.
Amanda: Well . . .	+ Starts to respond.
Terry: Let's say I'm in the same job, so we stay in Austin. You don't like the suburbs.	− Interrupts her. + Acknowledges her preferences.
Amanda: No. I like the idea of living further out. You could set up a satellite office.	+ Agrees and expresses her feelings; problem solving.
Terry: Maybe. But what about your more recent ideas of just throwing away everything that we have?	+/− Expresses his fears, although in an exaggerated way.
(She frowns.)	+ Protests his exaggeration.
Terry: I don't mean that you . . .	+ Recognizes her distress and tries to repair.
Amanda: I think that's what you hear when I talk.	+ Expresses her feeling that he's being unfair.

What They Say	What We Notice
Terry: Well, when you say you want to move to Costa Rica, that's kind of what I hear. OK?	− Slightly defensive. + Expresses his fear.
Amanda: I'm saying Costa Rica to stress what I don't like in our current lifestyle. And sometimes I feel like you don't value things that I find increasingly important in terms of the way that we're raising our family. You know, being around all this commercialism and seeing our children influenced by all this stuff.	+ Expresses her feelings. − Blaming. + Expresses her worries.
Terry: I share your concerns, but I don't share your solutions.	+ Validates her worries. + Clarifies the conflict.
Amanda: But we need to get a break. To get a year away from all the noise and all the commercials and all the ugliness.	+/− Expresses her needs; tries to convince him, but she's stopped telling him how she feels.
Terry: I just don't think we're in a position where we can coast. Maybe in ten years we can do something like that. But I'm afraid to say, "Yeah, that sounds like a great idea," because you'll just go and do it.	− Resisting, not communicating. + Finally expresses his feelings.
Amanda: When you say that, I feel like you don't trust me. Like I've done all these terrible things in the past. But I've never done anything that led us to ruin.	+ Expresses how hurt she feels when he becomes so resistant.

continued

What They Say	What We Notice
Terry: No. *(Pauses, smiling.)* Thanks to me.	+ Repairs the interaction with a smile and humor.
Amanda *(laughing)*: I mean, I'm a risk taker, yeah.	+ Accepts the repair; lightens up. + Acknowledges his point of view; accepts their differences.
Terry: *(Laughs, smiles at her with absolute adoration.)* Yes, you are. That's one of the things I like about you.	+ Expresses affection, love, acceptance. + Validates her personality.
Amanda: I have all this energy about having adventures and experiencing life. And it keeps getting tamped down until I get these crazy thoughts of just driving off into the sunset—just to see what would happen. Do you understand where I'm coming from?	+ Expresses feelings. + Asks for his understanding, acceptance.
Terry: Yes, I do. I do.	+ Extends his understanding, acceptance.

"This was an extremely productive conversation," John tells Terry and Amanda. "Not that it was fun or easy—you were talking about some tough issues. But you shared a lot of humor, affection, and respect for each other."

Most important, they were no longer ducking the tough issues. "Terry, you were talking about what you really fear and what you really need," John adds.

Amanda agrees. "It was definitely helpful to hear Terry say, 'I want the same things you do, but I'm afraid.' When he says that, I don't feel that we're on opposite sides anymore."

In addition, Terry and Amanda have openly acknowledged that their conflict is based on personality traits that they love in each other. Terry wishes he could "embrace change" like Amanda does. Later on, when he talks about what a "live wire" his daughter Danielle is, he just beams. It's clear that the little girl takes after her lively, adventurous mother, and that's what Terry loves in both of them. By the same token, Amanda says she wishes she could be more like Terry; she can see the merits of calmly settling down into this comfortable life they're building.

"I call this a 'delicious conflict' because it's bigger than just the conflict between the two of you," says John. "It's about a conflict that each of you carries *within yourselves.*"

Therefore, the more Terry and Amanda seek to understand each other, the more they'll each grow as individuals, John explains. "As long as you keep talking to each other this way, your conflicts are going to enrich your lives rather than drive you apart."

We offer Terry and Amanda a few more pointers. First, Terry needs to be aware of his tendency to interrupt Amanda—especially when he's feeling anxious. We notice that this domineering behavior results in Amanda shutting down and then fantasizing about getting away. Our advice? Be sure that Amanda has plenty of freedom to express herself in the relationship. Don't cut her off. Listen to what she's saying.

We also encourage them to keep expressing their appreciation and gratitude for the lives they're building together. (See the "Thanksgiving Checklist" on pages 268–270.) Doing so will warm the environment for more romance and intimacy.

And finally, as we do with all couples with small children, we strongly urge them to take time in their lives for sex and romance. (See the section in chapter 9 titled "Busting the Myth of Spontaneity in Romance.")

Two Years Later

When we check back with Terry and Amanda two years later, we find out that Terry has made partner in his law firm—a change that guarantees they'll stay in Austin for quite some time. In fact, they're still living in the same house—the one that Amanda felt certain they would have sold years ago.

Does all this stability still bother Amanda? "Not as much as it used to," she says. Maybe that's because she's had a few adventures on her own in recent years. For example, she and Danielle recently took a trip to Costa Rica as part of a cultural exchange program Amanda helped to organize through their church.

Still, Terry says he expects Amanda's restlessness to reemerge as a source of conflict in the future. "Maybe not this year or the next—but soon she'll feel she's in a rut and she'll shake things up somehow," he predicts.

"Our struggles are always changing and evolving," Amanda adds. "As soon as we get something resolved and put it behind us, we come to a place where we're facing some deeper struggle. In fact, sometimes I'm afraid that we're just working ourselves up to the mother of all marital conflicts."

At the same time, both partners say they're growing more confident in their ability to handle their conflicts as the years go by.

"We've certainly had our up and downs, both before we got married and after," says Terry. "I don't know what the next set of problems is going to be, but after all we've experienced, I'm pretty confident that we're going to get through them."

Don't Get Gridlocked over Perpetual Issues

Every marriage has perpetual issues—that is, conflicts based on personality differences or preferences in lifestyle that never go away. Common examples include disagreements over spending, where to live, or how to handle household chores. Our research shows that the happiest couples can live peacefully with their perpetual issues as long as they keep talking about them in an open, productive way. However, perpetual issues that become gridlocked conflicts can be harmful to a marriage.

In gridlocked conflict, couples

- *express little amusement or affection when they discuss the problem*

- *take the issue very personally, and feel rejected by each other when it comes up*

- *make each other "villains" in the conflict; one partner is completely right and the other is completely wrong*

- *become entrenched in their positions, never compromising*

- *spin their wheels, digging themselves deeper and deeper into conflict*

- *eventually become emotionally distant, disengaged*

To keep a perpetual issue from becoming gridlocked, you can

- *make dialogue your goal rather than finding the perfect solution*

- *see the problem as a third party outside your relationship; the problem is not your partner*

- *recognize that there are no "right" and "wrong" solutions*

- *accept that the conflict may never go away, but you can live together peacefully anyway*

- *look for humor in conflict*

Quiz: What Are Your Perpetual Issues and What Are Your Gridlocked Problems?

Every marriage has perpetual issues—those conflicts that just keep recurring, no matter what. But just because the same conflict keeps popping up again doesn't mean it has to harm your marriage.

Below is a list of common perpetual issues. There's also room at the bottom to fill in some of your own issues if they're not listed here.

In the first column, circle the issues that ring true for you and your partner. Then, looking back at each of the issues you've circled, ask, "Can my partner and I can still talk about this issue and find ways to compromise? Or are we gridlocked?" Make a check mark in the second or third columns as appropriate.

Is this issue a source of a perpetual conflict in your marriage	If so, do you talk and compromise?	Or do you gridlock?
1. Neatness and organization Partner A: Thinks it's important to be neat. Partner B: Doesn't think neatness matters that much.		
2. Emotional expression Partner A: Explores emotions and expresses them freely. Partner B: Is less comfortable with expressing or talking about feelings.		
3. Independence versus togetherness Partner A: Wants to spend more time together, to be more dependent on each other.		

Is this issue a source of a perpetual conflict in your marriage	If so, do you talk and compromise?	Or do you gridlock?
Partner B: Wants more time apart, to have more autonomy.		
4. Frequency of sex		
Partner A: Wants sex more often.		
Partner B: Wants sex less often.		
5. Sex and emotional intimacy		
Partner A: Wants to feel emotionally close before initiating sex.		
Partner B: Wants to have sex as a way to get emotionally close.		
6. Finances		
Partner A: Spends carefully, tries to save.		
Partner B: Spends freely, saves less.		
7. Family ties		
Partner A: Wants independence and distance from relatives.		
Partner B: Wants to spend time with and feel close to relatives.		
8. Household chores		
Partner A: Wants an equal division of labor.		*continued*

Is this issue a source of a perpetual conflict in your marriage	If so, do you talk and compromise?	Or do you gridlock?
Partner B: Does not want an equal division of labor.		
9. Disciplining children		
Partner A: Is stricter with the children.		
Partner B: Is more permissive with the children.		
10. Being on time		
Partner A: Thinks it's important to be on time.		
Partner B: Thinks being on time is no big deal.		
11. Socializing		
Partner A: Is extroverted, wants to spend more time with other people.		
Partner B: Is introverted, would rather spend time alone or as a couple.		
12. Religion		
Partner A: Places more value on religious practice.		
Partner B: Places less value on religious practice.		

Is this issue a source of a perpetual conflict in your marriage	If so, do you talk and compromise?	Or do you gridlock?
13. Ambition Partner A: Is more interested in success at work. Partner B: Is less interested in success at work.		
14. Romance and passion Partner A: Wants more romance and passion in life. Partner B: Doesn't care that much about romance and passion.		
15. Adventure Partner A: Wants more adventure and excitement in life. Partner B: Doesn't care that much about adventure; thinks life is exciting enough.		
16. Perpetual issue _____ Partner A: _____ Partner B: _____		
17. Perpetual issue _____ Partner A: _____ Partner B: _____		
18. Perpetual issue _____ Partner A: _____ Partner B: _____		*continued*

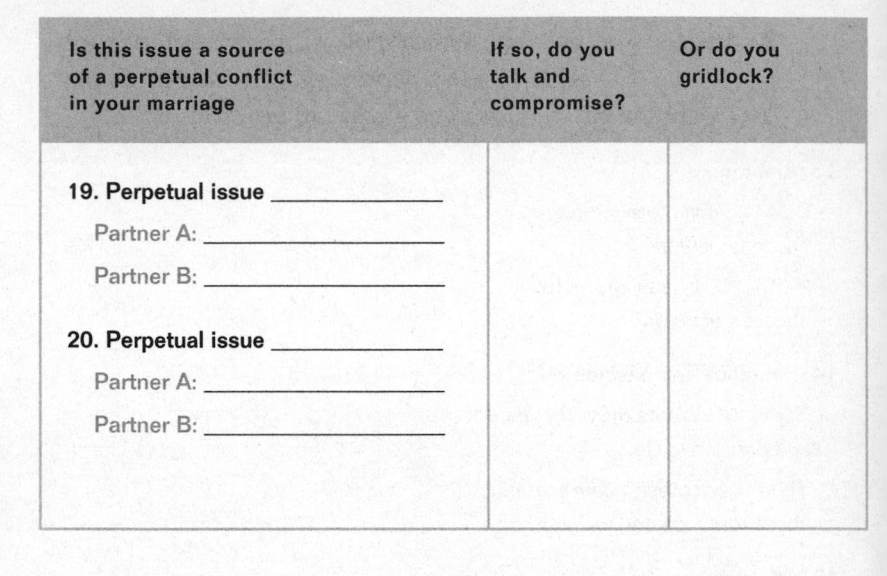

Is this issue a source of a perpetual conflict in your marriage	If so, do you talk and compromise?	Or do you gridlock?
19. Perpetual issue _____ Partner A: _____ Partner B: _____		
20. Perpetual issue _____ Partner A: _____ Partner B: _____		

As you review your check marks in the second column, consider how you and your partner can keep your minds and hearts open to each other around this issue. How can you keep talking, keep compromising, and keep stretching to find common ground?

As you review the check marks in the third column, consider whether there's any room for new dialogue or compromise on this issue. If you come up blank, look back at the section in Chapter 5 titled "Your Hidden Dreams and Aspirations: The 'Prairie Dogs' of Marital Conflict." As the material in this chapter explains, gaining a better understanding of each other's hopes and dreams is often the best way to break through gridlock.

Exercise: Creating a Culture of Shared Values and Meaning

Like Terry and Amanda, many couples are attracted to each other by their "opposite" natures. While this can be the basis of a vibrant marriage, it also requires lots of sensitivity and vigilance as you learn to accept and honor each other's points of view. By doing so, you create a culture of shared values and meaning in your marriage. This isn't something that happens automatically or overnight. Rather, it's a process that occurs as partners find ways to live side by side, respecting each other's goals, dreams, and perspectives. This exercise is a series of questions designed to encourage that process.

We recommend that partners each get a personal notebook. Then select one or two questions from the list that you'd like to think about. Write down your answer to the question. Then share what you've written with your partner. Discuss your answers, looking for areas of common ground, agreements you can build upon. Talk about your differences as well, finding ways to honor values and philosophies that both of you hold.

Some of these questions are big enough to stimulate hours of conversation, so don't feel that you need to tackle these questions all at once. In fact, you may want to come back to these pages time after time, selecting just a few questions that seem most important to you at various phases of your life.

- *What goals do you have in life, for yourself, for our marriage, for our children? What would you like to accomplish in the next five to ten years?*

- *What is one of your life dreams that you would like to fulfill before you die?*

- *We often fill our days with activities that demand immediate attention. But are you putting off activities that are great sources of energy and pleasure in your life? What are those activities?*

- *Who are we as a family in the world? What does it mean to be a _____ (insert your family's last name)?*

- *What stories from your family history are important to you?*

- *What does the idea of "home" mean to you? What qualities must it have? How is this like or unlike the home where you grew up?*

- *How important is spirituality or religion in your life? How important is it in our marriage and in our home? How is this like or unlike the home where you grew up?*

- *What's your philosophy of how to lead a meaningful life? How are you practicing (or not practicing) this philosophy?*

- *What rituals are important to you around mealtimes?*

- *What rituals are important to you around holidays?*

- *What rituals are important to you around various times of day (getting up, leaving the home, coming home, bedtime, etc.)?*

- *What rituals are important when somebody in our family is sick?*

- *How do we each get refreshed and renewed? How do we relax?*

- *What rituals do we have around vacations?*

- *What does it mean to be to be a husband or a wife in this family?*

- *What does it mean to be a mother or a father in this family?*

- *How do you feel about your role as a worker?*

- *How do you feel about your role as a friend? As a relative? As a member of our community?*

- *How do we balance the various roles we play in life?*

Exercise: Thanksgiving Checklist

We have learned that couples rarely improve their marriages by trying to change each other. Rather, partners find happiness by focusing on each other's positive attributes. Expressing gratitude and appreciation for these qualities creates a loving, accepting atmosphere between you—an optimal environment for building understanding around perpetual issues and finding ways to compromise.

For this exercise, take turns selecting three items from the following list that you really like about your spouse. (You can add your own items if you'd like.) Tell your spouse which three items you've selected for him or her. Describe in detail how you see these qualities expressed, and talk about the way they make your life better. Then thank your spouse for being this way.

I am grateful for:

- your energy

- your strength

- the way you take charge

- the way you let me direct things

- how sensitive you are to me

- how you support me and respond to my needs

- your ability to read me

- how I feel about your skin

- how I feel about your face

- how I feel about your warmth

- how I feel about your enthusiasm

- how I feel about your hair

- the way you touch me

- how safe I feel with you

- how I feel about your tenderness

- how I feel about your imagination

- how I feel about your eyes

269

- the way you move

- how I can trust you

- how I feel about your passion

- how you know me

- how I feel about your gracefulness

- the way you kiss me

- your playfulness

- your competence as a spouse

- your competence as a parent

- your sense of humor

- your friendship

- your loyalty

- your sense of style

- _____

- _____

- _____

- _____

Index

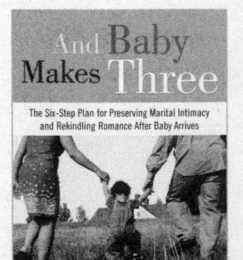

How I Became a Ghost

A Choctaw
Trail of Tears Story

The How I Became A Ghost Series
Book 1

Tim Tingle

THE ROADRUNNER PRESS
OKLAHOMA CITY

Published by The RoadRunner Press
Oklahoma City, Oklahoma
www.TheRoadRunnerPress.com

First Edition July 2013
Third Trade Paper Reprint August 2015
by Maple Press, York, Pennsylvania
This book is available for special promotions, premiums, and group sales.
For details e-mail Director of Special Sales at info@theroadrunnerpress.com.

Publisher's Cataloging-In-Publication Data
(Prepared by The Donohue Group, Inc.)
Tingle, Tim.
　　How I became a ghost : a Choctaw Trail of Tears story / Tim Tingle. — 1st ed.

　　p. : ill., map ; cm. — (The how I became a ghost series ; bk. 1)

　　Summary: A Choctaw boy tells the story of his tribe's removal from the only land its
people had ever known, and how their journey to Oklahoma led him to become a ghost—
one with the ability to help those he left behind.
　　Interest age level: 009-012.
　　Issued also as an ebook and an audiobook.
　　ISBN: 978-1-937054-53-3 (hardcover)
　　ISBN: 978-1-937054-55-7 (trade paper)
　　ISBN: 978-1-937054-54-0 (ebook)
　　ISBN: 978-1-937054-56-4 (audiobook)

　　1. Choctaw Indians—Relocation—Juvenile fiction. 2. Indian Removal, 1813-1903—Juvenile fiction. 3. Ghosts—Juvenile fiction. 4. Choctaw Nation of Oklahoma—Juvenile
fiction. 5. Choctaw Indians—Fiction. 6. Ghosts—Fiction. 7. Historical fiction. I. Title.

PZ7.T489 Ho 2013　　　　　　　　　　　[Fic]　　　2013935579

10 9 8 7 6 5 4

To my mentor Charley Jones,
who taught me the power of humor
in the Choctaw story

How I Became a Ghost

A Choctaw
Trail of Tears Story

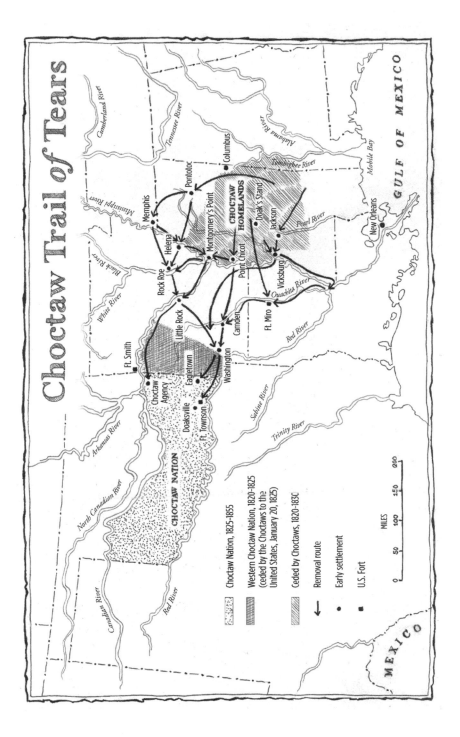

Choctaw Trail of Tears

CHOCTAW HOMELANDS

CHOCTAW NATION

Cumberland River
Tennessee River
Alabama River
Tombigbee River
Mississippi River
Black River
White River
Ouachita River
Pearl River
Red River
Sabine River
Trinity River
Arkansas River
North Canadian River
Canadian River
Red River

GULF OF MEXICO

Mobile Bay

New Orleans

MEXICO

Columbus
Pontotoc
Memphis
Montgomery's Point
Doak's Stand
Jackson
Helena
Rock Roe
Point Chicot
Vicksburg
Little Rock
Camden
Ft. Miro
Ft. Smith
Washington
Choctaw Agency
Eagletown
Doaksville
Ft. Towson

Choctaw Nation, 1825-1855

Western Choctaw Nation, 1820-1825
(ceded by the Choctaws to the
United States, January 20, 1825)

Ceded by Choctaws, 1820-1830

→ Removal route

• Early settlement

■ U.S. Fort

MILES
0   50   100   150   200

Chapter 1

Talking Ghost
Choctaw Nation, Mississippi, 1830

MAYBE YOU HAVE never read a book written by a ghost before. I am a ghost. I am not a ghost when this book begins, so you have to pay very close attention. I should tell you something else. I see things before they happen. You are probably thinking, "I wish I could see things before they happen."

Be careful what you wish for.

I'm ten years old and I'm not a ghost yet. My name is Isaac and I have a mother and a father and a big brother, Luke. I have a dog, too. His name is Jumper and he is my best friend. We go everywhere together. We swim in the river together; we chase chickens together.

"Make sure Jumper does not catch any chickens!" My mother always yelled this from the back porch.

"Why can't Jumper catch chickens?" I asked my father one evening, as we sat on the porch watching the stars.

"That's your mother's rule," he said.

"But *why?*"

"Because Jumper won't wait for the chickens to be cooked," he said. "He'll chew the chickens and choke on the bones and bloody feathers. Would you want to eat bloody feathers?"

"No," I said. "Good rule."

"Then make sure Jumper follows it."

"*Hoke,*" I said, which means "okay" in Choctaw.

Jumper and I, we take long walks in the woods together, we tug weeds from the corn stalks together, and we spend the day and night together.

"No dogs in your bed!" This was another rule of my mother's, but Jumper was smart. He waited until my mother fell asleep, then he climbed under the covers with me. In the morning, when he heard my mother making noise in the kitchen, he jumped out of bed.

Maybe she knew Jumper broke the rule. Maybe she smiled and let him get away with it. She was a good mother and we had a happy life, mostly. I had too many chores and too little free time, but I knew if I could just wait till I grew up, I'd have all the free time I wanted.

Then came the day that changed everything. Without any warning, I saw the ghosts. I also saw things before they happened.

My father rose early that morning, long before sunrise.

He left the house while it was still dark. He carried his shotgun and his bag of shotgun shells, so I knew he was going hunting.

I finished my chores and started tossing mudballs against the barn wall. Jumper barked and chased the mudballs, but only for a little while.

"I'm bored," Jumper said. "Let's chase chickens!"

We were on our way to the chicken pen when I saw my father coming home from the woods. He was carrying only his shell bag and his shotgun, so I knew something was wrong.

Usually he returned with a wild turkey or sometimes a deer. He never returned from a hunting trip with nothing. He walked through the back door and I followed him. He didn't say a word to me, just held up his hand to let me know I should stay outside.

I listened through the door.

"We must move," my father told my mother.

"What do you mean 'we must move'?" my mother asked. "You better move! Go back to the woods and catch us something to eat!" She was laughing.

"No," said my father, and he was not laughing. "There is Treaty Talk in town. We must move."

I was only ten, but I knew what Treaty Talk meant. It meant the *Nahullos* wanted something. *Nahullos* were people that lived a few miles away. They were not Choctaws, like us. We were nice to them and they were nice to us. But Treaty Talk always meant something else, and that something else was never nice.

3

My father took my mother by the hand and she gave him a strange look. He led her to their room, closing the door behind them. I was afraid of Treaty Talk and I didn't want to listen, not anymore.

Maybe it will all go away, I thought. You never know when your life is about to change. Treaty Talk is why I became a ghost.

Chapter 2

Treaty Talk

THE SUN ROSE HIGH in the sky, and I knew mother would have lunch ready soon. I was wrong. Everything about this day was wrong.

My father and mother kept talking, and I even thought I heard my mother crying. I waited on the front porch till Luke came home for lunch. He was twelve years old and never helped around the house. I had to do everything.

Hoke, sometimes he helped, but never enough.

"What's going on?" Luke asked.

"Mom and Dad are talking. Dad said there is Treaty Talk."

"Oh no," said Luke. "That means lunch will be late today. I'm not waiting around." He left to play stickball with his friends. *See what I mean?*

I circled the house and sat beneath the window of my parents' room, so I could hear what they were saying. My mother was crying, and she never cried.

"We have to be ready to go," my father said.

"Where will we go?" my mother asked.

"A long way from here. The Treaty has already been signed. We have till spring. But we should get ready to move."

We had no lunch that day. I fell asleep on the porch and Jumper rolled into a ball against my belly. When my mother finally stepped outside, the sun was peeking over the pine trees, ready for the moon to take over.

"Come with me," she said, taking my hand. Jumper trotted beside us.

"Where are we going?" I asked.

My mother said nothing. We walked through our garden of tomatoes and winding bean vines. We crossed the cornfield, where all the stalks were brown and dying. The evening air was already crispy cold and winter was coming. As we entered the woods, we met Luke walking from the river. He seemed upset.

"Luke, take Jumper home," my mother said. "Tell your father we will be home soon."

Luke nodded without saying a word.

He already knows what this is about, I thought.

We stepped from the woods and came upon a gathering of twenty old Choctaw men, scattered up and down the riverbank. I knew these men. They were the oldest men in town and they were our friends. We had supper at their homes and we knew their families.

One of the old men was Mister Jonah. He lived with his wife not far from us. As we watched, Mister Jonah took off his shirt and rubbed his back against a tree trunk. The tree was old, older than he was, and the bark was sharp and cracked.

Mister Jonah moved up and down, rubbing his back against the tree bark. His skin was dry and wrinkled. The bark cut into his skin and he started bleeding. Blood dripped from his back and covered the ground at his feet. His face was still as a stone, as if he didn't feel the pain, but I knew it had to hurt!

"Mother," I asked, "what is he doing?"

"Shhh," my mother whispered. "Don't talk. Just watch."

Soon all of the old men started rubbing their backs against the trees. When their backs were ripped open and bleeding, they sat in a puddle of their own blood. One man patted dirt on a friend's back to stop the bleeding. But the bleeding never stopped.

Hoke. *I should tell you this. Do not be afraid. This is how things are. When you will soon be a ghost, sometimes you see people before they are ghosts. You see how they will die. I didn't know it yet, but whenever I felt a warm shiver, I was about to see something no one else could see.*

I felt the warm shiver. I closed my eyes. When I opened them, Mister Jonah was sitting by the tree.

Suddenly, his hair burst into flames! He screamed and

7

waved his arms. He fell rolling to the ground. His arms were skinny logs and flames shot from his fingers.

No one moved to put the fire out.

I tried to run to him, but my mother held me tight. I jerked my arm free, took two steps, and stopped.

Mister Jonah sat with his back against the tree. His back was bleeding, like before, but his white hair fell over his shoulders. No burns on his arms. No burns anywhere.

The flames were gone. I looked at my mother. I was the only one to see the flames. They were flames for another day, a day that soon would come. If I was already a ghost, I might expect to see something like this. But I was not a ghost. Not yet.

"Mother, please tell me what is happening," I said.

"These men are saying good-bye to their home."

"They live in town. Their homes are in town."

My mother gripped my hand tight. "Come on," she said. "There is more to see."

Chapter 3

Dancing on the Stones

MY MOTHER LED ME to another spot on the river, where old Choctaw women were sitting on a pier. Some were the wives of the old men and some were widows.

I knew this pier. It was a long wooden pier with shallow water all around it. I fished from this pier, but very carefully, for the bottom of the river was covered with sharp stones. When I was only six, I went fishing by myself with my new cane fishing pole. I walked to the end of the pier and flung my line into the river. My cane pole slipped from my hand and I jumped in after it.

When I hit the river bottom I exploded in pain. The stones cut deep into the soles of my feet. I started jumping up and down, a stupid move, as every step I took meant more cuts.

I swam to the shore, leaving a bloody trail in the water behind me. I lost my first fishing pole that day and limped home in pain.

Yes, I knew this pier. While my mother and I watched, the old women sat on the edge of the pier, with their feet hanging over the water. Ten women sat on one side of the pier and ten sat on the other side. Four of the oldest women sat on the very end of the pier.

"They better be careful," I said.

"They know what they are doing," said my mother.

The sun peeked over the hills for one last look. Night was near. I leaned against my mother. The women started singing an old Choctaw song, rocking back and forth to the rhythm of the song. My mother joined them, singing in a whispery voice.

When the song was over, one woman shouted, "To the water!"

All at the same time, the old women jumped from the pier to the water. The stones must have cut their feet, but the women didn't seem to notice. They lifted their feet up and down and turned in circles in the water.

I could not believe what I was seeing. I gripped my mother's hand and looked up at her. Blood rose from the bottom of the river, and still the women danced. Their faces were the strangest thing of all.

The water was blood red, but the women showed no pain. They didn't squeeze their faces tight, like people do when they step on a sharp stone or stub their toe against a rock. The old women stared ahead like they were blind, like they saw nothing and felt nothing.

Missus Jonah was there. Her hair didn't turn to fire, like her husband's, not at first. I watched her dance with the others, till I felt the warm shiver again and closed my eyes.

"No," I whispered to myself. I shook my head. I didn't want to open my eyes, but I did.

Missus Jonah stopped dancing. The flames started at her feet, under the water. She screamed and tried to stomp out the flames. The fire climbed above the water and soon she was covered in flames.

The other women kept dancing on the stones. No one moved to help her.

Suddenly, just like before, the flames were gone. A few women limped to the shore. I looked to my mother. I knew she didn't see the flames.

As we left the pier, I looked over my shoulder at these tired old Choctaw women. Some were still dancing in the water.

"Mother, please tell me what is happening," I said.

"These old women are saying good-bye to their home," she said. "There is one more thing I want you to see. Then we can go. I will cook a good supper for you tonight."

We followed the river around a curve. The hills were lower here and the sun snuck through the trees. We came to my favorite swimming spot, where the river bottom was soft sand. A weeping willow tree hung over the water. My father once told me this tree was more than a hundred years old.

"It is the oldest willow in Choctaw country," he said.

11

The branches of the tree were long and thin and the leaves were light green. They hung over the river, like lime green walls of a small room.

In the center of this river room sat a Choctaw woman and her husband. They were the two oldest people in our town. Old Man and Old Woman, that is what we called them. They were both almost a hundred years old, and people spoke to them with respect.

My mother and I stood in the shadows and watched.

They sat in the shallow water, facing each other. Old Man dipped his hands in the river and lifted a double handful of wet, dripping sand. He smiled at his wife. She laughed and shook her head.

"No," she said, but she was smiling, too. He nodded his head up and down, then clapped his sandy hands to her face!

"Oh!" she squealed. She laughed and wiped the sand from her face. Then she scooped up two handfuls of sand and smacked him. These two old people acted like children. They laughed and played. They sat in the river and splashed and threw sand all over each other.

I knew what would happen next. The warm shiver came and I closed my eyes. After what I had already seen, I was afraid to look. I didn't want to see Old Man and Old Woman covered in flames.

What I saw was even worse.

When I opened my eyes, Old Man was covered in sores. His face was swollen and his eyes were closed. He shook as if he were freezing to death.

He turned to me, begging me to help him.

Old Woman had ugly yellow sores on her neck and face. She fell into the river and bubbles floated from her nose. She kicked and trembled, rolling her head from side to side.

Old Woman looked at me and tried to speak. A stream of bubbles rose from her lips. Then she stopped moving.

I closed my eyes again. When I looked up, everything was like before. Old Man and Old Woman were laughing and playing, like children in the river.

I did not have to look at my mother. I knew she hadn't seen the sores on Old Man and Old Woman. On our way home, I asked her again, "Mother, what were the old people doing?"

"They are saying good-bye to their home," she said.

"Their homes are in town."

"No," said my mother. "Their houses are in town. This river, this dirt, this is their home. This is our home. Your father was right. There is Treaty Talk and we must move. It is time to say good-bye to our home."

Chapter 4

Fire in the Hair

WE RETURNED FROM the river. While Luke and Jumper and I played in the backyard, Mother cooked supper. Everybody was quiet while we ate. No one said anything about the old men and women at the river. No one said anything about Treaty Talk, but the silence spoke louder than words. Soon after supper we went to bed.

It happened after midnight.

I felt no shiver. This was real.

I smelled smoke and jumped out of bed. The room was dark, but I could smell the smoke. It was behind me so I turned around. The smoke was still behind me. I turned around again. The smoke was still behind me. I turned around and around. I was scared now.

Why couldn't I see the smoke? I wanted to scream.

I felt the skin of my neck burning. My long hair was in flames! I heard a loud *crack* and fire fell from the ceiling. I grabbed my blanket and wrapped it around my shoulders, smothering the flames.

When I opened the door, a cloud of fire hit me in the face. I ran through the flames and out the front door. My mother and father and Luke stood in the yard. Jumper was there, too. He leapt in my arms.

"We thought you ran out back," my mother said. "We called for you. The smoke was so thick."

The roof of our house was burning. Bright specks of fire floated in the night sky.

"Run next door and wake the neighbors!" my father said. "They can help us put the fire out."

Luke and I ran to the neighbor's house, but it was burning, too. We flung open the door and ran inside. Everybody was still sleeping.

"Wake up!" Luke shouted. With squeals and screams our neighbors jumped out of bed and fled their burning house.

"Run to the church and ring the bell!" said my father. "Wake everybody up!"

Luke and I started for the church, but my father stopped us.

"Wait! Look there." He was pointing to the river. Men rode horses from the river, *Nahullo* men, and they carried burning torches. While we watched, they rode to the church. They leapt from their horses and threw the torches high, aiming for the house where the missionaries lived.

We stood in the street watching, my family and our neighbors. The torches made slow circles, turning over and over, followed by a trail of sparks. Like fiery comets, twenty flaming torches fell from the sky. They landed on the roof of the house and the dry cedar boards burst into flames.

The missionaries were visiting another Choctaw town that week, but the *Nahullos* didn't know that. They would have burned the house down with the missionaries inside asleep.

A *Nahullo* man ran into the church and climbed the ladder to the bell tower. He dropped his torch on the roof and soon the church was a swirling mass of flames.

What about the Bibles? I thought. *And the songbooks?*

The men shouted and pointed to us. One man took his shotgun from his horse and aimed it at my family. My father threw himself over us and we fell to the ground.

Pow! The noise from the shot was loud.

"Ohhhh," a neighbor shouted.

My face was covered in blood, the blood of our next-door neighbor. His shoulder was bleeding. My father took off his shirt and wrapped it around him.

"Run," my father said, "and stay together." We hurried to the deep woods at the end of town. The *Nahullo* men jumped on their horses and followed us.

When we entered the woods, my father pushed us into a clump of bushes. We knelt and huddled close together. My father whispered in my ear.

"Take a deep breath and do not move." I nodded and sucked in the cold night air. Jumper climbed under my shirt. My father put his hand behind my head and pushed my face to the ground. He did this to protect me.

I lay with my face on the wet ground. A man rode his horse into the woods. He was so close. I could have reached out and touched the hoof of his horse. Even Jumper knew to be quiet. I felt him warm against my belly.

"I don't see them!" the man yelled.

"Let them go," said another man. "They will wander around in the swamps till we find 'em. No place else for them to go. Their homes are burning."

"We should have done this a long time ago," he whispered to himself, but we were close enough to hear him.

We stayed in the bushes all night and watched the houses burn. The flames made a crackling sound and by morning every house had fallen to the ground.

I learned something about houses that night. This will sound strange. On the night I almost became a ghost, I learned something about houses.

Houses are alive.

Every house shook before it fell. Like Jumper shaking water after a swim, every house shook. Every house shouted, too. As loud as the thunder, every house also shouted. One by one, every house shouted and fell.

I lay on the ground with my father, my mother, my brother Luke, and Jumper. Our neighbors crouched on the ground nearby. We watched our houses shout and shake and fall.

"I wonder if anyone burned in their house," Luke said.

"The Jonahs," I told him. "Mister Jonah and Missus Jonah."

"How do you know that?" Luke asked.

I did not answer him.

My mother looked at me. Of course, she knew. She knew everything.

"There is nothing we can do," my father said.

"We can stay together," said my mother.

Chapter 5

Swamp Choctaws

"WE SHOULD GO NOW," my father said. "If we wait till morning they could find us."

We walked deeper into the woods, far away from town. We knew where we were going. For Choctaws, the safest place was the swamp. *Nahullos* never came to the swamp. We hunted there. We fished there. Whenever we wanted to be safe we always went to the swamp.

All night we walked the muddy ground. The trees were thick and covered with vines and thorny bushes grew everywhere. We arrived at the swamp as the sun was rising.

We were not alone. Every Choctaw from our town, those who were still alive, had come to the swamp. The old women were limping as they walked, and I remembered their dance on the stony river bottom.

The swamp water was green and sticky. I carried Jumper, and we crossed the swamp on logs and old wooden planks.

"Let me swim!" Jumper said.

"No," I told him. "The water is dirty green. You can't shake swamp water off."

By morning, a hundred Choctaws gathered on the island in the middle of the swamp. My father led us to a thick pine tree. Old Man and Old Woman from the sandy river bottom sat at the base of the tree. Old Man stood up and everybody hushed.

"We can talk about last night later. Now we go to work. Young men will get the meat. Deer and squirrels are all around us. The swamp is full of fish.

"Young women will look for wild onions and berries. Older men will build houses, lean-tos. Winter is coming. We will spend the day working and have our first meal tonight."

"What will the older women do?" a young man asked. Everyone grew very quiet. No one looked at him. They were too embarrassed. Old Man smiled.

"The older women do not need me to tell them what to do," he said.

When the gathering was over, my father spoke to Luke and me. "I'll build us a lean-to. You two see what you can catch for supper."

I was only ten years old, but I could catch a squirrel with a blowgun. Luke and I hollowed out two long stalks of river cane. Using a sharp stone for a knife, we carved darts from tree limbs and tied bird feathers to one end.

"I think we're ready," Luke said. "Let's see if they work. You go first."

I stuck a dart in my blowgun and lifted it to my mouth. Aiming at a skinny pine tree twenty feet away, I took a deep breath and blew. The dart stuck in the tree trunk!

"Good shot," Luke said.

"See how close you can get to my dart," I challenged him.

Luke got a serious look on his face. He loaded his dart, took his breath, and blew. The dart missed the tree, didn't even come close, but I didn't fall for it. I knew Luke was a better shot than that.

"You did that on purpose," I said. Luke laughed and slapped my shoulder.

"*Hoke*," he said. "You're a smart little brother, Isaac. Let's go hunting."

"I've been waiting for this," Jumper said.

Jumper dashed to a clump of trees on the far end of the swamp island. Luke and I hurried after him. Jumper circled a tall pine and jumped up and down, growling and scratching the tree trunk.

"Good boy, Jumper," said Luke. We heard a scattering of leaves and the chirping of squirrels.

By suppertime we had enough squirrels to feed the family.

While we were hunting, my father and his friends had built the lean-tos. They cut pine limbs, tied the limbs together with vines, and leaned them against the giant cypress trees. By nightfall, every Choctaw family had a home. Not real homes, not like before, but when it rained we could stay dry.

With blowguns we caught our food. With lean-tos we had a place to sleep. Young women found wild onions and leafy green vegetables, while the older women dug cooking holes. They covered the holes with green branches so the *Nahullos* couldn't see our cooking fires.

That is how we lived. A week later, winter came. Night and day we shivered from the cold wind and icy rainfall.

And every day I grew closer to being a ghost.

Chapter 6

Men with Blankets

WE WERE NOT AFRAID of the *Nahullos* in the swamp. *Nahullos* didn't know the swamp. Snakes and alligators lived in the swamp, and it was hard to tell the ground from a mudhole. We Choctaws knew to be careful, with every step, but the *Nahullos* didn't know the swamp.

But winter changed everything. The swamp froze in the winter. Snakes slept underground and even the deepest mudholes turned to ice. The *Nahullos* could ride their horses over the frozen swamp.

One morning I woke up and the world was white.

Even before I opened my eyes I felt the white. Everything was quiet, and I peeped through the branches of our lean-to. Ice hung from the trees and mounds of snow covered the ground.

This was a warning. On this white day, many people would become ghosts. Many of the old men and women would become ghosts, and many children, too.

"Be very quiet," my mother said. "*Nahullos* are coming." I looked for my father, but he was gone. I held Jumper close.

I heard the horses first. They snorted and wheezed, and soon I heard the wagons. The wooden wagon wheels crunched and cracked the ice. I was afraid. Everyone was afraid. My father came into the lean-to.

"Stay here," he said.

The wagons slowly crossed the swamp and came into our lean-to town. Everyone hid. We were so quiet. We looked through the branches.

The men on the wagons were *Nahullo* soldiers. They wore uniforms. They jumped to the ground and reached for something in the wagons.

"Guns," Luke said. "They will shoot us."

"Shhhh," my mother whispered.

When the men turned around, they didn't have guns. They had blankets and they smiled. We were all freezing from the cold and the *Nahullo* soldiers had blankets.

"The blankets are for you!" a soldier shouted.

At first no one moved.

"Come and get the blankets!" another soldier yelled.

Old Man was the first Choctaw to leave his lean-to. Old Woman followed after him. The soldier smiled and gave Old Man a blue blanket. Old Man wrapped himself in the blanket and turned around for everyone to see.

"Nice and warm. *Yakoke*," said Old Man.

Old Woman took the second blanket and threw it over her shoulders.

"*Yakoke*," she said. She buried her head in the blanket and shook with joy.

Many Choctaws ran for the blankets. Mothers and children took the blankets. Fathers took enough blankets for everyone in their lean-to.

"*Yakoke!*" they told the soldiers. "Thank you!"

When I tried to leave our lean-to, my mother grabbed my arm and pulled me back inside.

"Sit down," she told me.

"I want a blanket," I said.

My mother held my head on her shoulder. She ran her hand through my hair, and I felt warm next to her. "We do not need their blankets," she whispered in my ear.

Luke tried to run for a blanket, but my mother pulled him back, too. She drew him inside the lean-to.

"Sit next to me," she said.

Luke sat on one side of my mother and I sat on the other. My father stood over us and watched. No one left our lean-to that morning.

"We do not need their blankets." My mother whispered this. Over and over she whispered, "We do not need their blankets."

After the soldiers left, everyone was happy. For a few days, everyone was happy.

"We don't have to be afraid anymore," Old Man shouted.

"We can build our fires high!" said Old Woman.

Our neighbors left their lean-tos and visited and laughed. Jumper barked and played with the other dogs. But my father and mother were not happy, not like the others. We were still freezing cold.

"Luke and Isaac, stay in the lean-to," my father said. "Do not go near anybody. Stay here."

While everybody else slept that night, my father and Luke went hunting. They returned with two small squirrels, and we cooked them over the fire for breakfast.

Old Man saw the smoke from our cooking fire and stuck his head under our lean-to.

"Come outside," he said. "I'll share my blanket."

I looked at his face. I felt the warm shiver from inside, like before. I closed my eyes, and when I opened them, Old Man was not smiling. His face was red and swollen and a red sore lay next to his nose. Then another sore appeared, on his lip. Soon his cheeks were covered in sores.

Old Man fell to the ground. He rolled out of his blanket and buried his face in the snow.

"I don't want to see this!" I shouted. I covered my face with my hands.

"What is wrong with you?" Luke said. He pulled my hands apart. When I looked up, Old Man was staring at me. The sores were gone.

"Are you all right?" he asked.

"Yes," I said. "I am sorry. I am cold, that's all." I didn't want to lie, but I couldn't tell him what I knew. I knew that Old Man and Old Woman would soon be ghosts.

I almost became a ghost that day. If my mother hadn't pulled me back, I would have become a ghost.

How could my mother have known?

Years later, after I did become a ghost, I asked myself. *How did she know?*

Chapter 7

Snow Monsters

HOKE. *EVERYTHING WAS sad, rotten sad. I was ten years old. This was no way to live! In many ways, when you are ten years old, you are smarter than grown-ups. But sometimes your parents are smart, too.*

The very next day, my father and mother were smart. After breakfast (more squirrel), they looked at each other for a long time. I knew they had something planned.

"Luke, Isaac, we are going for a walk, without your mother," my father said. "Isaac, carry Jumper. Hold him tight and don't let him go."

We climbed out of the lean-to and walked away from the camp. We crossed the icy swamp, on the far side of the island.

"Careful," my father warned. "Do not fall through the ice!"

Jumper wiggled, trying to get free.

"I want to run," Jumper said. "Let me go!"

"Not yet," I told him.

We walked for almost an hour.

"Now," my father said, "let Jumper go. He's ready to run."

"You heard your father," Jumper said. "Let me down!"

I dropped him and Jumper took off running.

"I am faster than you are," Jumper called over his shoulder. I had to laugh. Of course, he was faster than me! I ran after him anyway. I tripped over a log covered in snow and rolled and tumbled.

"Be careful!" my father shouted.

When I came to my feet, my face was covered in snow. Luke laughed and pointed at me.

"You are a snow monster!" he said.

I didn't know what a snow monster was. I just knew I didn't like being called one. I grabbed a handful of snow and rolled a snowball.

Hoke. You are smart enough to know what I did next. I threw the snowball at Luke. He ducked and the snowball hit my father — in the face!

This was bad, real bad. I had never hit my father with a snowball. I stood and waited.

"Uh-oh," Luke said.

"Uh-oh," Jumper said.

We waited to see what my father would do. First he

stepped behind a tree. Luke and I looked at each other.

"This is strange," Jumper said.

The tree was covered in icicles and we heard cracking sounds. My father was breaking icicles from the branches. We stood still for a long time. What happened next was scary, really scary.

"Grrrr!" A low growling sound came from behind the tree.

"Grrrrrrrr!" The sound grew louder.

"I don't like this," Jumper said.

Without warning, something jumped from behind the tree!

"I am the real snow monster!" the thing yelled.

The snow monster wore my father's clothes. He had no hands. Icicles poked from his sleeves, where his fingers should be. And his head was made of snow.

The snow monster ran after us. He waved his arms and icicles flew all around us. He tackled Luke. They both rolled in the snow.

"Grrrr!" the thing yelled.

"Where is your father?" Jumper asked.

"No time for talking," I said. "Run!"

"Help!" Luke shouted.

"You are on your own," said Jumper. "I do not fight snow monsters!"

I thought the snow monster *was* my father, but Jumper and I didn't wait to see. We hid behind a big rock and clung to each other. The snow monster dragged Luke behind the tree. We heard more cracking sounds.

"Grrrrr!" That was the snow monster growling.

"Grrrrrrrr!" That sounded like Luke, growling *like* a snow monster.

"This has gone far enough," Jumper said.

I knew what was about to happen. Big Snow Monster jumped out: "Grrrr!"

When Little Snow Monster appeared, I laughed. It was scary, but I laughed anyway.

"Grrrrrr! I am Son of Snow Monster!" Little Snow Monster yelled.

Little Snow Monster was wearing Luke's clothes! His fingers were icicles and his head was a giant snowball.

"Hey, I want to be a snow monster!" I said.

Big Snow Monster looked at Little Snow Monster. I never knew snow monsters could shrug their shoulders. These two did.

"Come on," said Big Snow Monster.

We all went behind the tree, but Jumper stayed behind the rock. He was still scared and didn't want to be close to any snow monster.

My father (*hoke*, he was not a real snow monster) broke icicles from the tree. Luke (Little Snow Monster) scooped up enough snow to make me a snow monster head. I knew what we were about to do.

"Jumper likes to run," my father said. "We'll give him a good reason to run."

Jumper jumped on top of the rock.

"What's going on?" he asked.

We didn't answer. Soon I was ready, with icicle fingers and a snowy head.

"Grrrrr!" we growled from behind the tree.

"Go," my father whispered.

We jumped into the open.

"Grrrrrr!"

Jumper did not move. He was so afraid he just stared at us. Then he leapt from the rock and started running.

We waved our arms and flung icicles. We shook our heads and snow flew everywhere.

"Help!" shouted Jumper.

We chased Jumper through the trees and up a hill. I knew Jumper was fast, but he ran faster than ever! That's what happens when you're a dog being chased by three snow monsters.

Finally, Jumper stopped. Our icicle fingers were gone. Our snow heads were gone.

"Hey!" said Jumper. "That is not funny. You are not snow monsters. You are Luke, Isaac, and Father."

"I'm sorry, Jumper," I said. "We played a joke, that's all."

"Let's go home, now," my father said. "Jumper, we will make you something special for supper tonight."

"I think I deserve it," said Jumper. He was already wagging his tail. I knew he forgave us.

I learned something important that day. Hitting your father in the face with a snowball is not a good idea — unless you want to spend the rest of the day with real live Choctaw snow monsters.

I learned something else, too. Being a snow monster was better than being a ghost.

Chapter 8

Walking People

LUKE AND MY FATHER went hunting that afternoon. They returned with a deer! We roasted our first deer since leaving home. My mother gave Jumper the first piece of deer meat.

The next morning Old Man and Old Woman stayed in their lean-to. Most of our Choctaw friends stayed inside, too, curled up in their blankets. No one laughed.

By afternoon Choctaw people from every lean-to moaned and cried. Old people, young people, everyone cried. As day turned to darkness, a young girl shouted, "I am burning." Her mother ran to the swamp and brought her a cup of water.

"We should get a good night's sleep," my father said. "We will be leaving in the morning."

"Where will we go?" my mother asked.

"Away," my father answered. "Far away."

"I hate to leave our friends," Mother said.

"So do I," said my father. "But there is nothing we can do to help them."

I had a bad dream that night. I dreamed of what would happen in a few days. Old Man and Old Woman were covered in sores. They itched and burned and the sores never went away. Everyone with a blanket had the sores.

How did my mother know? I asked myself. *How did she know the blankets carried smallpox?*

Smallpox was a dark secret. It climbed from the blankets and carried the sores. I had already seen smallpox, but I didn't know it.

A week earlier, when I saw Old Man and Old Woman playing like children in the river, I saw smallpox. With my ghost eyes, I saw it.

Some Choctaws became ghosts from the shotguns. Some became ghosts from the burning houses. But the blankets made more ghosts than any guns or fires. The smallpox blankets were ghost-making blankets.

Our days in the swamp were over.

Early the next morning we gathered our belongings and left the camp. We walked all day and slept in the woods.

The next morning we came to a road. As far as we could see, Choctaw people were walking. Soldiers drove wagons and Choctaws walked. The roads were covered with snow and ice.

Most of the Choctaws had blankets wrapped around their shoulders. When my father saw the blankets he pulled us close. We followed this band of soldiers and walking Choctaws for three days, hiding in the tree shadows, unseen by anyone.

I carried Jumper so he couldn't chase the walking people. But he didn't even try to get away. After the *Nahullos* burned our town, Jumper knew when to be quiet. He seemed to understand about the ghosts, too, so I asked him.

"Do you see the ghosts, Jumper?"

"Do you promise not to tell?" he said.

"I won't tell anyone. I promise."

"Okay," said Jumper. "I see the ghosts. Maybe I will be a ghost soon."

"Jumper, no!"

Jumper just looked at me. I think he knew that I would soon be a ghost. We never spoke of it again.

On the morning of the fourth day, my father stepped out of the tree shadows and spoke to a friendly Choctaw man passing by.

"My family has no place to go," my father said. "Our town was burned and we have been living in the woods."

"You can come with us," the man said. "My name is Gabe. We are going to a new home, a home they will never take from us."

"The blankets?" my father asked. "Did the soldiers give you the blankets?" I knew what he was thinking. He was remembering the ghost-making blankets.

"Yes," Gabe said. "They are thick and warm."

35

My father nodded. "I am Zeke, and this is my wife, Ochi. These are my sons, Luke and Isaac."

"This is my wife, Ruth," said Gabe. "You are welcome to join us."

Ruth lifted her hand from under her blanket and waved. I couldn't see her face, but I could hear her laughing under her blanket.

"I am cooooold!" she said.

Ruth was short and round, and I knew she would be a funny friend. I saw something wiggling under her blanket.

"Momma!" a tiny voice said.

Ruth lifted her blanket and a little girl stood next to her.

"This is Nita," Ruth said.

Nita buried her face in the blanket.

"She is shy," said Ruth. "She is five years old."

"*Halito*, Nita!" we all said. She didn't look at us, but she waved.

"Just like her mother," Gabe said, and everybody laughed.

My family joined the walkers that day. After the burning of our town, the days in the swamp, and the blankets with small pox, my family joined the walkers. We were on our way to a new home.

But we were not alone.

Mister Jonah came to me the first night.

After sundown, Gabe and my father built a campfire close to the road. We had dried corn for our first night's meal. I was so hungry that I would have eaten the corn uncooked. But with wild onions, roasted over a log fire, it was delicious!

After supper we sat close to the fire.

"Do you want me to get you blankets?" Gabe asked my father. "The soldiers have blankets in the wagon."

"Not yet," my father said. "We will wait a few days."

We all slept close together. It was warmer that way. Sometime after midnight, when everyone else was asleep, I felt the warm shiver and sat up. The ghost of Mister Jonah sat next to me.

"We are waiting for you," he said.

"Did you die in the fire?"

"Yes, I did," he said. "But I am not alone. Missus Jonah is with me. Are you ready to come with us?"

"No," I told him. "I want to be with my family."

"You will be with us soon," he said, and stood to go.

"Wait," I said. "I want to ask you something."

"What?"

"Are the blankets safe?"

Mister Jonah smiled.

"Your mother was smart not to let you take a blanket in the swamp."

"But these new blankets," I asked, "are the new blankets safe?"

"Yes. The new blankets are safe."

"Thank you," I said. "I am glad you came."

After he was gone, I woke my father up.

"The blankets are safe," I whispered.

"How do you know?"

"I saw Mister Jonah. His ghost told me the new blankets are safe."

"I will ask for blankets in the morning," my father said.

Chapter 9

Nita and the Ghost Walkers

"HERE THEY ARE!" said Gabe. He plopped the blankets in front of my father. We still sat by the morning fire.

"*Yakoke*," said my mother. (*Yakoke* means "thank you" in Choctaw.) She unrolled the blankets and wrapped one around me.

"Here's one for you, too, Luke," she said, handing one to my brother. "And one for your father, and one for me!"

We sat looking at each other. My blanket itched, but I didn't care. I was with my family and we were warm. For the first time since our home burned, we were warm.

As we started the day's walk, the sun shone and the sky was clear and cloudless. The road was frozen and my feet were cold, but the sun felt good on my face.

We walked through a thick forest and melting icicles

fell all around us. A tree branch broke and fell to the ground. Nita squealed and jumped under my blanket!

"Can I walk with you?" she asked. Her tiny voice was so soft and muffled by the thick blanket.

"Yes, little Nita, you can walk with me," I said, giving her a big smile.

"I never had a big brother," she said. "Will you be my big brother?"

"Of course," I said. "I'd be happy to be your big brother."

That night at the campfire Nita suddenly stood. She walked close to the fire and turned to look at us.

"What are you doing?" her mother asked.

"I have something to say . . . to everybody," Nita said.

"What is it?" her mother asked.

"I have a big brother. Isaac is my new big brother."

I hung my head and hoped nobody would make fun of me. I thought this big-brother-thing would be a secret. I didn't look at Luke. If anybody laughed at me, it would be him.

I was wrong.

"Isaac will be a good big brother for you, Nita," Luke said. "I like being his big brother. He will like being yours."

I looked up. Luke was smiling at me.

"*Yakoke,*" I said softly.

I looked around the circle. Everyone was staring at me, waiting for me to do something. This was a special time, but I didn't know what to do. I finally stood and walked over by Nita.

"I am proud to be your big brother, Nita," I said. "I will

take care of you." Everyone nodded and smiled, and Ruth started singing the Choctaw friendship song. We all joined in, and for the first time our two families felt like one.

I hoped I could keep my promise, my promise to take care of Nita. Later that night, just before I fell asleep, I had a funny thought.

If I am a ghost, how can I take care of Nita? I asked myself.

By morning, I knew what to do. I could take care of Nita, as best I could, while I was still alive. I ate my breakfast in a hurry, and while everyone else was eating, I found a sharp stone. I cut two small pieces from my blanket.

"Nita, let me see your feet," I said. Nita lay back on her mother's lap and lifted her feet high. I tied the blanket pieces on her feet.

"Now," I said, "your feet will be warm when you walk. No more walking on icy roads, not for *my* little sister!"

I was glad Nita now had warm blanket shoes. That afternoon the wind blew hard and the sky was covered with mean, icy clouds.

"We should find a tree to sleep under tonight," Gabe said. "I think bad weather is coming."

We built our campfire under an old oak tree with thick branches.

Gabe was right. The next morning a hard rain fell. A clap of thunder woke me up, but my blanket was already soaking wet. I stood under the tree and shivered. I tried shaking the water from my blanket.

A soldier rode his horse into our camp.

"No time to build a fire," he said. "Breakfast will have to wait. We need to move. Start walking. If the rain stops, you can build the cooking fires."

"Careful!" my father shouted. "The roads will be slippery!"

I could barely hear his voice above the pounding rain. Soon the rain turned to ice. By late morning, the world was covered in ice. We walked without stopping all day, with nothing to eat.

An hour before sunset the sleet stopped. The woods were thick on both sides of the road. Long icicles hung from every tree branch. The soldier rode up and down the line of Choctaw walkers, shouting, "Let's make camp here!"

We found a small clearing in a clump of trees and started building our evening fire. By now we were like one big family. Gabe, Ruth, and Nita were more than friends. They were family. We shared the work and then we shared the food.

A soldier dropped off a bag of corn for our supper.

"Milk will be here, soon," he said. In a few minutes, another soldier brought a jug of milk.

"Thank you," Gabe said. "Where did you get the milk?"

"We bought it from a nearby farmer," said the soldier.

"I hope that farmer has a lot of cows," Gabe said, after the soldier left. "We need milk for a thousand Choctaws!"

We had Choctaw corn soup for supper that night. *Pashofa*, we call it. Soft corn in milk chowder. Yummm!

The next morning I remembered what Gabe had said: "a thousand Choctaws."

As we started to walk, I felt the warm shiver. I was afraid to open my eyes. My two families surrounded me, and I didn't want to see anybody die.

"I do not want to know," I whispered to myself. Then I felt a warm hand on my cheek.

"It is me, Isaac." It was Mister Jonah's voice. I opened my eyes.

"I was scared," I told him. "Sometimes I know too much."

"I understand," said Mister Jonah. "I want this to be easy for you."

"How can dying be easy?" I asked.

"I cannot give you a good answer," he said. "But there is something you should see. Go ahead, look all around."

I pulled back my blanket and stretched my neck high. As far as I could see, Choctaws were beginning their walk for the day.

"I see this every day," I said.

Mister Jonah laughed. "You are not looking close enough."

I squinted my eyes. The shiver was so warm I felt as if I was sitting close to a fire. I saw the Choctaw walkers, like before. But now I saw hundreds more Choctaws. Choctaw ghost walkers.

"Where did these people come from?" I asked.

"They came from all over Choctaw country," he said. "They died from the fires. They died from sickness and they died from hunger. But they will never leave."

"They are like you?" I asked him.

"Yes, son. They are like me. We are here to help you. Our lives are over, but we can still help the living."

"Can I ever call for your help?" I asked.

"Isaac, I will be there when you need me." As soft and quiet as the moon rising, Missus Jonah appeared at his side.

"I am here for you, too," she said.

"Now," said Mister Jonah, "we should be going. Today will be hard for you. Know that we are here." I closed my eyes and they were gone.

"Isaac!" my father shouted. "Catch up!"

This day was the coldest day of our walk, colder even than our days in the swamp. Freezing rain fell all day long, and I could not forget what Mister Jonah had said.

"Today will be hard for you."

I wondered what he meant.

I soon had my answer.

Chapter 10

Bloody Footprints

WHEN WE STOPPED for our noon meal, everyone huddled close to the fire. Everyone but me. I wasn't hungry and I was so cold I couldn't stop shaking. I stood under a tree, away from the icy rain.

"You should warm yourself by the fire," my mother said.

I was too cold to move.

"It is dry here," I said.

"Lift your feet," my father said. "You should move. You will never get warm standing there."

I covered my head with my blanket and leaned against the tree. I was standing in a pool of ice. I looked up and the snow was so thick I could not see the tree limbs. Nothing but white falling snowflakes.

"Come on!" my father shouted. "Time to walk."

I didn't move. *Maybe now is my time*, I thought. *Maybe that is what Mister Jonah was telling me. Maybe today I will become a ghost.*

I felt a tug on my hand.

"Come with us," Nita said.

"You better walk with your mother," I said. If I was about to be a ghost, I didn't want Nita to see.

I wiped the snow from my eyes. The camp was empty and everyone was gone. I took a step. I had been standing for an hour. My father had warned me.

"Lift your feet!" he had said.

I should have listened.

Mister Jonah had warned me, too.

"Today will be hard for you."

I tried to walk, but my feet were frozen to the ground. I pulled and tugged, and when I finally lifted my right foot, the skin tore away.

"Owwww!" I hollered. Pain shot up my leg and hot tears filled my eyes. I rocked back and forth, but the pain wouldn't go away.

"Come on, Isaac," Luke called to me. "You are falling behind!"

I clenched my jaw and raised my left foot, as gently as I could. I had sunk so deep in the ice, the skin of that foot ripped away, too. I jumped from one foot to the other. My feet were freezing cold and burning hot at the same time. I never knew pain could hurt this bad.

"Please make this be over," I said out loud. I felt the warm shiver.

"If you are ready," Mister Jonah said.

"You are welcome with us," Old Man said.

"It is warm here," Old Woman said.

I closed my eyes and wished everything to go away.

When I opened them, I saw everyone who had taken a blanket: Choctaw children, boys and girls, and men and women, too. They all stood before me, floating in a puffy white cloud. No one wore any blankets and their sores were gone. The sun shone on a beautiful blue sky. I knew I was seeing a ghost world.

"You will like it with us," said a young man.

"No!" I shouted. "No! I am not ready!"

I shook my head and they were gone. One step at a time I started walking. The snow was thick and my feet stung with every step. I looked behind me.

I was leaving bloody footprints in the snow. Mounds of snow covered the road. The snow fell in soft white flakes, but now the snow behind me was dotted red. I walked ahead, but I could not stop myself from looking over my shoulder.

Ten steps, ten bloody footprints. A hundred steps, a hundred bloody footprints trailing after me. I wanted to run, to leave the footprints behind me.

I did run, but the footprints followed me. The faster I ran, the more footprints.

"Make them go away!" I shouted.

"It is time," said Mister Jonah.

"No! I don't want to go with you!" I shouted. My voice was hoarse from shouting.

Then another voice cut through the snow.

"Son!" It was my father's voice.

The Choctaw ghosts vanished. Far ahead my father waited. I stumbled and fell and my father ran to meet me. He picked me up and held me close.

"Isaac," he said, "take one last look behind you."

I turned my head and saw my footprints in the snow.

"Son," he said, "you cannot keep your eyes on the bloody footprints you have left behind you. You must keep your eyes on where you are going."

I took a deep breath. I nodded. From that moment on, even though my feet burned, I refused to look behind me. I looked where I was going and forgot about the pain. I was stronger than the pain.

Three days later my feet healed. But the healing began when I heard my father say those words.

"You cannot keep your eyes on the bloody footprints you have left behind you. You must keep your eyes on where you are going."

Chapter 11

Nita's Walk

THE NEXT MORNING Nita woke me up, while the rest of the camp was still asleep.

"I have a gift for you," she said. She took her blanket shoes off and tied them to my feet.

"You need the shoes," she said. I had learned long ago never to refuse a gift.

"*Yakoke*, Nita," I said, smiling at my little sister. "You are sweet." Nita ran to the campfire and hid behind her mother.

"Nita, where are your shoes?" her mother asked.

Nita pointed to me.

"She wanted me to have these," I said. Her mother beamed with pride. I ate my breakfast quickly, then I cut Nita another pair of shoes.

"Here," I said to her. "Now big brother and little sister both have blanket shoes!"

"I like that!" she said.

Nita stayed near me all day. Once she jumped under my blanket and giggled. The cold was easier to endure with Nita close by.

At sunset the wind blew hard and rattled the ice in the trees. I drew my blanket over my head. Our day's walk would soon be over, and I was glad.

The shiver came swift and warm. I opened my eyes and Nita smiled at me. As I watched, her face swelled till her lips were puffy and her eyes were tiny slits. She stared at me without moving.

At first I didn't notice the small spider by her nose. It was a tiny black spider and it crawled across her face. I reached out a finger to flick it from her cheek, but my hand went right through her!

Nita was a ghost.

"It is her time," Mister Jonah whispered in my ear.

When I opened my eyes, Nita was still alive, walking beside her mother. We stepped from the road and into the woods. Luke and I gathered wood, while Gabe and my father started the cooking fire.

We all slept close to the fire. Nita slept by her mother and I found a dry spot on the ground next to Luke. When everyone else was asleep, I spoke to him. I had to talk to someone.

"Luke, are you awake?" I whispered.

"Yes," he said.

"Tomorrow will be a bad day."

"How do you know?" he asked.

"I just know," I said. "I am afraid for Nita."

"Can we help her?" he asked.

"No. I don't know how to help her."

"I am your brother, Isaac," Luke said. "Whatever happens, we are strong. We have seen many people die. We are some of the lucky ones. We still have our family."

"You are a good brother, Luke," I said, and drifted off to sleep.

The next morning, Ruth's cries woke everyone. Sometime during the night, Nita had rolled out of her blanket. She now lay covered by a blanket of snow, with only her face showing. I saw the tiny spider crawl across the face of my little sister, Nita.

"No," Ruth sobbed. "My sweet Nita, my little girl. No!"

My mother ran to help and wrapped Nita in her blanket. Nita did not move. She would never move again.

Ruth's cries carried far beyond our camp, and soon a dozen women circled Nita and her mother. The older women broke bark from the trunks of cedar trees. They burned the bark and waved the smoke over Nita. They sang the Choctaw death song.

No one built a cooking fire that morning.

A soldier rode his horse into camp.

"Time to walk!" he shouted. He looked at Nita and the women.

Another soldier pulled his horse to a stop.

"What's the hold up?" he asked.

"Another one died," the soldier said.

"One less to feed," said the second soldier.

They rode away.

I was glad Nita's family did not hear the soldiers' talk. But I had heard them, and Luke and my father heard them. We would never forget what they said.

Chapter 12

Disappearing Daughter

I HAD NEVER SEEN anybody as sad as Ruth and Gabe were that morning. Nobody said a word. Ruth knelt on the ground and wrapped Nita in her blanket. Gabe helped her to her feet and Ruth took the first step, carrying her little girl's body.

Gabe clung to her arm, as if he was afraid of falling. The women followed and the walk began.

I had never seen a parent lose a child before. I was seeing something else, too. I now knew what my parents would feel when I became a ghost. I felt the warm shiver coming.

"No, not now," I said. I closed my eyes tight and shook my head.

"Do not be afraid," a tiny voice said to me. "You are

still my big brother." I opened my eyes and Nita stood before me.

"I am sorry," I said. "I wanted to help you."

"You can help me," Nita said. "You can help my mother and father, too. You can make them happy again."

"How can I do that?"

"You can find my sister."

"Your sister?" I asked. "I didn't know you had a sister."

"Ask my father about her," Nita said. She smiled at me and reached for my hand. "He will tell you." Then she was gone.

Nita had another sister? If she was lost, why weren't they looking for her?

I knew this was a secret not even my mother or father knew.

I had to be very careful.

We made camp early that day. Ruth and Gabe traded carrying Nita, and they barely lifted their feet when they walked. Their feet left a sad trail on the road. Sometimes they sang the death song; sometimes they sang *Amazing Grace* in Choctaw. It is our song.

After our corn soup supper, I watched Gabe. I knew it would be easier to talk to him alone. When he stood up to go to the woods, I followed.

"Gabe, can we talk?" I asked.

"Yes, if you want to."

"I want to help."

"What can you do?" he said. I knew he was not listening, not yet.

"I want to help you find your other daughter."

The look on his face changed. He looked almost angry.

"We do not have another daughter," he said. "Do not speak of this!"

"Gabe, I know this is a secret. I have told no one."

"What are you talking about?" he said. I saw that he was no longer angry. He was afraid.

"Nita told me."

He started crying and moaning. "Go away, please."

"I want to help," I said. "Nita told me about her. Gabe, I have a secret, too. This is a secret my mother and father do not know."

"What is your secret?"

"I will be a ghost," I told him. "Soon, I think."

Gabe grabbed my shoulder. He turned me around and looked me in the eyes. "I am listening," he said.

"I see ghosts. They tell me things. Nita came to me this morning after she died. She wants me to find her sister. She wants you to be happy again."

"Nita told you this?"

"Yes."

"I cannot talk to you about Nita's sister. Not yet. I need to ask Ruth. Then maybe we can talk."

"What can I tell Nita?" I asked. "You know she won't let this go."

For the first time since Nita died and became a ghost, Gabe smiled. His body shook and his eyes filled with tears, but he was smiling.

"You are right," he said. "She is a determined little girl.

Tonight we can talk. All of us, your family, too."

"*Yakoke*. Gabe, I miss her, too." He patted me on the shoulder and we walked back to camp. I couldn't stop myself from listening as he spoke to Ruth.

"No, no, we cannot do this," Ruth said. He pulled her close and they spoke in whispers, till Ruth looked at me with a question in her eyes.

The wind blew strong that day. The snow swirled in circles and we were blinded by it. As I walked, I looked to my feet and pulled the blanket over my head.

If I walk off the road I'll bump into a tree, I thought. *That's how I will know I'm off the road.*

When you cannot see, your mind tells strange stories.

Maybe that's how it happens, I thought. *That is how I become a ghost. I bump into a tree and icicles fall all around me. I slip and fall. Then one long dagger icicle waits for its turn to fall. Everybody in the world stares at that one giant icicle. They hold their breath. I look at the icicle, too.*

I realize I am lying right under it.

"No," I whisper. The icicle responds.

It shakes, but it keeps everybody waiting. It is a very cruel icicle; anybody can see that. Then, as if it has nothing better to do, the icicle falls. I close my eyes. The icicle stabs me in the heart!

"No!" I shouted.

I was in the real world.

"Isaac," my father said, grabbing me. "Are you *hoke*?"

"Yes. I just had a bad dream while I was walking."

"That's okay," he said. "I have been having bad walking

56

dreams all day, too. Stay strong. This will be over soon."

Not until I am a ghost, I thought.

But I couldn't tell him that.

Not yet.

Chapter 13

The Coming of My Final Day

BY NIGHTFALL THE snow stopped, but the air turned bitter and cold. After supper, Gabe scooted close to the fire and everyone gathered to listen.

"We should talk about something," he said. Ruth had her blanket wrapped tight so no one could see her face. She began to shake and sob.

"Ruth is afraid," Gabe said. "But we have nothing to fear now. They can't hurt us anymore."

My mother and father looked at each other but said nothing.

"Now that Nita is gone," Gabe continued, "they can't hurt us."

"Who would want to hurt you?" my father asked.

"The soldiers. They said they would take Nita away if

we told anybody what I am about to tell you. We have another daughter. Her name is Naomi and she is twelve years old."

"Where is she?" my mother asked.

"The soldiers took her," Gabe said. "They rode into our camp one morning. They were looking for someone to do their cooking. A soldier spotted Naomi and threw her on his horse. Naomi is a strong young girl. She kicked and screamed. I ran to help her, but the soldier knocked me to the ground with his shotgun. 'We are taking her!' the soldier shouted.

"Then he fired his shotgun at a branch over my head. I jumped away just in time and the branch fell at my feet. The soldier didn't care. 'She is ours now,' he said.

"Then he looked at Nita. 'If you want to keep your other daughter, say nothing about this. If you say a word to anybody, we will come for this little girl, too. You will never see either of them alive again.' "

No one said anything for a long time. Ruth buried her face in her hands and cried quietly. Finally, my mother spoke.

"Do you know where Naomi is?" she asked.

"No," Gabe said. "We have been afraid to look, afraid to ask or tell anyone what happened. But now that Nita is gone, they cannot hurt us anymore." Then he looked at me.

"Isaac has something to tell you," he said.

Everybody was looking at me. I was embarrassed, but I knew that the time had come for me to tell my mother and father, and Luke, too, my own secret.

"Please don't anybody be mad at me," I began. "I don't want to upset anyone. Losing our home was bad enough."

"What do you need to tell us, son?" my father asked.

"I will soon be a ghost."

There. I'd said it. I closed my eyes. I felt the warm shiver. When I opened them, I was surrounded by Choctaw ghosts. Nita, Mister and Missus Jonah, Old Man and Old Woman. They stood in a circle around me. But there were more, at least a hundred other ghosts, many I did not know. They smiled and nodded.

"We are proud of you, Isaac," Old Man said. "We know this is not easy, but they needed to know."

I closed my eyes again. When I reopened them, everybody was waiting and the ghosts were gone.

"I don't know how, but it will be soon." I looked at my mother. She was trying hard not to cry. I knew she wanted to be strong for me.

"Ghosts come to me," I said. "They show me things, things that are about to happen. That is how I knew Mister and Missus Jonah burned in the fire. I saw their hair on fire that day by the river. I saw Old Man and Old Woman covered in sores. But I don't know what happened to their grandson, Joseph.

"Nita came to me yesterday," I continued. "She told me about her sister. She said she would help me find her."

I looked at Gabe and Ruth. "She wants you to be happy again," I told them.

"What can we do to help?" my father asked.

"I don't know," I said, "but the ghosts will tell me. If I have to leave camp to find her, you must understand. Please don't try to stop me."

"Will you be safe, son?" my mother asked.

Her question floated above the campfire. No one wanted to say what everyone was thinking.

He can be safe, but it will not matter. Isaac will be dead soon. He will join the others. He will be a ghost.

No one said it, but that is what everyone was thinking.

I did not have long to wait. I thought the ghost world was full of surprises, but the biggest surprise of my life woke me up that night.

"Isaac," a voice whispered. I rubbed my eyes. The sky was dark, and morning was still several hours away.

Somebody was leaning over me, but all I could see was a shadow surrounded by the bright moonlight. This was not a ghost. I was sure of that.

"Who is it?" I asked.

"It's me, Joseph. Old Man and Old Woman were my grandparents," the shadow said.

I sat up. Jumper sat up, too. He didn't bark. He knew who it was, and now that I could see him better, I recognized Joseph. He was older than me, maybe thirteen or fourteen.

"Where have you been?" I asked.

"It's a long story," Joseph said. "I'll tell you later. Right now, we need to find Naomi."

"Do you know where she is?" I asked.

"Yes, and she is still alive," he said. "The soldiers still

have her. But getting her back will not be easy. They are the meanest soldiers of all. They are the soldiers that brought the bad blankets."

I was afraid now, more afraid than ever. If these soldiers still had the blankets, we could all die.

"What can we do?" I asked.

"First, let your mother and father know you are leaving. We don't want them to be worried when they wake up and you are gone. Then let's go somewhere where we can talk."

I crawled to my father.

"Dad, wake up," I said in a quiet voice. I didn't want to wake my mother.

"What is it?" my mother asked.

She never sleeps, I thought. *No keeping secrets from her, not for a minute.*

My father rolled over and mumbled something.

"Wake up," my mother said, shaking my father.

"I have to go now," I told them. "I think I know where Naomi is. Don't worry. I'll come back as soon as I can."

"Be careful, son," my father said.

"I will. I promise," I said, but I was worried. I knew I might never see them again, not as a living person. My day of becoming a ghost grew closer, I could feel it.

Chapter 14
Joseph's Story

I FOLLOWED JOSEPH to a small clearing in the woods.

"Now," he said. "It's safe to talk. We have to be very quiet. No one can know where we are, not even Choctaws. This will be dangerous. You should know that."

"I understand," I said.

"Good. The soldiers took Naomi to a wagon, one of the wagons that brought the blankets into the swamp that morning."

"Did you take a blanket that morning Joseph?" I asked. I had to know. If he took a blanket, if he had wrapped himself in the blanket, we might both be dying soon.

"No," he said. "I was hunting that morning. When the soldiers left the swamp, they saw me. I had caught three squirrels and was headed back to camp. I tried to run, but I slipped on the ice." He pulled back his hair. "Look at this."

Over his right ear was a deep cut.

"Does it hurt?" I asked.

"Not anymore, but it bled for a long time. The soldiers let me lay there, bleeding in the snow. They made their camp for the evening, and by the time I woke up, they were cooking my squirrels for their supper. Then one of the soldiers saw I was awake.

" 'Are you cold, Indian?' he asked me. I told him, Yes. He brought me a blanket. It was one of the bad blankets, the ones that made everybody sick. I would have taken it. But another soldier stopped him. I guess the second soldier saved my life.

" 'Wait,' the second soldier said. 'This boy can help us. Let's keep him alive.'

"They threw me in the rear of the wagon. They tied my hands and feet together. 'If you try to get away, we will shoot you,' they said.

"I knew the time to escape would come, but I wanted to win their trust. For several days I did everything they asked me to do. I built their cooking fires.

" 'If you set me on a rock by the water, I will catch fish for you,' I told them. 'You can keep my feet tied. I won't run away.'

"I caught enough catfish for everybody. They even let me have a few bites. I was starving.

"After a week, they started to trust me. I could tell. They let me eat with them. They didn't yell at me in their mean voices. One night after supper, a soldier asked me,

'Do you want to go home to your parents?'

" 'No,' I said. 'They are fine without me.'

"The soldiers laughed at me. 'You are so dumb!' they said. 'Your parents are dead. The blankets we gave them had smallpox. It kills. All the Choctaws are dead, boy. You are the only one left alive.'

"They laughed and laughed. They meant my grandparents, but they didn't know. And that did not matter. They had just told me that everyone in my town was dead, and they were laughing."

Joseph paused. I knew he was ready to stop talking for a while. I knew he was remembering his grandparents, Old Man and Old Woman.

"How did you escape?" I finally asked him.

"I told the biggest lie of my life," Joseph said. "I told them, 'Thank you for saving my life.' I did not feel grateful to them. I didn't know if I wanted to stay alive or not. I was so angry. I wanted to kill them."

Joseph grew quiet. He closed his eyes and I knew he was lost in his own thoughts. He moved closer to me and put his hand on my shoulder.

"Can I trust you?" he asked.

"Yes," I said. "Why are you asking me that?"

"Because what I am about to tell you is known by very few people. My grandparents knew, and they kept the secret."

"I will tell no one," I promised.

"Then I'll tell you how I escaped. The next day they took me fishing again. They had to carry me to the river. My feet were still tied, tight. They checked the ropes several times a day. I caught enough fish for everybody and limped back to camp, carrying the fish. I also carried something else, a sharp stone.

"I knew the best time to escape was at night. After supper, I waited till I heard snoring. I had to make sure everybody was asleep. I knew they would kill me if they caught me. I cut the ropes with the stone and I ran.

"I didn't look over my shoulder. I ran faster than I had ever run in my life. I ran first to the river. The moon shone bright and I could see where I was going. I didn't stop running till morning. Then I hid in a small cave, on a hill overlooking the river.

"They must have followed my footprints in the snow. I thought I was free, but no. I heard the horses snorting below me. Just as the sun was rising, I peeked from the cave and saw the soldiers climbing the hill on horseback. I knew the time had come. My life depended on it."

Joseph paused and took a deep breath. "I made the change," he said, in a low whisper. "I closed my eyes tight shut. I wrapped my arms around myself. I felt claws digging into my ribs. My claws. I was the panther. I was still myself. But now I had the body of a panther."

Joseph waited for me to say something. I dropped my jaw. I didn't know what to say. I had heard of panther people, but I had always thought the stories were not real. When he saw I believed him, he continued.

"The soldiers rode closer, almost to the mouth of the cave. I saw them reach for their rifles, and I knew I couldn't wait any longer. I leapt from the cave and knocked a soldier from his horse. I stood on my hind paws, waved my claws at them, and growled. I showed them my sharp teeth.

"They froze for just a moment, long enough for me to jump back in the cave.

" 'Let's get out of here!' shouted a soldier. 'If the boy is in the cave, he's dead by now.'

"They turned down the hill and rode away. I waited till dark, then I ran some more. I ran like only a panther can run. I didn't know where to go. I only wanted to be as far away from the soldiers as I could get. I was so afraid. That night I dreamed about my grandparents.

"The next day I became myself again. I stumbled through the woods to the road. I saw the wagons and the Choctaws walking ahead of me. I followed behind, keeping to the woods. I have been following the Choctaw walkers since that day."

"Is that how you found Naomi?" I asked.

"Yes. I walked up and down the trail, hiding in the trees. I wanted to be able to see the soldiers before they spotted me. I knew they would kill me on sight. One night I located their wagon. I crept close.

"They were all sitting around the campfire, laughing about the dumb Indian boy that thought he could get away. 'He ran right into the cave of a panther!' they said. 'By now that panther is gnawing on his bones!'

"I ran to the rear of the line. I followed from the shadows of the woods, and no soldiers knew I was there. Of course, some Choctaws saw, but they said nothing.

"I walked close to Gabe and Ruth's family, long before you came. They had two daughters, as you know, little Nita and her big sister, Naomi. One morning the soldier who had caught me rode into their camp. You know what happened next. They took Naomi. They told Gabe and Ruth that they would take Nita, too, if they tried to get Naomi back."

"So now that Nita is gone," I said, "they can't hurt her anymore."

"That's right," said Joseph. "We have nothing to fear."

He smiled when he said that. Of course, we had everything to fear. The soldiers could kill anybody they wanted, at any time they wanted. But we didn't fear for Nita. She was a ghost. She could take care of herself now.

Chapter 15

The Bending Branch of Treaty Talk

"I LEARNED SOMETHING else," Joseph said. "Our leaders are with us."

"What do you mean?" I asked him.

"Not every Choctaw is walking. Behind the lead wagons, there is another wagon. Choctaw councilmen ride in this wagon. It is not big enough for all of them, so some walk while the others ride. They switch out several times a day, when someone is too tired to walk.

"They can't know everything the soldiers do, but they watch them. That is why the soldiers bring us milk and corn. They have to feed us. They have to keep us safe."

"Why?" I asked.

"That is what the treaty says," Joseph said. "They have to take us safely to our new home in the west. That was what they agreed, at the Treaty Talk."

"I wish I never heard of Treaty Talk," I said. "Before Treaty Talk, we had our homes. With no Treaty Talk, Old Man and Old Woman would still be alive, and Nita and Mister and Missus Jonah, too."

Joseph lowered his eyes and looked away without responding. I wished I hadn't mentioned his grandparents, Old Man and Old Woman. I could see it made him sad to think of them, burning in the fire.

"What should we do?" I finally asked.

"We should help Naomi escape. The soldiers cut her hair. They make her wear boy's clothes. She does everything for them, just like I did. She cooks their meals. She washes their clothes. She feeds their horses."

"Do you have a plan?"

"Yes," Joseph replied. "The best plan of all. We wait. We stay close and watch and we wait."

"We wait for a sign," I said.

"Yes," he said. "You are a smart young man."

"Do you know about me?" I had to ask him.

Joseph smiled and nodded. "Yes," he said. "Why do you think I wanted your help? Your brother, Luke, is bigger and faster. I asked you to help because you see ghosts. And a ghost will bring you a sign."

We did not have long to wait.

I followed Joseph to a creek a half-mile from camp. We found a tree with thick limbs hanging almost to the ground. He grabbed the lowest limb and swung himself from one limb to the next till he was out of sight.

"Come on up," he said. "Nobody can see us here." I gripped the limb and was about to climb, when the warm shiver came.

"Come on," Joseph said. "Here, I'll help you."

His hand reached down for me, but all I could see was a cloudy mist. Old Man appeared before me.

"Isaac, I am worried for my grandson. You must warn Joseph. He must be very careful. The soldiers are waiting for him. They know he is here."

"We want to find Naomi," I said.

"You must go alone, Isaac. They will not hurt you. Go to the Choctaw Council wagon. Tell them your father sent you to help them. Joseph can stay in the woods. He can look out for you, but he must not be seen."

"What should I do?"

"While you are working, keep an eye out for Naomi. I will be there." As suddenly as he appeared, Old Man was gone. I looked at Joseph, sitting on a tree limb.

"You saw a ghost, didn't you?" he said.

"Yes. It was your grandfather."

"What did he say?"

I climbed the tree before I spoke. What I said was too important to yell out loud, for anyone to hear. When I sat next to him, I spoke in a whisper.

"Joseph, your grandfather is scared for you. He told me to warn you. The soldiers know you are here."

"How can they know that?"

"I don't know, but your grandfather is speaking the

truth. He is a ghost. He sees thing people can't see."

"We are going to rescue Naomi," Joseph said. "Did you tell him that? I wish I could talk to him."

"Yes, I told him. He has a plan." I told Joseph about me helping the Choctaw councilmen, in the wagon close to Naomi.

"I'll stay close, as close as I can," Joseph said. Then he bowed his head and spoke in a quiet and serious voice.

"I know these soldiers," he said. "I know what they will do. Isaac, when you see them, when you get close to them, remember they are the same men who burned our houses down while we slept inside. They tried to burn us all, burn us alive. And when that didn't work, they acted so kind and gave us blankets. The blankets killed most of our friends."

"I know. I remember," I said. "I try not to be afraid, Joseph, but I am more afraid than I've ever been in my life."

"And you are smart to be," he said, lifting his eyes to mine.

We climbed down the tree and made our way through the woods. Thinking of Joseph's warning, I stayed in the shadows, moving as quietly as I could from one clump of trees to the next.

"Be careful how you step," Joseph whispered. "The soldiers send out patrols. If they hear the leaves rattle, they won't wait to see what it is. They'll fire their shotguns. Nothing would make them happier than to kill two Choctaw boys sneaking through the woods."

The forest was thick with snaking vines and bushes at

the base of the trees. I knew no Choctaw farmers had ever lived here. By nightfall we neared the council wagon.

"*Hoke*," Joseph said, pointing to the wagon. "Here's where you take over."

"Joseph, don't say that! I need you now more than ever."

"Sorry," he said. "I'll be right with you, invisible as a ghost," he joked.

I stepped from the woods to the camp. Ten older Choctaw men and women sat by the fire, eating bowls of *pashofa*. A thin man with gray hair stood when I entered the camp.

"*Halito*," he said. "Welcome to our camp."

"*Yakoke*," I replied.

"I am Nani Humma, and these are my fellow Choctaw councilmen," he said, gesturing to the circle of people.

"My name is Isaac," I replied. "I am from a small town in the swamps to the south. I would like to offer my help. I can gather wood, make a fire. I can hunt and fish if you need me to."

The councilmen laughed.

"We get our food from the supply wagon," said Nani Humma. He was smiling, but I could see he was trying his best not to laugh at me. I liked him already. "Do you have family on the walk?" he asked.

"Yes, my mother and father and a big brother."

"They will be worried about you, Isaac," Nani Humma said. "You should let them know where you are."

"My parents gave me permission to leave our camp," I said. I hated lying to Nani Humma. And although I hadn't really told a lie, I was not telling him the whole truth. I decided to tell him everything, as soon as I could.

"Isaac," said Nani Humma. "*Yakoke* for your kind offer. If you will wait by the wagon, we need to talk for a few minutes."

I moved to the road and stood by the wagon. I watched as the councilmen huddled together. They spoke quietly, and I knew they were deciding what to do about me. After only a few minutes, Nani Humma stood and waved.

"*Hoke*, Isaac," he said. I stood before the Choctaw Council. I knew this was an important day for me.

"We have decided that you can join us," Nani Humma said.

"*Yakoke*," I said, nodding to everyone. "I will show you every respect."

I was greeted with warm smiles as I walked from one to another. They each took my hand and said nice things to me. I felt welcomed.

"Have you had supper yet?" Nani Humma asked.

"Let me get you a bowl of soup," said a councilwoman.

"Please," I said. "I am here to help you. Let me serve myself."

The councilmen laughed again, a laugh that let me know they were glad I was there. After supper, I took the bowls to the creek and washed them clean. I scattered the logs and put out the fire. I even helped a very old man to his feet.

Nani Humma gave me a thick blanket. "You can sleep by the fire," he said. "If it rains, we have a small tent by the wagon. Climb inside and sleep by the door."

For a brief moment, I wished everything was different. I wished I was not on a mission to rescue Naomi. I wished I were the helper of the Choctaw Council, not a boy who would soon be a ghost. *Maybe I can be a Choctaw councilman someday*, I thought.

Then I returned to the real world. *I could never be a Choctaw councilman. They would never elect a ghost to be a councilman.*

I hoped that my first night with the Choctaw Council would be peaceful. But that was not to be. Nani Humma was smarter than I thought. He knew I had a secret, and it didn't take him long to learn the truth.

Chapter 16

Seeking Naomi

I THOUGHT everyone was asleep. I'd heard old men snoring. But not every old man snores. I thought I had fooled them all, and anyway I had to talk to Joseph. I climbed from my blanket and walked to the creek.

"Joseph?" I whispered. "Are you here?"

"Yes," he said, stepping from behind a big cypress tree. "Good job."

"Isaac, who is your friend?" In the quiet woods of night, the voice of Nani Humma boomed like a shotgun. I jumped like I was the target.

Nani Humma stepped from the shadows. I hung my head and said nothing.

"I already know Isaac, but we have not met," said Nani Humma, stepping to Joseph and offering his hand.

Joseph and I stood still, ashamed and caught.

"I won't wake up the council, not at this late hour," said Nani Humma. "But you will tell me what is going on, and you will tell me now."

Joseph and I told Nani Humma the whole story. For almost an hour we talked. We told him of the burning of our homes. Joseph told of his escape. We told him about Naomi and our mission to rescue her. We told him of the soldiers, and how Joseph's life was in danger. I even told him about seeing the ghosts.

When I saw that he believed us, I told him my biggest secret.

"I will soon be a ghost," I said in a whisper. I looked at Nani Humma, hoping he would believe me. He said nothing, but he nodded to let me know he understood.

When we finished talking, Nani Humma sat in silence for the longest time. Finally he stood up, brushed the leaves from his pants, and spoke.

"The hour is late and we need our sleep. Isaac, you can stay with us for now. Joseph, as long as you cause no trouble, you are welcome, too. I don't think I have to tell you how important it is that you stay out of sight."

"I understand," Joseph said.

"*Yakoke*," I replied.

The next morning Nani Humma told the Choctaw Council about our nighttime visit. I finished serving breakfast and sat down to listen. When Nani Humma came to the part about Naomi, and how she had been taken, the councilmen gave fire to their anger.

"They took a young girl from her family?"

"They use her like a slave!"

"Her family thought she was dead! How horrible."

When everyone had had their say, Mister Tibbi stood to speak. He was the head of the council and a large man, thick as a tree trunk. Gray hair fell about his face and down his shoulders.

"If we approach these soldiers and accuse them of keeping this girl against her will, they will lie," he said. "The girl will be afraid of what they will do to her and her family if she tells the truth. She might never see her family again, or worse, she might disappear."

"What do you suggest we do?" Nani Humma asked.

"If Naomi is ever to return to her family, I think her best chance lies with these young men, our new helper, Isaac, and his friend Joseph. We can lend a hand when needed. We can keep an eye out for the girl. But we must do these things in secret. We cannot endanger our people."

There were nods all around.

Joseph and I stood a little straighter. Rescuing Naomi gave us all a purpose. I noticed it right away.

The councilwomen walked faster than usual that morning, leaving our wagon behind. When we stopped for our noon meal, the women kept walking. They waved to the soldiers, saying, "We know there are berries in these woods. If we find any, we'll make berry pudding. It's an old Choctaw recipe. You will love it!"

The soldiers smiled and waved back.

"We'll hold you to that promise!" the soldiers shouted.

I knew better than to follow the women, not on my first full day with the council, but I listened and heard the friendly talk.

These councilwomen are smart, I thought. *They are gaining the soldiers' trust.*

While I built the fire that evening, the women reported to the council.

"We saw her," said Stella. She was the eldest, a white-haired, thin woman. "We saw Naomi. When she heard us speaking to the soldiers, she peeked around the back of the wagon. She was curious, but I could tell she did not want us to see her."

"She is afraid for her family," said Nani Humma. "The soldiers said they would harm her little sister if she caused any trouble."

"She was dressed like a boy," Stella said, "just like we expected. But anyone who looked closely could see she is a strong young girl."

"A terrified young girl," said another woman.

"What do you think we should do now?" Nani Humma asked.

"Let the boys do their job," said Mister Tibbi.

Chapter 17

Good-bye to My Family

WHEN I BROUGHT Joseph his supper that night, Nani Humma followed me. We sat in the shadows till Joseph finished eating. Nani Humma was waiting for the evening report.

"Did you see Naomi today?" he asked.

"Yes," Joseph said. "She stayed close to the wagon. A soldier gathered firewood and lit the fire. Naomi cooked the meals."

"Does she ever go to the woods, maybe to the creek to wash the dishes?" Nani Humma asked.

"No, never," said Joseph. "They brought a bucket of water from the creek for dishwashing. During the day she stays inside the wagon. She never walks with the others. After supper, she climbed in the wagon to sleep. I saw a soldier climb in after her. He had a rope. I am sure she is tied up every night and released every morning."

"Is there a guard?" Nani Humma asked.

"Yes," Joseph said, "but he fell asleep sometime around midnight. The soldier that relieved him saw that he was sleeping. He kicked him awake and they laughed about it. They are not worried about us."

"And why should they worry?" Nani Humma said. "They have the guns."

"I can sneak past the guard," Joseph said. "This will not be as hard or dangerous as we thought. I still have my sharp stone, good for cutting ropes."

Nani Humma did not reply. Finally, he leaned in my direction. "What do you say, young Isaac?"

I knew what I thought, but I didn't like disagreeing with my best friend.

"Go on," Nani Humma said. I knew we were thinking the same thing.

"Well," I stammered, "I am worried about Naomi. If we try to rescue her, she might not want to go."

"Why not?" Joseph asked.

"She thinks Nita is alive," I said. "She is afraid of hurting her. She could scream and fight and wake the soldiers up."

"Then I am one dead Choctaw," Joseph said.

Nani Humma laughed softly. "Between the two of you, I think Naomi will be fine. I am impressed. And let's meet again tomorrow night. Be very careful tomorrow. Joseph, you stay away from the soldiers' camp. We don't want to risk you being seen. Isaac, why don't you and Joseph walk backwards tomorrow?"

We laughed for the first time in days!

"Why would we want to do that?" I asked. "It's a long enough walk without doing it backwards!"

"I think he means we should visit your folks tomorrow," said Joseph.

"Good thinking," Nani Humma said over his shoulder on his way back to camp. "It's been a long day for everyone. Let's get some sleep."

I liked Nani Humma. He was a powerful and important Choctaw, but he still had a sense of humor.

Joseph snuck into camp long before sunrise.

"Time to go," he whispered. I rolled up my blanket and put it in the back of the wagon.

"What about breakfast?" I asked. "I need to start the fire."

"Nani Humma will tell them where you are. Come on!"

I followed him to the river. We walked in the trees so no one would spot us. With Joseph in the lead, walking backwards was faster than I thought. After only an hour, we saw my family.

I was so happy to see them! My mother and father looked strong, and Luke looked very bored.

That's a good sign, I thought. *That means there is no trouble.*

"There they are," I told Joseph. "But where is Jumper?"

"Right behind you," Jumper said.

I turned around and Jumper jumped in my arms.

"What took you so long?" he said, licking my face with his sloppy wet tongue. I lifted Jumper over my head.

"I missed you Jumper," I said. "But I did not miss your tongue!"

I set him to the ground and Jumper ran circles around us, barking.

"Look at you," my father said. Joseph stayed in the shadows while I hugged my family, even Luke.

"I'm glad to see you're safe," Luke said.

"Are you here to stay?" my mother asked.

"No, only for a short visit," I said. "I made friends with the Choctaw councilmen. I'm their helper."

I had no way of knowing how short this visit would be. This was the last time I would ever see my family. At least, the last time *the living me* would see them.

We stopped at noon and Luke and I built a fire. We had *pashofa*, just like before. It was the best bowl of corn soup I'd ever had. I told my family about Joseph, and everything we'd seen and done.

"Where is Joseph?" Luke asked.

"He is waiting by the river. I should bring him a bowl of soup."

"Let me do it," Luke said. "I want to see him." Luke carried his blowgun in one hand and the bowl of *pashofa* in the other.

I wished Joseph could join us, but I knew it wasn't safe. When Luke returned, the bowl was empty.

"I gave him my blowgun," Luke said. "He's already making darts. I told him to take care of you. Joseph is a good friend."

"Maybe he can live with us when we reach our new home," my mother said. I held Jumper close to me and smiled. I knew my family would like Joseph. He was a strong Choctaw, one of us.

The day went by too fast. Soon the sky streaked red and the sun dipped below the hills. I knew it was time to go. I knew I would soon say that word again, and hear my family say it.

Chi pisa lachike.

Choctaws never say "good-bye." There is no word for it. We say "*chi pisa lachike,*" which means, "I will see you again, in the future." Even though I was nearing the day when I would never see my family as a living person, I would never leave them. Choctaws never go away.

Chapter 18

Trail of Tears

MY MOTHER HELD me for the longest time.

"*Chi pisa lachike*," she whispered. I think she knew.

But I didn't know. How could I? I had not seen a ghost for days, it seemed. I thought they would at least warn me. There was no warning.

We were halfway to the council wagon when Joseph held up his hand. "Stop!" he said. "Did you hear that?"

I shook my head.

"There," he said, pointing to a small deer on the other side of the river. He quietly slipped into the water, holding his blowgun high.

"Don't wait for me," he said over his shoulder. "I'm going hunting."

I watched as Joseph climbed from the river and then

disappeared into the woods. I took a few steps, circled a fat tree trunk, and froze in my tracks. I knew something was wrong. I heard leaves flutter above me, and when I looked up, the wolf pounced.

He was so big. He knocked me to the ground and jumped on top of me. I tried to fight him off. I grabbed him and shook my head back and forth, so he couldn't bite my face.

I felt a sharp cutting pain. He sank his teeth into my neck. The wolf growled and threw his head back. His fangs dripped with blood.

My blood.

Soon the pain was gone. I closed my eyes. My body shivered and floated in a warm cloud. When I opened them, I was surrounded by so many Choctaws. Every Choctaw I had ever known who had died. They all were there.

The men and women sang the Choctaw friendship song, a song to welcome me. Young Choctaws waved at me. Each one held something, a blowgun, a boat paddle, a stickball bat, a cane fishing pole.

They wanted me to know that we were still Choctaws, always Choctaws, and that games and hunting and fishing still happen, even in the world of Choctaw ghosts.

I felt no ground beneath my feet. I felt lighter than air. I took a step to join the young ones.

"Noooo!" A scream pierced the cloud. I was alone again, back in the world of the living.

Joseph threw the deer to the ground and ran to help me. It was too late, but he didn't know. The wolf was carrying my body in his teeth. Joseph ran at him, left his feet, and sailed through the air. Before he struck the wolf, he was the panther.

I stood in my ghost body and watched them fight. The panther tore into the wolf, slashing him with his claws. The wolf dropped my body and fled into the woods.

The panther crouched beside me. He lowered his head and licked the blood from my face. As I watched, the black coat of the panther went away, like dark grass fading into the ground. I saw patches of skin, Joseph's skin, until finally it was only him, staring at my blood-covered body.

"No, no, no," he cried, over and over. "Why did you have to go? Not now. We have so much to do. You are my friend, my only friend, and I need you."

I felt helpless. I hated seeing Joseph so sad. I closed my eyes and felt the warm shiver. When I opened them, Old Man stood before me.

"You need to let him know," he said. "Joseph needs to see you."

"How can I do that?" I asked.

Old Man said nothing. He smiled and took me by the hand. Old Woman appeared beside him. They led me to Joseph.

"Speak to him," Old Man said, "and he will see you."

"Joseph," I whispered. My voice sounded like it always did. "I am still here."

Joseph turned his face to me.

"I am sorry," he said. "I should never have left you. I wish I had never seen that deer."

"Joseph, we both knew this was going to happen," I said. "Now that it's over, we can get to work. Naomi needs us."

"*Hoke*," he said. "But this will take some getting used to. I've never seen a ghost before."

"Just think of me like I think about you," I said. "I know you're there, even though I can't always see you."

"I can do that," Joseph said. "But promise me this. If you have to go away, let me know. I don't want the soldiers to capture me, tie me to a tree, and I'm not worried because I know you'll cut me loose, but you can't because you're off in the land of Choctaw ghosts! Can you promise me that won't happen?"

"I promise," I said.

Joseph was trying his best not to cry.

"Isaac, I have to tell your parents that you are dead," he said. "They have to take care of your body."

"This will not be easy." I was thinking of my mother. I followed Joseph back to my family. The snow had melted and the sun shone bright overhead. My family walked in the lead, and right behind them came Gabe and Ruth. Gabe held Nita's body, wrapped in her blanket.

Joseph stepped ten feet in front of them. When my mother saw him, she grabbed my father's arm and pulled him close.

"What is it?" my father asked. "Where is Isaac?"

Joseph hung his head. I could see he still blamed himself. My mother started crying, a soft muffled cry that turned the blue and sunny day into one of quiet mourning.

"What happened?" Luke asked.

"A wolf," Joseph said. He raised his head and looked at my father. "I am sorry. I fought the wolf but I wasn't quick enough. Isaac is gone."

My father pulled both families together and they sat beneath an old pine tree. He wrapped his arms around my mother and Luke and whispered a Choctaw prayer. They all cried, even Luke.

The passing walkers heard my family's sobs. They slowed down, bowed their heads, and said not a word, out of respect for the grieving family.

My father finally stood and threw a blanket over his shoulder. "Joseph, take us to his body," he said.

For the first time I realized what a burden I would be for my family. They would never leave my body behind, for animals to fight over my bones. Choctaws never leave their family's bones behind.

"I am going, too," said my mother.

No, please, I thought. I did not want my mother to see what the wolf had done to me.

As they neared the river, my father wrapped his arm around her and they walked so slowly, like a holy parade. Every step drew them closer to a sight they had hoped to never see.

Joseph circled my body and stood facing my parents. He didn't point or say a word. He bowed his head and looked at me, the face and chest and arms that used to be me. My eyes stared at the sky. The blood was dark red and covered the ground around me.

I felt a strong urge to end this grieving sadness. I wanted to leap into my body, to smile at them, to wipe away the blood and lift my arms. I wanted to stand up and let them know I was *hoke*.

Yes! I can do this, I thought. *I can float into my body and be with them again.* Then I remembered my father's words:

"You cannot keep your eyes on the bloody footprints you have left behind you. You must keep your eyes on where you are going."

I took a deep breath and watched.

My mother took the blanket from my father and laid it on the ground, away from the puddle of blood. My father rolled my body inside the blanket, wrapped his arms around me, and lifted me over his shoulder.

As Joseph waited in the woods, alone, they returned to the road and began their saddest day yet, carrying my body and walking on the Trail of Tears.

Chapter 19

Naomi Meets the Ghost

MY FATHER IS a hunter. So is my brother, Luke. They know the tracks of every animal and beast in the woods and swamps. As they left the woods with my body, I saw Luke tap my father on the shoulder and point to the ground. My father nodded.

They both saw the panther tracks, mixed with those of the wolf. Joseph's secret was no longer a secret to my family. They knew Joseph was the panther.

While my family began their slow walk, Joseph and I returned to the Choctaw Council wagon. At nightfall, while the others finished their meal, Nani Humma ambled to the river. He was looking for us.

"I'm over here," Joseph said, from his hiding spot in the bushes.

"Where is our friend?" Nani Humma asked.

"Isaac is dead," Joseph said. "A wolf attacked him. His family is carrying his body."

"Oh, Joseph," Nani Humma moaned. "Will the suffering ever be over?"

"Before you tell the others, know this," Joseph said. "Isaac always knew he would never reach our new home alive. He knew he would become a ghost. Now that it has happened, he is not afraid. His pain is over. He is with us now, and will stay with us till we rescue Naomi."

"You are a brave young man," Nani Humma said.

When we were alone again, Joseph lifted his palms, and asked, "Are you with me?"

"Yes," I assured him, and floated into view.

"No reason to wait. Let's go," he said.

The river curved way from the road. We left the riverbank and entered a thicket of oak trees. Joseph crept quietly, till we saw the flickering light of the soldiers' campfire.

"She's in the middle wagon," Joseph said.

Easier to keep an eye on her there, I thought.

"Isaac," he said, "the soldiers would see me before I reached her wagon, or they'd catch me when she cried out. She doesn't know me."

"She doesn't know me either," I said. But I knew what he was thinking.

"No," Joseph said, "but you can climb into the wagon without being seen. And you can whisper so soft, she'll listen to you. No Choctaw would scream to drive a ghost away, you know that. This is a job for you."

I knew he was right. *"Hoke,"* I said. "But stay close!"

"I'll be right here, but what are you worried about?"

He was right. *What did I have to worry about?* That's when I realized, for the first time, that the soldiers couldn't hurt me. I was already dead! Maybe being a ghost wasn't so bad after all.

With my newfound courage, I walked to the soldiers' campfire. I sat down next to the man who had passed out the smallpox blankets. He could not see me, of course.

A young man was scooping beef stew from a large kettle and filling their bowls. He was Luke's age, more or less, but his arms were long and thin. His black hair was cut short, and I could see he was Choctaw.

Where is Naomi? I asked myself. *I thought she was their helper.*

Dumb me! Of course, this was Naomi, dressed like a teenage boy, with short-cut hair. *I have to be smarter than this*, I told myself.

"Hey, don't be so stingy," shouted a skinny soldier with a long pointy nose. "Gimme more stew! And where's the bread?"

Naomi took his bowl and refilled it. She hurried to the breadbasket and then handed over thick chunks of cornbread to every soldier.

"That's better," said Pointy Nose.

I waited and watched. The steam rose from the stewpot, but I couldn't smell a thing. Once Naomi tripped and splashed stew on my face. I jumped, out of habit. But I didn't feel anything, no blistery, burning skin.

When supper was over, the lead soldier stood up. He had curly black hair and a thick chest. I knew he would be a tough man to beat in a fight. He also had a serious look on his face.

"All right, we have another long day tomorrow," he said. "Let's get to bed." The others finished off their remaining stew and unrolled their blankets. I saw that some slept in the wagons; others, on the ground by the fire.

Those must be the guards, I thought.

"Who's got first watch?" Leader asked.

"Not me," said Pointy Nose.

"I'll take it," said a short, round soldier.

The other guards took off their boots and slipped under their blankets. Roundman rolled a log by the fire and sat down. His shotgun lay across his lap.

Moving among the soldiers should be easy, I knew that. But I also knew I had to be careful. If I knocked anything over or made too much noise, they would look for somebody sneaking around their camp.

I knew these men wouldn't care if they shot the right man or not. The closest Choctaw to their camp might end up dead because of me. It might be Nani Humma, wandering by the river at night.

I couldn't live with myself if that happened.

Naomi gathered the dirty bowls and stood by the campfire. The logs burned low and embers sparkled in the dark night air. I heard frogs calling from the river. Pointy Nose brought her a bucket of water, and Naomi washed the bowls.

"Let's go," Leader said to Naomi. She followed him to the middle covered wagon, and they climbed aboard.

He's tying her up with a rope, I thought.

I decided not to wait. When everyone was sleeping, any noise would alert the guards. Now was the time.

I tiptoed to the middle wagon. The wagon bed was high off the ground. Normally, I would have grabbed the rear board and swung my legs onto the wagon bed. But that would make too much noise.

I slid one arm over the rear board and scooted on my belly like a snake, trying to lift myself on the wagon. I fell through the wagon bed and hit the ground below!

I jumped to my feet and got ready to run.

Nobody moved. Nobody had heard me.

I tried to climb on the wagon again, but I kept falling to the ground.

"Isaac," Mister Jonah said, and he was laughing. "You need to remember, you are a ghost. You can't grab or move anything. You can't knock anything over; don't worry about that."

"How can I get inside the wagon then?" I asked. *Being a ghost was not so easy after all.*

"It's easier than you think," he said. "Just imagine where you want to be, and you're there."

"Do I close my eyes, like before?"

"You can if you want to," he said, still laughing, "but nobody else does."

"*Hoke*," I said, "I am inside the wagon." And I was! Mister Jonah was gone, and I floated above Naomi.

She lay curled up in a corner; her feet and hands tied to a thick nail. The ropes that bound her were short, forcing her to lie in the same spot. If she grew sore, she couldn't roll over, like everybody else does when they sleep.

I hovered above her and watched for a long moment. Her face was buried in her hands and she was crying.

"Naomi," I finally whispered.

"What took you so long?" she said.

Chapter 20

Naomi the Strong

"WHAT TOOK ME so long!" I said, far too loud. I clamped my hands over my mouth and listened. Nobody had heard me. Nobody *could* hear me.

"*Hoke*," I whispered. "What do you mean, 'What took me so long?' Do you know who I am?"

"No," Naomi said. "I do not know who you are. But I have been dreaming about you for a week. Every night you climb into my wagon. You are here to help me escape. But I cannot go with you."

I let her see me.

"Oooh," she said. Her voice was filled with wonder. "You are a ghost. I didn't know you would be a ghost."

"I have only been a ghost since this evening," I told her. "A wolf killed me, but I'm *hoke* now. Don't worry about me. We need to get you home to your family. We've been planning your escape for several days."

"Is that why the Choctaw councilwomen come by?"

"Yes. You see everything, don't you?" I said.

"I have to be watchful to stay alive," Naomi said. "But you must understand. I can't leave or the soldiers will take my little sister."

"I know Nita," I said. "And I know your family. They walk with mine."

"How are they?" Naomi asked.

"They are sad, Naomi. Nita is gone. She died four days ago."

Naomi shook her head. "No," she said. Fat balls of tears rolled down her cheeks. "Not my little sister. How did she die?"

"She rolled out of her blanket and froze to death," I said. "Nita is my little sister, too. She adopted me."

Naomi shook with sadness, and I waited for her to finish crying. Grieving is hard. Lives are changed forever by grieving.

"The soldiers can't hurt her anymore," she sobbed. "They already killed her." After a long time, she wiped the tears from her eyes and asked, "Can you talk to her?"

"Yes," I said. "It was Nita's idea that we bring you home. She said you would make your family happy again. That's why I am here, Naomi."

I should have known Nita would follow me. But I was as surprised as Naomi when I heard her voice.

"Naomi," Nita giggled. "Give me a big hug." Nita

shone like a pale moon. I could see through her. But there she was, wrapping her ghost arms around her big sister, Naomi.

"Nita," Naomi said. "I am so happy to see you!"

"See," Nita said. "You can make Mommy and Daddy happy, too."

I wanted to talk to Naomi about an escape plan. But that never happened, not on this night.

"Naomi!" A voice shouted from the rear of the wagon. Leader waved a bright lantern from one corner of the wagon to the other.

"Who's in there with you? I heard voices."

"No one," Naomi said, trembling. "I was having a nightmare. I must have been talking in my sleep. I am sorry I woke you."

Leader held the lantern close to the ground and circled the wagon.

He is looking for tracks, I thought. *I hope ghosts don't leave footprints.*

"Who were you talking to?" Leader hollered, louder than before.

"No one," Naomi said. "I was asleep."

He knew she was lying. He climbed into the wagon and untied her hands and feet. With one strong arm he lifted her and tossed her to the ground.

I jumped to her side and tried to drag her away. My hands passed through her. I could do nothing to help her.

This was all my fault.

I wanted to run to the river for Joseph, but I was afraid

to leave Naomi. Leader was so mad. I feared he would hurt her.

"Don't move!" Leader shouted. He took a rope from the wagon and tossed it over a strong tree limb. I froze at the horror of what I was watching.

No, please no. He is going to hang her! I thought.

Leader grabbed Naomi by the waist. The other soldiers stood watching. They knew better than to say a word, but I could tell what they were thinking. It was written on their faces: *When Leader is this mad, he'll strike anyone or anything in his way.* They stared without moving as Leader dragged Naomi to the rope, dangling on the ground beneath the tree.

"Give me your hands!" he said.

Naomi lifted her hands, and he tied the rope tight around her wrists. "I need some help!" he yelled.

Roundman and Pointy Noise ran to his side.

"Take this rope and pull it till I say stop," he ordered.

They tugged on the rope and Naomi rose to her feet, lifted by the rope tied to her wrists. She clenched her jaw tight shut. I saw by the wild look in her eyes that Naomi was afraid for her life.

They pulled on the rope till Naomi was standing, her arms high over her head.

"Keep pulling!" Leader shouted. "I didn't say stop!"

Pointy Nose and Round man yanked hard on the rope.

"Ohhhh!" Naomi screamed. Leader slapped her hard across the face.

"You will never lie to me again," he said. He moved

his face so close to hers, I could not hear what he was saying. It must have been horrible. Naomi closed her eyes and shook her head back and forth.

When Naomi's feet were at his waist, Leader turned back to his helpers.

"Now, you can stop," he said. "Tie the rope to the tree trunk." Naomi swung slowly, twisting and swaying. Her face was etched in pain.

"Now," Leader said. "It's getting late. We have a long day tomorrow. Men, let's get some sleep."

As if she were a dog tied to a stake, they left her. They left my new friend Naomi hanging from a tree. I heard a soft cry and knew without looking who it was.

"We did this to her. Didn't we?" Nita said.

"Yes, Nita, I think we did," I said. There was no reason to lie. "But we will not leave her here."

We hurried to the river, where Joseph was waiting.

"Joseph," I said, "you have to see this." I led him to the soldiers' campsite. By the light of the dying fire, Naomi hung.

"We can't wait any longer," Joseph said. "Naomi comes with us tonight."

Chapter 21

The Panther and the Fire

"DO YOU STILL HAVE your cutting stone?" I asked Joseph, as we hid behind the tree.

"Yes, always. I'll cut her down. I can slip up behind her, but once she's on her feet, the guards will come after us. And they don't have to outrun us. They have shotguns."

"I can lead her to her family," I said.

"We need some way to distract the soldiers," Joseph said, "some way to slow them down."

"I think a strong panther could handle the soldiers," I said. "You've done it before."

"What can I do?" Nita asked.

"You can wake up the Choctaw Council, the men and women, all of them. Let them know what happened. When the soldiers chase us, they can delay them.

Every minute is important," I said.

"I understand," Nita said. She disappeared into the night fog, a five-year-old Choctaw girl — a ghost — making her first appearance before the Choctaw Council. Her sister's life was at stake.

Joseph and I circled the camp. Pointy Nose and Roundman sat on a log by the fire, their shotguns close-by. We crept behind the tree and waited. The quarter moon cast a bright light through the naked branches of the tree.

Joseph pointed to the sky. A huge cloud moved across the sky. I understood. We would wait till the cloud covered the moon.

"You take first watch," said Pointy Nose. "I'm going to sleep."

"That's not a good idea," Roundman said. "You saw how mad he was. If something happens, we'll be hanging from that tree. And not by our wrists."

"He wouldn't hang us!" Pointy Nose said.

"Want to risk your life?" asked Roundman. "Not me. You stay here and I'll watch the girl." He rose and moved by the tree where Naomi hung. Roundman leaned against the trunk, three feet from us!

We sat so quiet, in fear for our lives. If Roundman stepped around the tree, all three of us would be dead. He held his shotgun ready to fire.

What happened next could never be planned.

Something licked me on the ankle. I looked at my feet. There stood Jumper, wagging his tail and ready to play! I froze.

Please don't let him bark, I thought. I wanted to ask him how he had found me, but there was no time. We needed a distraction, and Jumper was ready to play.

As quietly as I could, I ran to the river and Jumper dashed after me. At just the right moment, the cloud covered the moon and the sky turned dark. With a loud splash, Jumper dove in the river!

"What was that?" Roundman shouted.

"Something fell in the river," Pointy Nose said, and the two soldiers followed the noise.

Boom! Roundman's shotgun blasted and soon the camp was scrambling with soldiers.

"What's going on!" shouted Leader, as he hurried to the riverbank.

"Someone stay with the girl," said Leader, and a soldier stayed behind. He touched Naomi's feet with the barrel of his shotgun. Naomi jerked.

"Don't you worry," he said, with a cruel smile in his voice. "You're not going anywhere."

I hid behind the hanging tree. No one could see me, I was sure of that. Joseph was gone. I heard a clawing sound and looked above me. The panther crouched on the tree limb, gnawing on the rope.

Suddenly, Naomi fell to the ground. The panther leapt on the soldier and his shotgun went flying.

"We have to run," I said. "Can you make it?"

"Lead the way," she said. She was shaking, but I knew she was strong. Her wrists were still tied to the rope, but we had no time to stop. She dragged the rope behind her as she ran. The panther ran to the fire and slapped the burning logs, sending fiery embers all about the camp.

Boom! Boom! Boom! The soldiers fired at Jumper in the river.

"Let him be," shouted Leader. "It's only a dog."

"Look!" said Roundman. "The camp is on fire!"

The soldiers returned to camp, ready for battle. Panther Joseph was ready, too. He gripped a burning log in his teeth and jumped into a wagon. The cloth top of the wagon burst into flames.

The panther wasn't finished. He roared his panther cry and jumped under the burning wagon, hiding himself in the flames. When the wagon collapsed, he leapt to a tree, climbed up the trunk, and disappeared in the branches.

Two soldiers surrounded the tree and fired their shotguns overhead. A blast hit the limb where the panther crouched. Before it hit the ground, the panther jumped on the soldiers, knocking both of them off their feet.

With all eyes on the panther, Naomi and I were far from the camp before they realized she was gone. When we arrived at the Choctaw Council wagon everyone was wide-awake. They were expecting us.

Nita did her job, I thought.

"You are the captured girl?" a councilwoman asked.

"Yes," said Naomi.

"Here," she said, "let me help you." She hurried to the wagon and returned with a sharp knife. She sliced the rope and tossed it in the campfire.

"We don't want the soldiers to see that," she said.

"Now, you must leave. The soldiers will be here soon. Can you find your way to your family by yourself?"

"I am not by myself," Naomi said. I realized the woman couldn't see me. I floated into sight.

"Oh," the councilwoman said, "I see you are protected by our ghost friend. But you must hurry. We'll do what we can to stop them."

We ran without looking behind. I soon realized Naomi was faster than me. This was only my first day, I hadn't learned to run like a ghost!

The panther was faster than us both. The soldiers fired their guns at us, but we had a big lead. They returned to their camp and the burning wagon, while we hurried down the line of walkers, nearing my family's camp.

Luke saw us first. "You must be Naomi," he said. "We don't have time to talk, not now. You know you can't stay here. Your mother and father are with my family. This is the first place they will look."

My parents stood with Gabe and Ruth.

"Where can I go?" Naomi asked.

"We have a wagon ready," said Luke. "Follow me."

"Wait," Naomi said.

"There is no time," said Luke. "We have to go!"

"There is time for this," Naomi said. She stretched out her arms and her mother and father ran to greet her.

"We were so afraid for you," Ruth said.

"You know that Nita is gone?" asked Gabe.

"Hey!" Nita's sweet voice always came when least expected.

She floated into sight. "I'm not gone. I'm just a ghost, but I am still part of the family."

Only Nita could bring smiles on a day like today.

"Of course," said Ruth, "family stays together. Always."

"You better be going," Gabe said.

"*Chi pisa lachike*," they whispered. Both of my families waved when we left the camp.

"*Chi pisa lachike*," they said.

We followed Luke to a Choctaw wagon a half-mile down the road.

"They are waiting for you," he said. "We didn't know you would come so soon. But after Nita spoke to us, we told them everything. They are ready to hide you, Naomi."

Luke led us to the rear of the covered wagon.

Who would risk their lives by hiding Naomi? I asked myself.

I soon had my answer.

"We are here!" Luke called to the people in the wagon. An old woman with wrinkled skin and long white hair stuck her head through the curtain. She nodded and flung the curtain open. Three even older women smiled and welcomed Naomi into their wagon, into their world.

The world of the bonepickers.

I lifted my arms and passed through the wagon walls.

Chapter 22

Buried with the Bones

"WE HAVE BEEN waiting for you," said the woman. "Take your shoes off before you climb in the wagon. We keep everything neat and clean."

Naomi leaned against a wheel and slipped off her boots.

"Here," said the woman, "hand them to me. I'll hide them for you." She helped Naomi into the wagon and closed the flap. Once inside, Naomi was struck by the smell of dried rose petals.

"Mmmm," she said, "it smells nice in here." The women were silent, but Naomi thought she heard soft laughter.

"We are so used to the smells, we barely notice," said the woman. "But we try to keep everything nice for the others."

"What others?" asked Naomi.

More soft laughter floated from the rear of the wagon.

"Everybody else," said the woman. "Most people don't like to be around us."

"Why not?" The words had barely passed through Naomi's lips when she wished she had never uttered them. In a sudden flash, like a thunderbolt that shook her very being, Naomi realized where she was.

"I'm in the wagon of the bonepickers," she whispered.

Few Choctaws have ever seen the bonepickers, but everyone knew of them. Before the soldiers came, they lived in a thicket of trees, deep in the piney woods. They never left their tiny log house.

A small pond lay close to their back door, gushing warm water from far underground. A young man brought them food and supplies, so they never had to leave home. Their job was the hardest and most sacred in all of Choctaw country.

When a Choctaw died, the body was brought to the bonepickers. They carried the body to a wooden platform close to the spring, where animals came to drink. After days, sometimes weeks, when the wolves and buzzards had eaten the flesh from the bones, the bonepickers began their real task.

They carried the body inside and picked the bones clean. They washed and scrubbed the bones till they were shiny and white. With a thin rope made from the clothing, they tied the bones into a bundle. This bundle was now ready for burial.

This was the Choctaw way.

And now, with Choctaws forced to walk, the bonepickers had to leave their home, too. They were too old to walk. Urged by the Choctaw

Council, the soldiers gave them a wagon. This was the wagon Naomi had climbed into, a wagon sweetened by the smell of dried roses.

"Don't worry, dear child," the woman said. "Don't be afraid of us. This is the safest place for you now. If the soldiers search the wagon, we have a place for you."

Naomi's eyes adjusted to the darkness. She saw the three older women, curled together at the rear of the wagon. They surrounded a large wooden trunk.

"Here," said the woman, lifting the lid. "You will be safe in the trunk."

Naomi took a deep breath and froze. The trunk was filled with bones!

"Don't be afraid," the woman said. "You do not have to touch the bones. The men built a secret hiding place for you."

The woman piled the bones into two large sacks. While Naomi watched, they lifted the floor of the trunk.

"It has a secret bottom, a tiny place for you to lie and wait till the soldiers go away. Here, climb inside."

Naomi crawled into the trunk, lay on her back, and closed her eyes.

"Take this," said the woman, handing Naomi a blanket. "This will keep you warm."

The women settled the wooden plank on top of her, and emptied the bags of bones into the trunk.

Naomi heard the bones scatter and roll, only a few inches above her head. The air was stuffy, but she could breathe. She curled under the blanket and waited.

I hope I don't have to stay here long, she thought.

"I know what you're thinking," the woman said, and the bonepickers laughed. "We'll do our best to see that your stay is short."

"Oh, don't say that," said an older women, in a cracked and tiny voice. "She seems so nice. Maybe she can stay and help us."

Naomi felt the wagon move. The bones creaked and rattled above her. She listened while the woman spoke to Luke.

"Have your panther friend bring us a small animal from the woods, a possum or raccoon," she said.

"I'll tell him right away," said Luke.

"Tell him to gnaw the animal, make it good and bloody!" the woman shouted. "The more blood the better!"

Chapter 23

Naomi and the Bonepickers

I KNEW NAOMI needed me, now more than ever. I slipped through the walls of the trunk. I was learning when to disappear and when to be seen. I let my body give off a soft glow, slowly coming to life before her eyes.

"Do everything they say and you will be safe," I whispered. "Joseph will be nearby, to warn us when the soldiers come. They'll never find you here."

"Why do they want a bloody animal?" Naomi asked.

"I don't know. We'll have to wait and see."

We didn't have long to wait. After only a few minutes, Panther Joseph caught a fat raccoon. He dragged the dead raccoon across the ground, then crouched and leapt into the wagon, dropping the raccoon before the bonepickers.

I lifted my arms and floated through the top of the trunk. I wanted to see what the woman would do with a bloody dead raccoon. Panther Joseph had done what she asked. The raccoon was slashed and cut from head to tail.

Panther teeth cuts, I thought.

A thick trail of blood stretched across the floor of the wagon. The woman took the raccoon by the neck and flung it in a circle over her head. Blood flew everywhere, on the walls, the trunk, and all over the woman. She lifted the lid of the trunk and held the raccoon over the pile of bones.

As I watched, the woman squeezed the raccoon tight and wrung it out, like she was squeezing water from a wet towel.

Blood dripped on the bones.

"Oh!" Naomi shouted.

I returned to the trunk and hovered over Naomi.

"I'm here, Naomi," I said.

"Help me," Naomi whispered.

Blood dripped through the cracks in the floor and fell like raindrops on Naomi's face.

"Nooo," she cried.

"Shhhh," said the woman. "We have to do this. Once the soldiers look in the trunk, they'll leave us alone."

"She's right, Naomi," I whispered. "Nothing scares *Nahullos* like bloody bones."

"I think I'd rather be a ghost," said Naomi.

"Don't think like that. What about your mother and father? One ghost daughter is enough."

113

"You're right," she said. "*Hoke*, just get me out of here as soon as you can."

"I'll do my best, but I have to leave you now."

Luke and Joseph waited for me by the river. The snow fell thick and they were shivering cold. Bits of blood and raccoon fur dotted Joseph's face and hair.

"You should wash up before anybody sees you," I told him.

"Oh, sorry," said Joseph. He grabbed a handful of snow and washed himself clean.

"How long will Naomi stay with the bonepickers?" he asked.

"Till it's safe," Luke answered. "Remember they are looking for a girl with short hair, cut like a boy's. The women have a plan to hide Naomi in plain sight. They are weaving a long hairpiece for her to wear."

"It might work," said Joseph. "For now, Isaac and I will wait here. We'll let you know when anything happens," Joseph said.

"I'll do the same," Luke promised. "I need to get back to the family. *Chi pisa lachike.*"

"Don't go yet," a deep voice said.

Luke stopped in his tracks. He stood speechless, his eyes filled with wonder. A thick white cloud covered us, and when it lifted, Old Man stood among us.

I am the only ghost Luke has ever seen, I thought. *He's entering my world now, the living place of ghosts.*

"We want to tell you three young men how proud we

are of what you have done today," Old Man said.

He nodded and lifted his arms. In the dark of the woods the air trembled with light. One by one they appeared, until at least a hundred Choctaw ghosts encircled us.

They were the walking ones who never left us. In times of trouble they are there. We know this, but sometimes we must be reminded.

Our deeds touch not only the living. We did more than save Naomi today. We made our people proud. That is the highest honor a Choctaw can ever earn, to make the ancestors proud.

They spoke in a single voice and with a single word they honored us.

"*Yakoke*," they said. "Thank you."

As suddenly as they appeared, the ghosts were gone. Luke said not a word. He looked at Joseph and me, then turned quickly and started home. When he thought we weren't looking, he broke into a run.

"He'll get used to it," said Joseph.

"He'd better," I said, "now that his little brother is a ghost."

Sometime after midnight the wind grew angry and sleet replaced the friendly snow. Watching the ice fall, I was glad to be a ghost. I couldn't feel a thing. Joseph wrapped himself tight in my blanket, but I knew he was freezing. We couldn't risk a fire.

"The snow has covered our footprints," I said, "and the ice will slow them down in the morning."

"Yes, I'm glad for that," Joseph said, through chattering teeth. "Let's hope for more ice!"

As if in reply, a branch heavy with ice cracked and landed at our feet.

"Careful what you wish for," I reminded him.

Chapter 24

A Soldier's Vow

IN SPITE OF THE FREEZING cold, Joseph fell asleep
in minutes. His blanket was soon covered in snow. I
knew he was exhausted from the long day of rescuing
Naomi, setting fire to the soldiers' camp, rushing Naomi
to the bonepickers' wagon, and catching a raccoon with
his bare teeth!

I sat watching him sleep. I was neither tired nor cold.

Life is very different as a ghost, I told myself. I learned
something else that night: Without sleep, life as a ghost
can be boring!

That must be why ghosts know everything, I thought.
*While everybody else is sleeping, they float around and see
what's happening.*

I closed my eyes tight and imagined the soldiers' camp.

When I opened them, I stood by the burning wagon. The soldiers had tried to put the fire out with buckets of snow, but the wagon was destroyed. Piles of smoking embers were all that remained.

Roundman leaned against a tree, wide-awake, with his shotgun over his lap. The other soldiers were asleep in their wagons. I searched the wagons till I found Leader. He was tossing and turning, adrift in a nightmare of the fire and Naomi's escape.

"I will kill you for this!" he called out in his sleep.

His anger was strong, and I knew he would seek revenge in the morning. I returned to my family's camp. Everyone was safe and sound asleep. Nita lay between her mother and father. She smiled and waved at me.

"Where have you been?" Jumper asked.

"Jumper," I said, "I've missed you!"

"Yeah, life's not the same without you, either."

"Is everything *hoke*?" I asked.

"*Hoke* for now, but stay close in the morning. Trouble's coming. That's what everybody says."

"Well, everybody is right. The soldiers will be looking for you, you know."

"How'd you like my little act?" Jumper said with pride. "I jumped in the river and got their attention, so you and Joseph could save Naomi. That water was cold, but it was worth it."

"You were great, Jumper! But this battle is not over quite yet," I said. "Get some sleep, and I'll see you in the morning."

"*Chi pisa lachike*," Jumper said. When he saw the surprised look on my face, he added, "What? You never heard a dog speak Choctaw before?"

"Jumper, you have to be the smartest dog in the world!"

"*Yakoke*," said Jumper.

I waved good-bye as I floated away.

The light of day came slow and quiet that morning. No red streaks in the sky announced the sunrise. I circled the soldiers' camp till one by one they rolled out of bed and joined Leader by the campfire.

"Stay together today," Leader said. "We will find the girl. She and her family will pay. Feed the horses well and carry extra shotgun shells. If anyone runs, shoot them."

"Do you want anyone to guard the camp?" asked Pointy Nose.

"No!" shouted Leader. He grabbed his shotgun and walked slowly to Pointy Nose. "Ask me that again," he said, in a low and menacing voice.

"Do . . . you want anyone . . . to guard the camp?" Pointy Nose stammered.

Leader tilted his hat to the back of his head and looked to the sky. Every soldier stared at him, unsure of what he would do next. Leader took a step back, lifted his shotgun to his shoulder, and swung it hard at the skinny soldier.

Pointy Nose fell to the ground, with blood flowing from a cut on his forehead.

"Do you have your answer?" Leader shouted. "No guards! You are not getting out of this!"

Roundman leapt to his friend and wrapped a cloth around his head. Blood soaked through the cloth, and Roundman packed the wound with snow to stop the bleeding.

"Now," said Leader, "saddle your horses and let's go. We will search every wagon, starting with the Choctaw Council's. Climb in the wagons and search in every corner. When you find the girl, bring her to me."

As the soldiers mounted their horses and stepped to the icy road, Leader shouted, "Someone will die today."

Chapter 25

A Day of Death

TWENTY SOLDIERS ON horseback rode behind Leader. As they approached the camp of the Choctaw Council, he held his hand high. The soldiers waited. Joseph crouched beside me, watching from the shadows.

"Shotguns!" Leader shouted. The soldiers lifted their guns to their shoulders.

"You are welcome in our camp," said Mister Tibbi. He rose from the campfire and stepped to the soldiers, who held their guns ready to fire.

"Take aim!" shouted Leader. He pointed to the tree limbs hanging over the council members, men and women both.

"Let us talk about what happened last night," said Mister Tibbi. Leader ignored the Choctaw councilman, as if he were nothing more than a patch of snow on the road.

"Fire!" shouted Leader.

Boom! Boom! Boom! Twenty shotguns exploded, shattering the treetops. Ice-covered branches fell all about the camp, destroying the fire circle and toppling the cooking pot. A large tree limb ripped through the roof of the wagon. Joseph quickly turned into the panther and growled with anger.

"Joseph, no," I shouted. "The soldiers will shoot you. You can't escape twenty men in daylight. Stop, please. Naomi needs you alive."

The panther turned to look at me.

"After you burned the wagon last night," I said, "they would love to parade your body for everyone to see. You don't want that. Naomi could die, too." The panther paused at the mention of Naomi. His dark coat receded, and soon Joseph knelt beside me.

At first glance, the Choctaw council members appeared to be safe, but soon a low moan rose from beneath a heavy branch.

"Stella," a woman shouted. "Help me, someone!"

Two councilmen rolled the limb away, and elderly Stella lay unconscious. A large purple bruise covered one cheek and her eye was swollen shut.

Mister Tibbi stood his ground.

"We did nothing to deserve this," he said, in a quiet but strong voice. Leader leaned from his saddle and, for the first time, spoke to Mister Tibbi.

"You are lucky no one died," he said. "But the day is

not over yet. Find the girl and bring her to us."

Mister Tibbi turned to his camp. Nani Humma dragged the tree limb from the wagon and the women circled fallen Stella.

"Let's move!" shouted Leader. The soldiers tugged the reins and moved their horses down the road.

As Joseph and I watched, something changed among the uniformed horsemen, some new cloud of fear hung in the air. Since they had left their campsite, only a short while ago, they had become deeply afraid of Leader. They had stood and stared, helpless to stop him, as he struck Pointy Nose with his shotgun.

He might have killed him, they realized. Privately they wondered, *What might he do to me?*

But seeing how helpless the Choctaw council members had been, with no guns or weapons, the soldiers also felt a new power, the power of life and death. They reloaded their shotguns as they rode, eager for the day. By the time they reached the next camp, their fear had turned to anger.

"No walking!" Leader shouted at the next group of Choctaws, sitting quietly around their morning fire. "You," he said, pointing to a young Choctaw man. "Run to the others and tell them to stay where they are. No walking today."

He turned to his waiting soldiers. "Turn the camp inside out. Burn the blankets," he said.

The soldiers leapt from their horses and invaded the camp. They tore blankets from women and children huddled from the cold. They threw the blankets into the fire. If a man stood in their way, they knocked him to the ground.

Word soon spread up and down the line of Choctaw walkers.

"The soldiers are coming!"

When the soldiers arrived at every camp, they found Choctaws standing away from the fires, clinging to their children. As they rode from the camps, flames lifted high from the burning blankets. Curls of smoke filled the air, as closer and closer the soldiers came to my family.

"Joseph, I have to warn them," I said. "They'll come after Naomi's parents. I'm going." In a moment I stood by the campfire where my two families gathered. I closed my eyes and came to life before their eyes.

"Are we safe?" my father asked.

"Yes," I said. "Let them have your blankets and say nothing."

"They are looking for Naomi, aren't they?" Gabe asked.

"Yes, and they are angry," I said. "They don't know Nita is dead. They'll be looking to take her."

"What should we do?"

"Show them her body," I said. "Unroll the blanket and let them see that she is dead."

"I do not want the soldiers to cast their eyes on my little girl," Ruth sobbed. "They might take her body from us; they might try to burn it."

"Mother," said the tiny voice we had come to expect. Nita appeared. "I am here. I am with you. My body is not me. Whatever the soldiers do, let them do."

"Nita is right," I said. "When the sun sets on this day, we want everyone to be safe. If they scatter Nita's bones, we will gather them. If they burn her bones, we will gather the ashes. We are Choctaws. We are stronger than the soldiers."

I could not believe I had spoken those words.

For a long moment, everyone stared at me in silence. A warm yellow cloud rose from the fire and filled the air. Old Man appeared in the cloud. Soon he was joined by every Choctaw from our town, the living and the dead. Our tiny camp was filled with hundreds of people.

The living people looked confused, not knowing where they were or how they came to be here.

Finally, Old Man spoke.

"The young man is right," he said, nodding to me. "Every Choctaw needs to hear his words."

Though my lips didn't move, my voice filled the air, and I heard myself say once more, "When the sun sets on this day, we want everyone to be safe. If they scatter Nita's bones, we will gather them. If they burn her bones, we will gather the ashes.

"We are Choctaws. We are stronger than the soldiers."

Chapter 26

Choctaw Rattlesnake

"THERE THEY ARE!" Leader shouted. "The girl's family! They know where she is." The soldiers circled the camp, staying on their horses.

"My daughter isn't here," said Gabe, stepping forward. "We do not know where she is. Search all you like, you will not find her here."

"She can't be far," Leader said, turning to the soldiers. "If she tries to run, don't shoot her. She needs to suffer for the trouble she's caused."

"What about you?" Leader said, pointing to my father. "Have you seen a girl with short hair, dressed like a boy?"

"I do not know where she is," my father replied.

"Then I must believe you," said Leader. His voice was evil and his face was hard. "What reason would you have to lie? I guess you've heard by now, this girl has escaped. But we don't need to find her. We have a promise to keep."

He turned to Gabe. "Where is your other daughter, the little one?"

"She is no longer with us," Gabe said.

"You are lying!" Leader hissed. "Bring her to me now!"

I expected Ruth to cry, but she did not. Instead, she carried Nita's body, wrapped in the blanket, and laid it by the fire.

"Here is my daughter," she said, and unrolled the blanket. Nita looked so small and helpless. Her face was swollen and her eyes were shut tight.

The soldiers stepped back and looked away. I felt the warm shiver creep through my skin. I closed my eyes and hoped. I did not want to see how anyone would die, not today.

When I opened my eyes, I saw children hovering close to their fathers. Boys and girls clung to their soldier fathers. Many were the same age as Nita, whose body now lay before them.

The soldiers have children, I thought, *and they are hoping this never happens to any of them.* Thinking of their children, the soldiers hung their heads and waited for their orders.

"What would you like us to do?" Pointy Nose asked. I knew by his manner that he had no children. Nita's death meant nothing to him. He was more concerned with winning back Leader's trust.

"Well," said Leader, "I am glad to see that one of us

is not afraid of death. Roll her up and take her with us!"

"Be glad to," Pointy Nose replied, with a thin smirk on his face. He stooped to Nita's body.

I saw Gabe look at my father. My father nodded, so slightly the soldiers didn't see.

They share a secret, I thought. *What do they know?*

Pointy Nose reached for the blanket, but something stopped him. His eyes grew large and a look of fear replaced the smirk. A soft sound filled the silence, a soft whirring sound. It grew louder and louder till the air around us shook with the sound.

Whirrrr! Whirrrr! Whirrrr!

The head of a rattlesnake weaved back and forth over Nita's body.

"Sir," said Pointy Nose, "I can . . . not . . . please don't make me do this."

"Shut up!" Leader said. "Get back on your horse. We can't waste our time here."

He turned to Gabe and Ruth.

"You have lost one daughter already," Leader said, "so I cannot keep my promise. But I made a vow this morning. Someone will die today. We will find the girl and she will die."

As the soldiers rode away, the snake lowered his head and coiled into a tight circle. Ruth looked at Gabe and my father, then knelt to Nita's body.

"*Yakoke*," she whispered. She bowed her head over her daughter, and the snake disappeared in a thin cloud of curling smoke.

Only later would I learn who cast the spell and brought the snake. On this morning I simply bowed my head like everyone else and whispered my gratitude.

"*Yakoke.*"

Chapter 27

Wagon of the Bonepickers

THE SOLDIERS CONTINUED their search, burning blankets and questioning Choctaws at every camp. By noon they arrived at the wagon of the bonepickers, the final stop.

I stepped through the walls of the trunk to warn Naomi. "They are here," I whispered.

"Did they hurt my family?" she asked.

"No, your family is safe, but Leader is furious. He wants to hurt you. Whatever happens, don't make a sound."

"I am ready for this day to be over," she said. "My body is stiff from lying here so long."

"You won't have long to wait," I said. The words had barely left my lips when the soldiers stormed into camp. I waited for Leader to bark his orders. I heard the horses shuffling around the wagon, but Leader was silent. I lifted myself from the trunk and floated through the wagon.

Leader waved his arms and motioned for the soldiers to dismount. The bonepickers huddled together in the wagon.

"Where is everyone?" Roundman asked.

Leader stared hard at him, moving his finger to his lips for silence. He stepped to the wagon and flung the curtain aside.

"Come out, now!" he yelled.

No one moved.

"Get out of the wagon!"

The bonepickers, one by one, climbed from the wagon. They were old and moved so slowly, stepping down with feeble, unsure legs. Leader grew impatient.

"Move!" he shouted. The oldest bonepicker was the last to leave. Her legs were so short her feet dangled in the air, searching a safe place to step. Leader grabbed her by the arm and threw her to the ground. A soldier moved to help her.

"Leave her alone," Leader said. His chest was heaving back and forth. "Someone will die today," he said in a mean, low voice, staring hard at the soldier. "It might be you."

The soldiers froze. They looked at the old woman lying at their feet. I felt the warm shiver washing over me and closed my eyes. When I opened them, I was surrounded by dozens of older *Nahullo* women.

They are spirit people, I thought. *Ghosts. They are the*

131

grandmothers, the mothers, and aunts of the soldiers.

The women wrapped their arms around the soldiers, and though their arms floated through the air, touching nothing, they smiled and talked among themselves. They were overjoyed to see their young men.

The soldiers could not see the ghost women, but their memories were strong. I could see it in their faces. They winced as they stared at the fallen bonepicker.

What if that was my mother? they seemed to be thinking. They looked at Leader, and saw for the first time the cruel man they were bound by law to follow.

Leader shouted at the bonepickers standing before him.

"Where is she? You are hiding the girl, I know it. Speak to me!"

The bonepickers moved to help their fallen friend. *They are frail but they are brave,* I thought.

"Leave her alone!" Leader yelled.

The bonepickers ignored him and he grew madder still.

"Drag everything from the wagon," he said. Two soldiers stepped forward and entered the wagon. I floated in beside them.

"There is blood everywhere," a soldier said. "Nothing here but an old trunk."

"Open it," Leader said, leaning inside the wagon. The soldier lifted the lid and stepped back in horror.

"The trunk is full of bones," the soldier said. "They are covered in blood."

Leader turned to the bonepickers.

132

"What are you hiding?" The bonepickers huddled together and spoke not a word. Nothing Leader did or said meant anything to them.

"I don't think they understand English," said Roundman.

"Maybe they will understand this," Leader replied. He stepped to the campfire, picked up a burning log, and handed it to Roundman.

"Burn the wagon," he said in a quiet voice.

No! I thought. *Naomi is still inside.*

"Please help her," Nita whispered in my ear. I entered the wagon and tried to lift the lid, but my hands passed through the trunk. Roundman tossed the burning log in the wagon. The dry wood and cloth caught fire and the wagon burst into flames.

From his hiding place in the cedar trees, Joseph saw everything. He leapt from a low hanging branch and landed near the wagon.

"Grab him!" Leader shouted. A soldier tackled Joseph and wrestled him to the ground.

"Well," said Leader, "we thought the panther killed you."

Joseph said nothing. Flames shot into the sky, and soon the wagon was a tower of fire. Scorching heat cracked the air. The soldiers covered their faces and stepped back. Joseph relaxed and the soldier loosened his grip, just enough.

Joseph wiggled free and dashed to the wagon. He leapt through the burning curtain as the soldier grabbed his legs.

"Let him go," said Leader. "My prophecy comes true. Let him burn."

Nita and I entered the smoke-filled wagon. Flames crept up the walls of the trunk. Joseph flung open the lid and tossed the bones aside. He lifted the false floor and pulled Naomi to her feet. She was covered in blood and looked more dead than alive.

"We are here for you," Joseph said. Naomi shook with fear, but her face looked strong. Somehow I knew she would live through this day.

"They are watching the rear of the wagon," Joseph yelled, over the sound of the crackling flames. "We'll jump through the cloth wall."

He ripped a piece of burning wood from the floor and held it to the cloth. The flames ignited and they waited for the circle of fire to grow. Naomi slapped embers from her hair and clothes.

"They are waiting too long," I said. "They will burn to death."

"No," said Nita. "They know what they're doing."

As the roof of the wagon collapsed in a mound of flames, Joseph took Naomi by the hand and they jumped from the wagon. By the time they were spotted, they were almost to the river.

"After them!" Leader yelled, but his voice was drowned out by the sound of the wagon crashing. All eyes remained on the burning wagon — and the bonepickers huddled together quietly and unafraid of death.

While the soldiers watched, the women kicked aside

the still burning boards, searching for any remaining bones.

Leader jumped on his horse and rode after Joseph and Naomi. They dashed to the river, with Leader close behind. It looked like he would catch them, but his horse slipped on a rock overhang and Leader jerked the reins. His horse bucked and sent Leader flying from the saddle.

His head struck hard against the rock. Blood gushed from a gash on his forehead, but he scrambled to his feet.

"They're safe for now, Nita," I said. I knew they could outrun him. Leader was staggering. He grabbed a tree trunk to steady himself.

Suddenly, Naomi stopped.

"Run," said Joseph. "Follow me. I know a place to hide."

Naomi shook her head and pointed to a dark cavern beneath the rock. I followed her gaze and froze in terror at what I saw. I closed my eyes, hoping this was all a ghost vision, a terrible vision that would go away.

Please, don't let this happen, I thought.

Chapter 28

Panther and the Wolf

WHEN I OPENED my eyes, the wolf that had killed me
was crawling from the cavern. He lowered his head and
stared at Naomi, then slowly turned his head to look at
Joseph. He bared his teeth and growled a low growl. He
lifted his head and sniffed the air.

"He smells the blood," Joseph whispered. "Don't
move, Naomi."

The wolf leapt on the stone overhang and spotted
Leader, leaning against the tree.

Someone will die today.

Leader's vow hung in the air. The wolf crouched, ready
to pounce.

"We cannot let this happen," Naomi said. She looked
to Joseph, but Joseph was no longer at her side. He was

now the panther. He lifted himself on his hind legs, swatted the air with his claws, and let fly a piercing scream.

Leader came to his senses. He saw the wolf crouched in front of him. He covered his face with his hands as the wolf leapt for his throat.

The wolf never reached him. The panther took two quick steps, caught the wolf in mid-air, and flung him to the ground.

The fight was over in a heartbeat. The panther sank his claws into the belly of the wolf. He locked his jaws around the wolf's head and lifted him off the ground, swinging him back and forth till the wolf was limp and lifeless. He dropped the dead wolf at the feet of Leader.

"Now," I said. "We have to go!"

"No," said Naomi. "He has to know who saved his life."

Following Naomi, we circled the tree. Leader sank to the ground. I came to life before him, and Nita joined me. Leader shook in fear.

"Who are you?" he said, trembling. We looked to the panther. Shiny black fur sank into his skin, his clothes appeared, and Joseph soon stood among us.

"You are the panther," Leader said. "That is how you survived that night in the cave."

"Yes," Joseph said. "I am the panther. And the boy you tried to kill."

"And you," he whispered, looking at Naomi. "I vowed that you would die today. Why did you save me?"

"It was the right thing to do," said Naomi. "It is the Choctaw way."

Leader looked hard at us. With the threat on his life gone, we saw his strength return. Leader kicked the wolf, and the carcass lifted from the ground. It fell at Naomi's feet, splattering blood in all directions.

Hearing the scuffle, the soldiers dashed to the river. They aimed their shotguns at Naomi and Joseph.

"One move and we will shoot you both," Roundman shouted.

"Put down your weapons," Leader said. "That is an order. We will return to our wagons now."

He turned to Naomi. "You have earned your life today," Leader said. "You can return to your parents. But there will be another day." For a moment that stretched into forever, we stood in silence and watched Leader walk away.

I felt a strong shiver and breathed a sigh of relief. Hundreds of Choctaw ghosts appeared, encircling us. A stout old Choctaw man stepped forward.

"I have heard of you young Choctaws," he said, casting a slow gaze at Joseph, Naomi, Nita, and myself. "I want you to know that I walk with you now."

"Who are you?" Naomi asked. "I think I have seen your face."

"I am Chief Pushmataha," the man said.

"My grandfather spoke of you," said Joseph. "You are General Pushmataha. You fought at the Battle of New Orleans."

"Yes," Pushmataha said, smiling. "I was a general in the United States Army. I come today to honor four young

Choctaw heroes. You are brave and you are honest. Young men, you rescued an innocent Choctaw. She will never forget how you risked your life to save her. Young lady, you saved a man's life today. You did the right thing."

We hung our heads, proud and embarrassed both.

"I hope you will never forget this day," Pushmataha continued. "Always remember, we Choctaws are a strong people, a good people. We fight to protect two nations, the United States of America and the Choctaw Nation."

"*Yakoke*," we said.

"*Yakoke* to you," Chief Pushmataha said, lifting his arms.

The gathered throng of Choctaws, a thousand strong, lifted their arms and whispered, "*Yakoke*," sending their thank you to the heavens. The trees rustled in the wake of a soft breeze.

Chapter 29

Pushmataha and the Choctaw Four

BY DAY'S END, the bonepickers had a new wagon and the burned blankets were replaced, as ordered by Leader. The soldiers delivered bags filled with ears of corn to every wagon of walkers. Naomi was reunited with her mother and father, and that very evening she insisted on helping with the cooking.

"Please," she said. "I can't sit still and be waited on."

"But this is your first day with your family," her mother said. "We are celebrating your return."

"Nothing will make me happier than to cook for my family, my bigger family," she said, looking at Luke and my mother and father.

"I want to help, too," said Joseph.

She and Joseph built a fire, fanning the sparks till yellow

and blue flames flickered and danced and warmed the air. Naomi and her mother, Ruth, boiled the corn to a thick broth, stirring the pot and smiling. Nita and I joined the gathering, in full view of everyone.

The Trail still lay before us. The winter was fierce and food was scarce, but our most feared enemy, Leader, left us alone to be with our families. We met a new friend and protector that day, as well.

We knew we would see General Pushmataha for many days and years to come.

"*Chi pisa lachike*," he told us, as he floated from our sight. "I will see you again."

Acknowledgments

I would like to acknowledge the following friends, researchers, and encouragers for helping bring *How I Became a Ghost* to life: The many Choctaws who have generously shared their family stories for the past two decades will always be remembered. Gone-before Choctaws include Jay McAlvain, Buck Wade, Tony Byars, Archie Mingo, Lizzy Carney, and Estelline Tubby. *Yakoke* to language teachers LeRoy Sealy and Richard Adams, and to Stella Long, Tom Wheelus, and Helen Harris for their panther stories.

Thanks to Steve Hawkins of the Oklahoma Historical Society's research division, for guiding us to a good map of the various Choctaw Trails of Tear routes. I also want to acknowledge fellow members of the Choctaw Literary Revival. Inspired by Louis Owens, they include D.L. Birchfield, Roxy Gordon, Ron Querry, James Bluewolf, Phil Morgan, Lee Hester, Jim Barnes, LeAnne Howe, Clara Sue Kidwell, Rilla Askew, Donna Akers, John D. Berry, Devon A. Mihesuah, and Greg Rodgers.

I am forever indebted to Dr. Joe Moore for supporting my efforts to record tribal stories. Special thanks to museum advocates Susan Feller, Mary Robinson, and Mississippi Choctaw Martha Fergusen. *Yakoke* to friends and fire-lighters Charley Jones, Geary Hobson, Joe Bruchac, and Les Hannah.

About the Author

Tim Tingle is an Oklahoma Choctaw and an award-winning author and storyteller. His great-great-grandfather, John Carnes, walked the Trail of Tears in 1835. In 1993, Tingle retraced the Trail to Choctaw homelands in Mississippi and began recording stories of tribal elders. His first book, *Walking the Choctaw Road*, was the result, and in 2005, it was named Book of the Year in both Oklahoma and Alaska. He lives in Canyon Lake, Texas.

Discussion Questions

1. In *How I Became a Ghost*, there are many ghosts who make appearances throughout the story. Can you name three of them? Can you say whose experience inspired the name of the book?

2. What do Isaac and his family mean by "Treaty Talk"?

3. How did the older Choctaws say good-bye to their home?

4. What does *chi pisa lachike* mean? Why is this phrase so important to Choctaws? Why is it important to the story?

5. Why does Joseph hide from the soldiers? Now tell his escape story as if you were the panther.

6. Why does Naomi refuse to try and escape from the soldiers? What happens to change her mind?

7. Have you ever met a dog like Jumper? What makes him so special? Describe the Snow Monsters and how they came to be.

8. Would you like to spend a day with Isaac before he becomes a ghost, or after? Why?

9. If you were to be a ghost for a day, what would you spend it doing?

10. Who is Nita and what does Nita want more than anything?

11. What role do the Choctaw bonepickers have in Choctaw country?

12. When Naomi has a chance to leave the soldier who threatened to kill her to the mighty jaws of the wolf, why does she step in and save the soldier's life?

13. Have you ever forgiven someone who wronged you? If so, why?

14. Who is General Pushmataha, and why does he appear in our story?